DYNAMIC PORTFOLIO THEORY AND MANAGEMENT

USING ACTIVE ASSET ALLOCATION TO IMPROVE PROFITS AND REDUCE RISK

RICHARD E. OBERUC

McGraw-Hill

New York   Chicago   San Francisco   Lisbon   London
Madrid   Mexico City   Milan   New Delhi   San Juan
Seoul   Singapore   Sydney   Toronto

The *McGraw·Hill* Companies

Copyright © 2004 by The McGraw-Hill Companies, Inc. All rights reserved. Printed in the United States of America. Except as permitted under the United States Copyright Act of 1976, no part of this publication may be reproduced or distributed in any form or by any means, or stored in a data base or retrieval system, without the prior written permission of the publisher.

1 2 3 4 5 6 7 8 9 0   DOC/DOC   0 9 8 7 6 5 4 3

ISBN 0-07-142669-8

McGraw-Hill books are available at special quantity discounts to use as premiums and sales promotions, or for use in corporate training programs. For more information, please write to the Director of Special Sales, Professional Publishing, McGraw-Hill, Two Penn Plaza, New York, NY 10121-2298. Or contact your local bookstore.

This publication is designed to provide accurate and authoritative information in regard to the subject matter covered. It is sold with the understanding that neither the author nor the publisher is engaged in rendering legal, accounting, or other professional service. If legal advice or other expert assistance is required, the services of a competent professional person should be sought.
—*From a Declaration of Principles jointly adopted by a Committee of the American Bar Association and a Committee of Publishers.*

 This book is printed on recycled, acid-free paper containing a minimum of 50% recycled, de-inked fiber.

Library of Congress Cataloging-in-Publication Data

Oberuc, Richard E.
   Dynamic portfolio theory and management : using active asset allocation to improve profits and reduce risk / by Richard E. Oberuc.
     p. cm.
    Includes indexes.
    ISBN 0-07-142669-8 (hardcover : alk. paper)
    1. Portfolio management. 2. Investment analysis. I. Title.
HG4529.5.O24 2003
332.6–dc21   2003007821

To Patricia
My Wife and Muse

Other Titles in the Irwin Library of Investment and Finance

CONTENTS

Over a half century has elapsed since the dawn of modern portfolio theory (MPT). During this time a wealth of techniques has evolved to aid the investor in creating rational portfolios of multiple investments. The Markowitz mean-variance model has become a universally understood technique within the investment world for generating the trade-off of changes in risk for changes in expected return called the efficient frontier. Despite the acceptance of MPT and its derivatives, there is still a nagging feeling that the value of the results obtained from MPT is limited by the uncertainty of the inputs required to implement the model. How should the needed expected returns, standard deviations, and correlation matrix be obtained? Ten skilled financial analysts charged with determining the required inputs for an identical list of investments will in all likelihood generate ten different sets of assumed inputs. This will, of course, lead to ten different asset allocation results using the same MPT model. The problem is no longer how to estimate the optimal asset allocations. Harry Markowitz gave us the solution to that problem in the 1950s. The problem is how to determine the required inputs. Selecting a slice of history and using the average values of the investment performance for that time period is a poor way to predict future performance. The linkage between long-term past investment performance and short-term future performance is weak at best. Something more effective is required.

There are two purposes for *Dynamic Portfolio Theory and Management*. The first is to investigate a fundamental procedure to obtain more accurate estimates of future investment performance. This ultimately involves the determination of the factors that have an influence on investment returns, with special emphasis on the traditional markets of stocks, bonds, and interest rates. Chapters 3, 4, and 5 evaluate many factors considered by leading financial investigators to be fundamentally related to the performance of these three traditional markets. Some of these factors are found to be truly useful and others not quite so useful. Beyond the most frequently investigated factors, a number of new factors are considered. Some of these new factors are found to be effective when combined with the more commonly applied factors. Additionally, for the world of alternative investments, factors influencing the performance of hedge funds are evaluated in Chapter 6. Many individual investors will find that Chapters 3 to 6 are all they will need from this book. Simply knowing what factors to monitor will provide enough insight to confidently reduce allocations to those assets heading toward lower performance and increase allocations to those headed up.

The second purpose of this book is to present a new asset allocation model that sidesteps the need for determining expected returns, standard deviations, and the correlation matrix in the first place. This new model, called DynaPorte, links the asset allocations directly to the values of macroeconomic factors without the need to calculate the expected performance of the investments. The major advantage is that DynaPorte adapts to changing market conditions as they occur. Furthermore, as more historical data are used to determine the needed relationships, the better the model becomes. Increasing the historical date range to form naive expectations for the Markowitz model makes the mean-variance model less sensitive to current conditions and less usable in defining an asset's future performance. With DynaPorte, more data simply make the relationships more robust.

Readers interested in the DynaPorte model are advised to read Chapter 1 on static portfolio theory to understand the problems suffered by static models and then review Chapter 9 for background on multiperiod portfolio theory. Chapters 10 and 11, describing DynaPorte itself, should then be read.

There is considerable effort under way regarding multiperiod portfolio optimization. This is covered in some detail in Chapter 9. While DynaPorte attempts to uncover relationships from multiple time periods from the past, it essentially optimizes performance for a single future time period. The DynaPorte methodology could have been embedded within a multiple future-period setting. This is not done because forecasting investment performance, or the factors that influence performance, more than 3 months forward will never be successful for the same reason that forecasting the weather is not successful more than 3 days forward. The persistence of the causative factors is simply too chaotic. Forecasting next year's average dividend yield is just as difficult as forecasting next year's total rainfall amount. An empirical justification for recommending the use of a single-period forecast is included in Chapter 9.

The investments suitable for optimization under the Dyna-Porte principles are not limited to just stocks, bonds, and interest rates. Any investment that is controlled by a set of causative factors and that has regularly monitored performance is suitable for investigation. This would include mutual funds, traditional money managers, real estate, certain classes of hedge funds, and commodity trading advisors. It would probably exclude venture capital investments and private equity since these asset classes are not marked-to-market and do not possess regularly measured rates of return.

DynaPorte does not use variance or standard deviation as the portfolio risk measure. The reason for this is a practical one. Most investors simply do not think about investment risk in terms of the volatility of performance. They certainly do not care about the volatility of positive-return months. They are much more interested in the size and frequency of the losing months. Furthermore, standard deviation alone cannot address the effect of skewness in performance returns found in so many investments. For these reasons mean absolute deviation below a target return is utilized as the measure of portfolio risk. Minimizing mean absolute deviation reduces both the size and the frequency of losing months. For a discussion of this risk measure including a comparison against the use of standard deviation, the reader is directed to Chapter 12.

This book is intended for use by both individual and institutional investors. For investors who study the factors affecting the markets detailed in Chapters 3 to 6, there will be ample reward for understanding which factors seem to control these markets and which other factors do nothing more than cause confusion. For investors, especially institutional investors willing to study the DynaPorte methodology, there is a further reward—a relatively simple quantitative procedure to calculate changing allocations as a function of fundamental macroeconomic factors. The financial industries seen benefiting from this book include:

Brokerage firms that must regularly update recommended holdings of stocks, bonds, and Treasury bills

Balanced money managers who shift allocations among several classes of stocks and bonds when conditions indicate it is prudent to do so

Mixed mutual funds that dynamically change allocations to stocks and bonds

Hedge fund managers who vary the amounts they invest in traditional and alternative investments

Pension plans, foundations, and endowments seeking to avoid large capital losses during market conditions that are unfavorable to traditional investments

All these financial institutions have something to gain by the patient application of the principles and procedures detailed in this book. The basic benefit from such application is to shift the investment odds in your favor. No guarantee is made or implied that the use of these techniques will result in positive portfolio returns in every single future month. The goal is to decrease the impact that any potential losing months might have on long-term portfolio growth.

Many of the ideas to achieve this goal were developed over the last half century by a host of finance academics and investment professionals. Homage should be paid to these giants of the financial research world whose shoulders I have stood on to complete this volume. This includes all those who have contributed to modern portfolio theory, the capital asset pricing model, arbitrage pricing theory, and multiperiod portfolio theory. The references cited throughout the book represent the thoughts and efforts of hundreds of researchers. I apologize in advance for not being able to include the entirety of their insights and conclusions. I have simply referenced or included portions of their efforts as background for reaching just a little further. For their enterprise in carrying modern portfolio theory and extensions to this point, I offer collective gratitude from myself and every reader of this book.

Finally, to the readers of what follows, I advise you not to be afraid of being painted with the brushes labeled *dynamic asset allocator* or *market timer.* These are not titles to fear. Either you believe that markets move because certain causative factors make them move, or you don't. If you do not believe this, you will suffer whatever performance your buy-and-hold portfolio metes out. If you do believe in such dynamic causes, then you have a choice of reacting to changes in these underlying factors or not reacting. If you are a believer and you react to the macroeconomic environment rationally, then you have some chance of confidently controlling your own investment future instead of passively being the subject of everyone else's future.

CHAPTER 1

Static Portfolio Theory

> There is always something to upset the most careful of
> human calculations.
>
> *Ihara Saikaku*
> *The Japanese Family Storehouse (c. 1670)*

Some would claim that the investment world is controlled by two
schools of thought. The first is a discretionary school that holds that
investing is best practiced by those with long experience in dealing
with marketplaces and investment instruments using their
intuitive skills to resolve problems. Decisions concerning the
selection of instruments and asset allocation are made based on
personal experience dealing with problems and opportunities in
the past. The reasons for making decisions are derived from having
seen similar situations before. Personal insight plays a large part in
the process. Once a situation is identified and properly evaluated, a
prudent but subjective course of action is implemented. The key
assumption of the discretionary school is that each problem
requires fresh thinking, resulting in a commitment to a possibly
new evaluation process that best deals with the problem.

The second school is the quantitative school that holds that
most problems are subject to rigorous analytical evaluation. This
school believes in the use of tools such as formulas, mathematical
models, simulation techniques, and, especially, optimization
processes to discover best solutions. There is a strong belief that a
problem should be expressible in a mathematical form based on
assumptions, parameters, input variables, and output variables.
Assuming a model is available, all that is required is to collect the

1

right input data and select any user-defined parameters, and the model will produce a workable answer. The key assumption of the quantitative school is that most repetitive problems can be resolved with a mathematical tool, either a new one or an existing one. Once the tool exists, if a string of similar situations meets the assumptions of the tool, then the tool can be applied over and over.

There is obviously a place for both schools in the investment world. Surely, there are many situations for which fresh thinking is required. This is certainly true for problems that have never been encountered before. And it is also true for problems not meeting all the assumptions of an existing model. Conversely, there must be many situations for which the assumptions of an existing model match a problem at hand. If a model fits a situation, then it would seem prudent to at least evaluate the model. This must be especially true for recurring problems with a history of having an established model applied to them.

Modern portfolio theory (MPT) is one of those established quantitative techniques. Specifically, the Markowitz mean-variance model has an established record of being applied to the asset allocation process. For 50 years, it has offered valuable insights and tractable solutions to the single-period asset allocation problem.

This book means to go beyond the Markowitz model and other static asset allocation models to allow for practical asset allocation in a fundamental, dynamic framework. This new framework, called DynaPorte, is fundamental because it employs macroeconomic and market-related factors to determine their impact on changing asset allocations. DynaPorte's structure is considered dynamic because the model allows an indefinite number of discrete historical time periods to be used to optimize the model fit. Once a model is established, an additional indefinite number of future time periods can be used for producing out-of-sample forecasts.

In order to set the DynaPorte methodology in context, it is worthwhile to review the status of modern portfolio theory for static models. The status of current approaches to dynamic portfolio models will be covered in Chapter 9 on multiperiod portfolio theory.

THE MARKOWITZ MEAN-VARIANCE MODEL

Before modern portfolio theory, the classical equity investment tool was the dividend discount model as typified by John Burr Williams (1938). This is a one-dimensional tool that only considers the expected return of an investment. There is no structure for dealing with risk. Carried to its logical conclusion, the dividend discount model could lead an investor to place all capital in the single equity with the largest string of expected dividends. If we were certain about the future performance of investments, this would be a correct solution. Since we cannot be certain about future performance, this one-dimensional approach is a formula for financial disaster.

The inauguration of modern portfolio theory came with the insight of Harry Markowitz (1991, 1993) that an investor should not simply seek the single highest-performing investment. An investor should create a portfolio of multiple investments. Each investment can be viewed as having a return that cannot be known with certainty. The return is a random variable with an expected value and an associated level of uncertainty or risk. Markowitz showed how to calculate the return and risk of any composite portfolio in terms of the individual investment return values, the risk values, and the asset allocation weights given to the investments. His final insight was that there is a way to determine optimal asset allocation weights in order to target some desirable portfolio performance characteristic. The investor has a choice. The portfolio return can be maximized at an acceptable level of risk, or the portfolio risk can be minimized at an acceptable level of return. Both options lead to the same mathematical process. If maximizing return and minimizing risk are considered co-objectives, only one at a time can be optimized. The other must be taken as an acceptable constraint. Both cannot be optimized simultaneously.

In his earliest work, Markowitz adopted the use of standard deviation as the measure of risk to be used. He recognized that other measures of risk such as semideviation were possible. Given the computing techniques available at the time, standard deviation was simply a practical choice as a risk measure.

The mean-variance portfolio optimization problem can be formulated in mathematical terms, assuming that there are n investments available:

For each investment i,

r_i = expected return of investment i
s_i = expected standard deviation of investment i
s_{ij} = expected covariance between investment i and investment j

For every portfolio,

x_i = portfolio allocation given to investment i
$xmin_i$ = minimum allocation allowed to investment i
$xmax_i$ = maximum allocation allowed to investment i
R_p = resulting portfolio return
S_p^2 = resulting portfolio risk expressed as variance

For every possible portfolio rate of return R_p, there is an optimal set of investment allocations x_i that will minimize the portfolio variance S_p^2. This is a mathematical programming problem that can be expressed as:

Find x_i such that

$$\sum_{i=1}^{n} x_i\, r_i = R_p \qquad (1\text{--}1)$$

$$\sum_{i=1}^{n} x_i = 1 \qquad (1\text{--}2)$$

And where, for each investment i:

$$0 \le x\min_i \le x_i \le x\max_i \qquad (1\text{--}3)$$

which minimizes the portfolio variance:

$$S_p^2 = \sum_{i=1}^{n} (x_i\, s_i)^2 + \sum_{i=1}^{n}\sum_{j=1}^{n} x_i x_j\, s_{ij} \qquad \text{for } i \ne j \qquad (1\text{--}4)$$

The solution to this mathematical programming problem requires quadratic programming techniques because there are second-order terms in (1–4), which is termed the objective function. Equations

(1–1) to (1–3) are treated as constraints that must be satisfied when minimizing the objective function. The objective function is just the square of the portfolio standard deviation. This choice of objective function indicates that the user wishes to minimize the square of the volatility of the portfolio returns. This applies equally to volatility above the average and below the average return.

The values of the investment expected returns r_i, the investment standard deviations s_i, and the investment covariances s_{ij} are all treated as inputs to the problem, having known values. The value of the target portfolio return R_p and upper and lower bounds on the allocations, $x\text{max}_i$ and $x\text{min}_i$, are treated as parameters to be selected by the user. The values of the allocations x_i are treated as unknowns to be solved for by the optimization process.

The beauty of the Markowitz model is that it establishes a clear quantitative investment objective. It is a formal procedure that will always give the same solution when presented with the same inputs and user parameter selections. Unless the inputs are changed or the model formulation is altered, the model itself is not subject to intuition or emotional reaction to current market conditions.

That being said, it is evident that the Markowitz model is a two-step process. Obtaining the inputs to the model is step 1. Solving equations (1–1) to (1–4) based on these inputs is step 2. Obtaining the inputs can be treated as a separate problem with its own set of difficulties. The Markowitz model can be viewed as a substitution of one problem for another. The original problem has the optimal allocations as unknowns. Given a set of n investments, we want to know what the allocations should be in order to make us comfortable with the expected portfolio risk. The best set of asset allocation values is not intuitively obvious. The Markowitz approach trades the set of asset allocation unknowns for another set of unknowns involving the expected future performance of each investment. The hope is that either these expected performance measures have intuitively obvious values, or there is some practical way to determine them.

Besides trading a seemingly complex problem for a less difficult problem, there are other advantages to using the Markowitz model. The model provides a formal structure in which the inputs can be individually evaluated. Sensitivity studies can be conducted by changing one input at a time and inspecting the change in the optimal solution. This can provide some insight about the effect of uncertainty in the inputs. Additionally, as time goes by, the values of the inputs are bound to change. The model makes it easy to adapt to the changing values of these inputs to obtain new solutions.

The Markowitz model is also capable of being adapted to other useful assumptions and constraints. Any linear combination of allocations can easily be treated as an additional constraint. If three of the investments considered come from the same investment class, such as technology stocks, then the sum of these three allocations can be controlled to have its own set of allocation bounds. For example, the sum of the technology stocks can be controlled to stay between 5 and 20 percent of the portfolio and never be allowed to range outside these bounds. Other constraints and model revisions allow for short selling, portfolio leverage, and consideration of risk measures other than standard deviation. The Markowitz model proves to be a useful formulation for including other practical concepts. For examples of the implementation of the mean-variance model under a range of additional constraints, see Pogue (1970) and Perold (1984).

The fact that there are mathematical procedures available that provide easy computerized solutions to the Markowitz model adds to its appeal. Except in certain degenerative cases, solutions are always attainable.

BASIC ASSUMPTIONS OF THE MARKOWITZ MEAN-VARIANCE MODEL

Every quantitative model is conditioned on a set of logical and structural assumptions. These assumptions have to do with the nature of the variables in the model or relationships among the variables employed. It is worth reviewing these assumptions because it is the very nature of the assumptions that leads us to go beyond the Markowitz formulation.

Variance as an Objective Function

The most basic assumption of the Markowitz model is the choice of the objective function. Variance or standard deviation is not the only measure of risk that could have been selected. Basically, it is chosen because it is a reasonable measure of risk and it has one attractive property. That property is we know how to calculate the portfolio variance from the individual investment variances and covariances. Not all risk measures have this simple property. It can be shown that variance is a suitable measure of risk if the individual investment returns are normally distributed or if the investor has a quadratic risk tolerance. Quadratic risk tolerance results if the investor always prefers less standard deviation to more without considering other return distribution characteristics.

Methods for Forming Expectations

The next assumption holds that there is a valid method for forming the investment expectations for returns, variances, and covariances. Four methodologies have been proposed for forming these expectations. The most common method is to calculate the three statistics from historical monthly or quarterly returns. The second method is to seek the judgment of one or more persons about what the future values of the statistics will be. A third method employed is the scenario method. In a scenario approach, past times in history are found having macroeconomic conditions similar to current conditions. Then the average performance of the investments is evaluated for all those instances when the same conditions were previously true. In a sense, this is a type of simulation methodology. A fourth, and more complex, approach is to develop a macroeconomic model of the factors that control the performance of each of the investments. A great deal of research has been done in this fourth area with regard to investment return means. For more detail, see Chapters 3, 4, and 5 on factors influencing stock returns, bond returns, and interest rates. Forecasting variances and covariances is another matter requiring special procedures. For an example of a conditional covariance matrix that is time-varying, see Flavin and Wickens (2001).

Special care must be taken when forecasting the covariances. Whatever method is used to determine the covariance matrix, the resulting matrix must be positive definite. This means that for every nonzero vector x and square matrix A, the matrix equation

$$x^T A x > 0 \qquad (1-5)$$

must be satisfied for the matrix A to be positive definite. For covariance matrices this means that the matrix must be symmetric and that the variance of the portfolio cannot be negative. It also implies that the covariance matrix can be inverted in order to solve for the asset allocation values. If the covariance matrix is ill-conditioned, then the Markowitz formulation will likely fail to have a solution. Covariance matrices formed by calculating variances and covariances from historical time series of returns are always positive definite. But covariance matrices with independent estimations of individual elements may be ill-conditioned.

Linear Constraints

Only linear constraints are allowed. While the objective function has quadratic terms, all of the constraint equations must be linear in order to use the Markowitz approach. Problems involving nonlinear constraints could possibly be solved using generalized mathematical programming, but there may be no guarantee of finding a global optimum solution.

Single Time Period

The portfolio optimization involves a single time period for which the expected returns and covariance matrix are defined. In its original formulation, the Markowitz model is only capable of calculating the optimal allocations for one time period. Furthermore, because the Markowitz model is defined for a single time period, there is no reason to explicitly deal with transaction costs, as this consideration only applies in a multiperiod setting.

Investment Availability

The Markowitz model also assumes that the investments evaluated by the model are actually available for purchase and may be obtained in any fractional amount. For many investment instruments this is not precisely true. One cannot easily buy a fraction of a share of stock. For portfolios of sufficient size involving most common investments, the practical effect of violating this assumption can be ignored. For investments like physical real estate, the large unit size can be a problem. Buying a fraction of a land parcel or a fraction of a house is not always feasible. Integer programming techniques are required to handle these types of size constraints in order to ensure holding integer units of the underlying investments.

Returns Independent of Allocation Level

An assumption of the Markowitz model frequently ignored is that the investment return is independent of the calculated asset allocation for that investment. If there is a limited amount of the asset available, supply and demand for the asset may require a nonlinear relationship between the price paid and the level of the desired asset allocation. This is likely to affect the rate of return itself. For example, acquiring a large percentage of a closely held company may not result in the same rate of return as acquiring a small percentage.

Despite any objection to these assumptions, the Markowitz model is still a powerful and effective tool under a wide range of real-world conditions. Its simplicity, elegance, and ease of implementation make it a very attractive tool.

PERCEIVED DIFFICULTIES WITH THE MEAN-VARIANCE MODEL

No matter how good a tool is, someone is bound to object to one of its design constraints and wish for an improved tool. Several features of the original mean-variance formulation have been questioned, leading to other related approaches. Some of these features are worth evaluating.

The Curse of Dimensionality

For a portfolio with n investments, the number of independent elements required for the Markowitz mean-variance formulation including means, variances, and the covariance matrix is $(n)(n + 3)/2$. For 3 investments this is a trivial number of 9 statistical values. For 10 investments the number jumps to 65 items. For 100 investments the number of required values expands to 5150 values. If the covariances were independently modeled, this would quickly become an unworkable approach. On the other hand, calculating many covariance terms from historical time series of returns is an easy proposition on a computer. It is only when the number of investments approaches 500 or more that the computation time and storage requirements begin to present problems for computerized implementations. For 500 investments, the number of calculated statistical values becomes 125,750.

Skewness and Kurtosis

The Markowitz model assumes that the portfolio risk is only dependent on the mean return and the variance, the second moment about the mean. Third and higher moments are ignored. It is especially skewness, the third moment about the mean, that has caused some concern. If the assumption that investment returns come from a normal distribution is satisfied, then the skewness value is zero and there is no issue. If the returns are not normally distributed and the investor has a non-quadratic risk preference, then the Markowitz formulation is not sufficient. Skewness, especially negative skewness, in the return distribution would concern many investors. The mean-variance model could give an unduly large allocation to an investment with a large negative skewness, presenting the portfolio with losses larger than expected. Markowitz (1991, 1993) recognizes this potential problem and suggests the use of semivariance as a solution. Semivariance deals with the lower partial second moment about the mean. A methodology termed downside risk deals with the lower partial second moment below a target return value. For example, only monthly returns below zero might be considered harmful and all returns above zero treated as benign. A body of work has developed around the use of semivariance and downside risk. A discussion of the desirability of using downside risk is contained in Balzer (1994). For an implementation of a mean-semivariance optimization model, see Markowitz's own approach in Markowitz, Todd, Xu, and Yamane (1993). Another related methodology is the mean absolute deviation portfolio optimization model described in Konno and Yamazaki (1991), as updated by Feinstein and Thapa (1993).

It is clear that the consideration of semivariance is important whenever there is significant skewness in the underlying investments. This is particularly acute when derivatives instruments are used. Option, hedge fund, and futures trader returns frequently involve highly skewed distributions.

In order to justify the need for semivariance portfolio optimization, we need to have a method to estimate whether an investment is not normally distributed. One way to establish nonnormality is to calculate estimates of skewness and kurtosis based on sample data. Skewness indicates whether one tail is stretched longer than the other. Kurtosis indicates whether the tails are very fat or very thin. We can conduct tests on samples for skewness and kurtosis to determine if they are significantly different from the values associated with a normal distribution. The following statistical definitions apply:

x_t = return for the investment in month t
n = number of months in the sample
s = sample standard deviation of the investment
$\bar{x}$ = average of the n monthly values of x_t
$\bar{x}^2$ = average of the squares of the n monthly values of x_t
$\bar{x}^3$ = average of the third powers of the n monthly values of x_t
$\bar{x}^4$ = average of the fourth powers of the n monthly values of x_t

Using these statistics, a test can be conducted on the skewness of a sample distribution to estimate if the sample could have come from a normal distribution. The required measures are shown in equations (1–6) to (1–8).

$$\text{Skewness} = \frac{n^2[\bar{x}^3 - 3\bar{x}^2\bar{x} + 2(\bar{x})^3]}{(n-1)(n-2)} \quad (1\text{-}6)$$

$$\text{Coefficient of skewness} = k_3 = \frac{\text{skewness}}{s^3} \quad (1\text{-}7)$$

$$\text{Standard error of coefficient of skewness} \approx \left(\frac{6}{n}\right)^{1/2} \quad (1\text{-}8)$$

The coefficient of skewness of a normal distribution is zero. A t-test to determine if the coefficient of skewness for a sample distribution is not zero is performed by dividing the sample coefficient of skewness by the standard error of the coefficient of skewness. If the absolute value of this ratio is larger than *Student's* t-statistic, typically 1.96 for large values of n, then the coefficient of skewness is not zero at a 95 percent confidence level, and the underlying distribution is judged not to be normal.

Similarly, it is possible to test the coefficient of kurtosis of a sample distribution to see if it is different from the value expected for a normal distribution. The kurtosis test, similar to the one for skewness, is performed using the equations shown in (1–9) to (1–11).

$$\text{Kurtosis} = \frac{n^2(n+1)[\bar{x}^4 - 4\bar{x}^3\bar{x} + 6\bar{x}^2(\bar{x})^2 - 3(\bar{x})^4]}{(n-1)(n-2)(n-3)} \quad (1\text{-}9)$$

$$\text{Adjusted coefficient of kurtosis} = k_4 = \left(\frac{\text{kurtosis}}{s^4}\right) - 3 \quad (1\text{-}10)$$

$$\text{Standard error of coefficient of kurtosis} \approx \left(\frac{24}{n}\right)^{1/2} \quad (1\text{-}11)$$

The adjusted coefficient of kurtosis of a normal distribution is zero. As before, a t-test to determine if the adjusted coefficient of kurtosis for a sample distribution is not zero is performed by dividing the sample adjusted coefficient of kurtosis by the standard error of the coefficient of kurtosis. If the absolute value of this ratio is larger than 1.96 for large values of n, then the adjusted coefficient of kurtosis is not zero at 95 percent confidence level.

There is a combined test called the Jarque-Bera test that evaluates whether the sample skewness and kurtosis values indicate together whether the sample is drawn from a normal distribution. The Jarque-Bera statistic, C, is distributed as a χ^2 distribution with two degrees of freedom.

$$C = \left(\frac{nk_3^2}{6}\right) + \left(\frac{nk_4^2}{24}\right) \qquad (1\text{--}12)$$

If the value of C is greater than 5.99, then the sample distribution is rejected as being normal at the 95 percent confidence level; or if C is greater than 9.21, then the sample distribution is rejected at the 99 percent confidence level.

Equations (1–6) to (1–12) give us the tools to test whether historical investment returns are normally distributed. Let us apply them to five different types of investments to see if their returns are normally distributed. The investments considered are long U.S. government bonds, the S&P 500 total return stock index, the NASDAQ total return stock index, the First Eagle hedge fund operated by Arnhold and Bleichroeder, and the Witter and Lester Commodity Trading Advisor (CTA) stock index program. The last two investments are included to test whether examples of derivatives products are normally distributed. Table 1–1 provides all the statistical measures required to test whether each of the investment historical performance samples could have come from a normal distribution. Each investment is evaluated using monthly data from October 1982 to June 2002.

All the investments have significant nonzero skewness except government bonds. All have significant nonzero kurtosis. All have significantly nonnormal distributions according to the χ^2 test at 95 percent confidence. The two stock indices and the hedge fund have strong negative skewness. The CTA program has strong positive skewness. While the government bonds did not exhibit significant skewness, extending the government bonds back to 1960 (not shown) does obtain strong positive skewness for this longer interval. Most of this evidence points to the likelihood of many types of investments having returns that are not normally distributed. Thus, it would seem that the normal distribution assumption of the mean-variance model would be violated for this particular selection of investments. It is likely that this assumption would also be violated for many other investments as well.

T A B L E 1-1

Tests if Investment Monthly Returns Are Normally Distributed

	Long Govt. Bonds	S&P 500 Index	NASDAQ Index	First Eagle Hedge Fund	Witter & Lester CTA
Average return	0.9156	1.2316	1.1270	1.3837	3.4181
Standard deviation	2.7635	4.4271	6.9539	4.6634	14.0283
Variance	7.6372	19.5989	48.3565	21.7469	196.7941
Skewness	5.23	−63.83	−196.31	−182.87	7684.13
k_3	0.2476	−0.7357	−0.5838	−1.8032	2.7834
k_3 standard error	0.1591	0.1591	0.1591	0.1591	0.1591
$t_{skewness} > ?\,2$	1.56	−4.62	−3.67	−11.33	17.49
Kurtosis	213.91	2291.92	11860.57	7347.34	670837.16
k_4	0.6675	2.9667	2.0722	12.5359	14.3218
k_4 standard error	0.3182	0.3182	0.3182	0.3182	0.3182
$t_{kurtosis} > ?\,2$	2.10	9.32	6.51	39.39	45.01
$C > ?\,5.99$	6.82	108.29	55.87	1680.28	2331.52

Standard Deviation as a Measure of Risk

Using the volatility of the investment returns as a measure of risk is subject to a number of criticisms. For example, the magnitude of the standard deviation is not very intuitive as a measure of risk. Is a 10 percent annualized standard deviation a good number or a bad number on an absolute scale? Is the utility of a 5 percent standard deviation twice as good as a 10 percent standard deviation?

Two investments with the same set of monthly returns have the same standard deviation. If one of them has all of its investment returns reordered so that the negative returns are in a sequence, would an investor see a difference between these two investments? The means of the two investments are the same, and the standard deviations are the same. Both arrive at the same terminal wealth. One just has its losses all in sequence. Only measures evaluating data sequence such as serial correlation or maximum drawdown (peak-to-valley loss) could distinguish between these two investments. Standard deviation and all other moments about the mean will not help resolve this issue.

But the biggest objection to the use of standard deviation comes from the fact that it considers volatility above the mean just as harmful as volatility below the mean. Most investors would have a much stronger reaction to excursions below the mean than above.

Other measures of risk which circumvent some of these difficulties must be sought. The most common class of risk measures that deals with both stretched tails and fat tails in investment return distributions involves lower partial moments below a selected target return. For a discussion concerning the types of lower partial moments that would apply, see Harlow (1991) and Balzer (1994).

In the end, if an investor is always willing to accept standard deviation as a measure of risk, the Markowitz mean-variance model produces the optimum asset allocations to achieve this goal. The question is whether the standard deviation should be the acceptable measure of risk. For example, in the case of skewed distributions, it would not seem prudent for an investor to settle for minimizing standard deviation as a goal. In this case, a different objective function is required to react to the shape of the skew.

Formation of Expectations

Many investors assume that the historical averages of the individual investments in a portfolio are the best estimators of future performance. There are two cases in which the past averages may produce poor expectations of the future. In the first case, the past performance sample may not be representative of the future population distribution. This could happen if the return-generation process changes. Such a change could occur if there is a fundamental change in the structure of the market or if there is a governmental regulatory change. Examples of such changes include shifts in population demographics affecting the demand for specific instruments or dramatic changes in investment tax laws affecting the willingness to hold certain instruments.

The second case in which past performance may give a poor indication of the future performance distribution occurs when historical samples have insufficient size. If the sample is too small, the random draw obtained could produce statistics very far from the true population measures. Stein (1955) shows that a sample average is not an admissible estimator of the true mean of a multivariate normal distribution. The simple average is not admissible because it can be demonstrated that other methods produce better estimates when there is a quadratic portfolio objective. Jobson and Korkie (1981) show that this problem directly applies to the Markowitz model if the historical sample size is fewer than 200 months. If something is not done about this problem, the mean-variance model could unduly overweight investments with randomly high mean return estimates and do the opposite for randomly low estimates.

When the sample size is too small, a number of suggested solutions exist for producing better estimates of the true population mean. In this case of small sample size, when there are a number of similar investments in the portfolio, James and Stein (1961) show that a better estimate of the individual stock expected return is the *shrinkage estimator,* which moves the sample average in the direction of the *pooled average* of all stock returns. Using the shrinkage estimator for each investment produces a more accurate portfolio mean than attempting to use the individual means formed from a too small sample.

$\hat{w}$ = shrinkage factor
$\underline{Y}$ = vector of all sample average returns
Y_0 = pooled average return of all investments
$\underline{1}$ = unit vector
N = number of investments in the portfolio
T = number of time periods in the sample
Σ = sample covariance matrix among the investments

Then the James-Stein estimator of the investment mean is

$$\mu_{JS}(\underline{Y}) = (1 - \hat{w})\underline{Y} + \hat{w}\,Y_0\underline{1} \qquad (1\text{--}13)$$

where the shrinkage factor is estimated as

$$\hat{w} = \min\left(1, \frac{(N-2)}{T(\underline{Y} - Y_0\underline{1})'\,\Sigma^{-1}\,(\underline{Y} - Y_0\underline{1})}\right) \qquad (1\text{--}14)$$

When the number of time periods is large, the division by T in (1–14) makes the shrinkage coefficient $\hat{w}$ approach zero. When T is small, the value of $\hat{w}$ will have a significant impact on the estimated investment mean.

In a similar approach, Jorion (1986) develops Bayesian estimates of the mean returns. The same variables apply as in the James-Stein approach with the following adjustments:

$\underline{x}' = \underline{1}'\Sigma^{-1}/(\underline{1}'\Sigma^{-1}\underline{1})$
  = weights of the minimum variance portfolio
Y_0 = grand mean at the minimum variance portfolio
λ = scale factor, which is a measure of the tightness of the prior

Then the Bayes-Stein estimator of the investment mean is still

$$\mu_{BS}(\underline{Y}) = (1 - \hat{w})\underline{Y} + \hat{w}\,Y_0\underline{1} \qquad (1\text{--}15)$$

where the shrinkage factor is determined as

$$\hat{w} = \frac{\lambda}{(T + \lambda)} \qquad (1\text{-}16)$$

and the estimate of the investment covariance matrix is

$$V[\underline{r}] = \Sigma\left(1 + \frac{1}{(T + \lambda)}\right) + \left(\frac{\lambda \underline{1}\,\underline{1}'}{T(T + 1 + \lambda)\,(\underline{1}'\Sigma^{-1}\underline{1})}\right) \qquad (1\text{-}17)$$

Using this estimator, the revised portfolio risk is a multiple of the sample portfolio risk. Kempf, Kreuzberg, and Memmel (2002) take another approach and assume that the estimation risk is a second independent source of risk that needs to be added to the portfolio risk. This risk has an impact on the level of the expected returns as well as on the covariance matrix.

For another method of dealing with the small sample problem, see ter Horst, de Roon, and Werker (2002), who employ a pseudo risk aversion in place of the actual risk aversion in order to account for the estimation risk.

Loss of the Time Aspect of Investment Performance

The final problem to be noted with the mean-variance model is the very fact that the model works with statistical moments of the distributions of historical performance data. The very nature of the time aspect of the performance history is lost. When the month-by-month performance history for multiple investments is reduced to statistics such as averages, standard deviations, and a covariance matrix, nuances of the data not captured by these statistics are lost. As already mentioned, these nuances can include such items as skewness, kurtosis, and serial correlation of losses. But any other time aspect of the data is also lost. Examples of other time-related measures of history include runs of losses or gains, time shifts of distribution shapes, and downside versus upside correlations. If investors care about such time-related performance measures, portfolio optimization methods that could deal with these measures might be worth the effort to develop.

OTHER STATIC ASSET ALLOCATION APPROACHES

A number of other portfolio optimization approaches within a single-period framework have been defined to deal with some of the objections to the Markowitz mean-variance approach. Some of these approaches involve the same structural model form as that of the Markowitz model but contain a replacement for the objective function. Other formulations involve a redefinition of the structural form of the model as well.

The Single-Index Model

If the number of investments is n, the total number of inputs required for the Markowitz mean-variance model is $n(n+3)/2$. When considering portfolios containing a large number of investments, forecasting, calculating, and storing this many inputs becomes burdensome. To alleviate this burden of dimensionality, Sharpe (1963) develops a single-index model that only requires $3n+2$ inputs.

Following Cohen and Pogue (1967), the single-index model assumes that the future performance of each investment in the portfolio can be represented by a linear relationship to a common index.

$$R_{it} = \alpha_i + \beta_i I_t + \varepsilon_{it} \qquad (1\text{--}18)$$

where for each investment i out of a total of n investments:

R_{it} = return of investment i at time t

I_t = return of an investment index at time t

α_i = constant coefficient of investment i relative to index I

β_i = slope of investment i relative to index I

ε_{it} = residual error of the linear equation fit of investment i at time t

V_i = variance of the error of the linear equation fit of investment i

The future performance of the index is modeled by its average value and a random component.

$$I_t = \alpha_{n+1} + \varepsilon_{n+1,t} \tag{1-19}$$

where:

α_{n+1} = constant term in the performance model for index I
$\varepsilon_{n+1,t}$ = residual error of the performance model fit of index I at time t
V_{n+1} = variance of index I

The expected value of the index is just

$$E(I_t) = \alpha_{n+1} \tag{1-20}$$

And the variance of the index is

$$E(\varepsilon_{n+1,t}^2) = V_{n+1} \tag{1-21}$$

For the individual investments the expected value of the investment return expressed in terms of the performance of the index is

$$E(R_{it}) = \alpha_i + \beta_i \, E(I_t) = \alpha_i + \beta_i \, \alpha_{n+1} \tag{1-22}$$

And the variance of the investment i is

$$E(\varepsilon_{it}^2) = V_i \tag{1-23}$$

Equations (1–18) to (1–23) describe the performance of the original n investments in terms of the index I. For n investments, the number of statistics to be estimated has been reduced to just α_{n+1}, β_n, and V_{n+1}. The covariance between investment i and investment j has been eliminated. Any relationship between investment i and investment j has been replaced by the individual relationships that the investments have with the index. This reduced set of statistics is the input to a revised asset allocation optimization model.

Sharpe (1963) shows that the single-index model can be viewed as investing in a set of n basic securities and investing in an $n + 1^{st}$ investment, the index. The allocation to the index is defined to be the weighted average responsiveness of the portfolio return to the level of the market index I. This allocation to the $n + 1^{st}$ index investment is just

$$x_{n+1} = \sum_{i=1}^{n} x_i \beta_i \tag{1-24}$$

The optimal asset allocations are the $n + 1$ values of the x_i that satisfy equation (1–24) plus the following constraint on the portfolio return R_p.

$$\text{Portfolio expected return} = E(R_p) = \sum_{i=1}^{n+1} x_i \alpha_i \tag{1-25}$$

that minimize the portfolio variance

$$\text{Portfolio variance} = \text{variance } (R_p) = \sum_{i=1}^{n+1} x_i^2 V_i \tag{1-26}$$

The single-index system of equations (1–24) to (1–26) is a quadratic programming problem, as is the original Markowitz mean-variance problem. But the single-index problem has fewer variables, resulting in faster solution times. Cohen and Pogue (1967) demonstrate that the solution to the single-index formulation obtains a mean-variance efficient frontier with very similar values to the original Markowitz formulation when the investments are strongly related to the market index I. They point out that the single-index approach would not work as well if the investments covered a wide range of asset classes, resulting in poor relationships with a single index.

The single-index model is typically used for portfolios consisting entirely of equities. The main advantage of the single-index model is that it can easily handle as many as 1000 investments in a portfolio. There are no other special advantages to this approach. It shares similar problems with the Markowitz mean-variance approach regarding skewness and difficulties in the formation of expectations.

The Downside-Risk Models

Semivariance is defined as the sum of squares of the performance deviations below the mean. Downside risk is defined as the sum of squares of the performance deviations below a target or benchmark value. Markowitz (1991, 1993) recognizes the potential of semivariance as a suitable risk measure for investment portfolios. There is a strong appeal to consider the lower partial moment about a central value, especially for skewed distributions. Markowitz, Todd, Xu, and Yamane (1993) show that the central value can be the distribution mean or an arbitrary benchmark value selected by the investor. They detail a critical line algorithm to calculate the optimal portfolio allocations for both types of lower partial moments.

Sortino and Price (1994) and Sortino and Forsey (1996) also describe a downside risk methodology designed to overcome the skewed distribution problem. Their approach starts by fitting a three-parameter asymmetric lognormal distribution to the tenth percentile, mean, and ninetieth percentile of the performance data. This procedure allows for both positively and negatively skewed distributions. A proprietary asset allocation methodology has been developed based on this asymmetric distribution approach.

In a groundbreaking study, Konno and Yamazaki (1991) propose a linear programming formulation to portfolio optimization using the mean absolute deviation about the mean as the objective function. This work was followed by a revised form of the same model in Feinstein and Thapa (1993). The revised model employs the following variables:

r_{jt} = return of investment j at time t
r_j = average return of investment j over all time
a_{jt} = difference between the return of investment j at time t and its long-term historical average
ρ = minimal rate of return required by an investor
M_0 = total asset size of the portfolio
u_j = the slack variable for t when the weighted sum of the a_{jt} is $\geq$ zero
w_t = slack variable for t when the weighted sum of the a_{jt} is $<$ zero
x_j = allocation to investment j

The mean absolute deviation optimization model for n investments is then:

Find x_j to minimize the objective function

$$\sum_{t=1}^{T}(v_t + w_t) \qquad (1\text{--}27)$$

subject to

$$a_{jt} = r_{jt} - r_j \qquad (1\text{--}28)$$

$$(v_t - w_t) = \sum_{j=1}^{n} a_{jt}\, x_j \qquad \text{for each time } t \qquad (1\text{--}29)$$

$$\sum_{j=1}^{n} r_j\, x_j \geq \rho M_0 \qquad (1\text{--}30)$$

$$\sum_{j=1}^{n} x_j = M_0 \qquad (1\text{--}31)$$

where

$$0 \leq x_j \leq u_j \qquad \text{for each investment } j \qquad (1\text{--}32)$$

and where

$$v_t \geq 0,\, w_t \geq 0 \qquad \text{for each time period } t \qquad (1\text{--}33)$$

For each time period t, either $v_t > 0$ or $w_t > 0$, depending on whether the return is above or below the mean. Both cannot have nonzero values at the same time. Both can equal zero when the return is at the mean. This model penalizes all deviations about the investment means, both positive and negative. It is a simple matter to convert this mean absolute deviation model to a mean semideviation model by removing the v_t term from the objective function (1–27). This will minimize the sum of the deviations below the investment means over all time periods.

Similarly, the model can be converted to a downside-risk model, using the value τ as the target return for every investment, where only those time periods with returns below τ are included in the objective function. To accomplish this, the value of τ is substituted for r_j in equation (1–28). This will minimize the sum of the deviations below the target τ over all time periods. The value of τ is commonly set to zero.

Konno and Yamazaki (1991) find that their mean absolute deviation model generates an efficient frontier quite similar to that of the Markowitz mean-variance model when optimizing three separate samples of 224 stocks from the Tokyo stock market. Their empirical investigations show that the two models produce very similar allocations in the underlying stocks. They prove mathematically that the two models should produce the same result if the performance histories are normally distributed. On the other hand, they show empirically that the Sharpe single-index model employing the same historical data produces significantly different efficient frontiers and asset allocations. The single-index model typically assigns nonzero weights to over 30 percent of the stocks. This is in contrast to the mean absolute deviation and mean-variance models, which only assign nonzero weights to less than 15 percent of the stocks. The single-index model also assigns a large number of small allocations under 1 percent. The disparity between the single-index model and the other two models is surprising given that the portfolio consists entirely of stocks from one market, for which one would expect a strong link of each stock to the market index.

The mean absolute deviation model has an advantage over the mean-variance model in terms of solution time for large problems. Furthermore, the downside-risk version of the mean absolute deviation model is capable of dealing with the impact of skewed distributions.

REVIEW

Static asset allocation models have become a workhorse of the investment industry for guiding investors in their selection of investments. If there has been any reservation in the use of these models, it has stemmed from the question of how to generate meaningful inputs. The expectations of future means, variances, and covariances are typically formed by observing their values over the last 5 to 20 years. This can give rise to two problems. The first has to do with historical samples being too small to form useful expectations. A second, and more subtle, problem has to do with establishing a procedure for updating expectations. If 20 years of monthly data were found to be sufficient to overcome the sample-size problem, what is the procedure for updating the expectations? A rolling average procedure that adds in one new month and drops off one old month as time goes by will hardly budge the expected values of the inputs. This procedure will not adapt quickly enough to changing market conditions.

Both these problems can be alleviated by the use of a procedure to form expectations of future performance or asset allocation characteristics as a time-varying function of causative state variables. The remainder of this book is devoted to procedures for forming such time-varying functions and then taking advantage of them in a portfolio optimization setting.

REFERENCES

Balzer, Leslie A. "Measuring Investment Risk: A Review." *Journal of Investing* (Fall 1994): 47–58.

Cohen, Kalman J., and Jerry A. Pogue. "An Empirical Evaluation of Alternative Investment Models." *Journal of Business* (April 1967): 166–193.

Feinstein, Charles D., and Mukund N. Thapa. "Notes: A Reformulation of a Mean-Absolute Deviation Portfolio Optimization Model." *Management Science* 39 (December 1993): 1552–1553.

Flavin, T. J., and M. R. Wickens. "Macroeconomic Influences on Optimal Asset Allocation." Working paper, National University of Ireland, Maynooth (March 2001).

Harlow, W. V. "Asset Allocation in a Downside-Risk Framework." *Financial Analysts Journal* (September/October 1991): 28–40.

James, W., and C. Stein. "Estimation with Quadratic Loss." *Proceedings of the Fourth Berkeley Symposium on Statistics and Probability.* Berkeley: University of California Press, 1961: 361–379.

Jobson, J. D., and Bob Korkie. "Putting Markowitz Theory to Work." *Journal of Portfolio Management* (Summer 1981): 70–74.

Jorion, Philippe. "Bayes-Stein Estimation for Portfolio Analysis." *Journal of Financial and Quantitative Analysis* 21, no. 3 (September 1986): 279–292.

Kempf, Alexander, Klaus Kreutzberg, and Christoph Memmel. "How to Incorporate Estimating Risk into Markowitz Optimization." *Operations Research Proceedings 2001,* edited by P. Chamoni, et al., Berlin, et al., 2002: 175–182.

Konno, Hiroshi, and Hiroaki Yamazaki. "Mean-Absolute Deviation Portfolio Optimization Model and Its Applications to Tokyo Stock Market." *Management Science* 37, no. 5 (May 1991): 519–531.

Markowitz, Harry M. *Portfolio Selection: Efficient Diversification of Investments*, 2d ed. Cambridge, Mass.: Basil Blackwell Publishers, 1991.

Markowitz, Harry, Peter Todd, Ganlin Xu, and Yuji Yamane. "Computation of Mean-Semivariance Efficient Sets by the Critical Line Algorithm." *Annals of Operations Research* 45 (1993): 307–317.

Perold, Andre F. "Large-Scale Portfolio Optimization." *Management Science* 30 (October 1984): 1143–1160.

Pogue, G. A. "An Extension of the Markowitz Portfolio Selection Model to Include Variable Transactions' Costs, Short Sales, Leverage Policies and Taxes." *Journal of Finance* 25, no. 5 (December 1970): 1005–1028.

Sharpe, William F. "A Simplified Model for Portfolio Analysis." *Management Science* 9, no. 2 (January 1963): 277–293.

Sortino, Frank A., and Lee N. Price. "Performance Measurement in a Downside Risk Framework." *Journal of Investing* 3, no. 3 (Fall 1994): 59–64.

Sortino, Frank A., and Hal J. Forsey. "On the Use and Misuse of Downside Risk." *Journal of Portfolio Management* (Winter 1996): 35–42.

Stein, C. "Inadmissibility of the Usual Estimator for the Mean of a Multivariate Normal Distribution." *Proceedings of the Third Berkeley Symposium on Probability and Statistics.* Berkeley: University of California Press, 1955: 197–206.

ter Horst, Jenke R., Frans A. de Roon, and Bas J. M. Werker. "Incorporating Estimation Risk in Portfolio Choice." Working paper, Department of Finance and CentER, Tilburg University, Netherlands (February 2002).

Williams, John Burr. *The Theory of Investment Value.* Cambridge, Mass.: Harvard University Press, 1938.

CHAPTER 2

Arbitrage Pricing Theory

> I am the only child of parents who weighed,
> measured, and priced everything; for whom
> what could not be weighed, measured, and
> priced had no existence.
>
> *Charles Dickens*
> *Little Dorrit (1857–1858)*

DESCRIPTION OF THE APT MODEL

In its simplest expression, the arbitrage pricing theory (APT) states that the return of a risky asset such as a stock is a linear function of a number of macroeconomic and financial factors. The values of the factors change over time. The value of the return then responds to the changing values of the factors. Without identifying the factors, Ross (1976) defines the following return-generating process as a linear factor model (LFM):

$$R_{it} = E_i + b_{i1}f_{1t} + b_{i2}f_{2t} + b_{i3}f_{3t} + \cdots + b_{in}f_{nt} + e_{it}$$

$$= E_i + \sum_{k=1}^{K} b_{ik}f_{kt} + e_{it} \qquad (2\text{--}1)$$

where:

There are $i = 1$ to n assets
R_{it} is a random variable representing the return on asset i at time t

E_i is the expected value over time of the return R_{it}

f_{kt} represents risk factor k with values at time t that influence the return R_{it}

f_{kt} are constructed so that they all have a zero expected return over time

f_{kt} are not required to be independent of each other

f_{kt} are not allowed to be predictable from their own past—no autocorrelation is allowed

f_{kt} must be unanticipated innovations

b_{ik} represents the sensitivity, or loadings, of investment i to changes in the factor f_{kt}

All the loading factors b_{ik} are unknown constants to be determined

e_{it} is an error term representing the portion of R_{it} that is not explained by the factors

The expected value of e_{it} is assumed to be zero, and e_{it} is independent of e_{jt} for all $i \neq j$

$R_{it}, f_{kt},$ and e_t are not required to be normally distributed or follow any other distribution

The number of assets n is much greater than the number of factors k

Each of the k factors is designed or transformed to have a zero mean. By defining the factors to have a zero mean, it is clear that when the factors all take values at their expected value, the influence of the factors on investment i becomes zero and the expected value of the return $R_{it} = E_i$. Note that the value of E_i is a constant over time. It is not the forecasted value of the return for investment i at time t. E_i is simply the mean return for investment i over the entire time interval for which data are available for R_{it}.

Determining the f_{kt} in such a way that they are true innovations can be a challenging problem. Most research uses a method of taking a first difference in a basic variable. Priestley (1996) evaluates three methods of forming these factors: first differences, autoregressive time series, and Kalman filters. He finds that Kalman filters provide the best results for creating factors used in the APT.

When Stephen Ross develops what he terms the arbitrage theory of capital asset pricing, it is clear that he considers it an alternative approach to the pricing of risky assets which had previously been idealized in the capital asset pricing model (CAPM). Because of the functional form of the APT, there are some who hold that this made the CAPM equivalent to the APT when a single factor is employed in the APT equal to the market index utilized by the CAPM.

Ross (1976) develops a second equation called a cross-sectional constraint which he terms the *arbitrage theory equivalent of the CAPM*. This equation defines E_i, the expected return of investment i, as a function of the risk-free interest rate and the values of the b_{ik}.

$$E_i = R_0 + b_{i1}P_1 + b_{i2}P_2 + b_{i3}P_3 + \cdots + b_{in}P_n = R_0 + \sum_{k=1}^{K} b_{ik}P_k \quad (2\text{-}2)$$

where:

R_0 = the risk-free interest rate
P_k = price per unit of risk, or factor risk premium, for the risk factor f_k
The P_k are not directly measurable, so they must be determined
The product $b_{ik}P_k$ is referred to as the risk premium for the risk factor f_k

Note that there is no error term in this equation.

The factor risk premium P_k can be interpreted as the excess return above the risk-free interest rate R_0 for each whole unit of risk from factor f_k for portfolios only containing the risk associated with factor f_k. Looking at it another way, P_k is the amount of additional excess return that justifies the added risk associated with each full unit of risk factor f_k. Note that it is assumed the P_k are constants across time and do not vary with each specific investment i. For each investment i evaluated using (2–2), the values of the P_k remain the same, and it is only the values of the b_{ik} which differ.

Roll and Ross (1980) provide a derivation of (2–2) based on an arbitrage portfolio approach. Consider an investor who holds a current portfolio of investments. The current portfolio can be viewed as a weighted sum of the included investments. Positive weights indicate long (purchased) investments. Negative weights indicate short (sold) investments. If the investor changes the weights in the portfolio without adding or removing any equity, the resulting new portfolio is termed an arbitrage portfolio if the portfolio return can be increased without taking on additional risk. It can be shown that such arbitrage opportunities do not exist whenever the investments all lie along a line.

Consider the example shown in Figure 2–1 involving investments 1, 2, and 3. Each investment i has an expected return E_i and a beta value of b_i. In this example, investments 1 and 3 could be sold to fund an additional purchase of investment 2, with the result of a higher portfolio return at the same level of risk. This arbitrage opportunity can only be avoided if investments 1, 2, and 3 all lie along the straight line represented by equation (2–2).

If the equation for E_i from (2–2) is substituted into (2–1), the result is

$$R_{it} = R_0 + \sum_{k=1}^{K} b_{ik}P_k + \sum_{k=1}^{K} b_{ik}f_{kt} + e_{it} \qquad (2\text{–}3)$$

where the values of R_{it}, R_0, and f_{kt} are all known and measurable, and the values of b_{kt} and P_k must be determined by a process that minimizes a function of the e_{it}.

If it were not for the quadratic term $b_{ik}P_k$, (2–3) would be a multiple linear regression equation that could be easily solved. Roll

F I G U R E   2-1

Arbitrage Opportunity Example

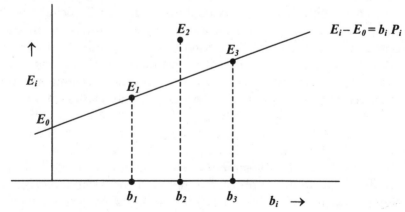

and Ross (1980) chose to solve equations (2–1) and (2–2) as a two-step process fully recognizing that this method presented some econometric difficulties. In the first step, the values of the E_i and the b_{ik} are determined using a factor analysis methodology. In the second step, the values of the P_k are determined using (2–2) and the estimates of the values of E_i and the b_{ik} determined in step 1.

FACTOR ANALYSIS APPROACH

Factor analysis is a statistical procedure that seeks to determine how many true factors there are when trying to relate the performance of a response variable, y, with many exogenous variables, x_k, through a linear relationship.

$$y = \alpha + \sum_{k=1}^{K} \beta_k x_k + e \qquad (2\text{–}4)$$

Factor analysis determines if there are a smaller number of independent exogenous variables, z_m, which are related to the x_k through the loading factors, δ_{mk}.

$$z_m = \sum_{k=1}^{K} \delta_{mk} x_k \qquad (2\text{–}5)$$

This approach is used to overcome the potential that could exist for multicollinearity among the x_k exogenous variables. That is, one or more of the exogenous variables could be linear combinations of some of the other variables. The names and meaning given to the individual z_m are arbitrary since they are linear combinations of the original exogenous variables. It is possible to determine the number of independent exogenous variables without actually identifying the specific z_m. Roll and Ross (1980) conduct empirical evaluations of 42 groups consisting of 30 stocks per group and determine that the apparent number of independent factors is five.

Subsequent research by others including Kryzanowski and To (1983) and Dhrymes, Friend, and Gultekin (1984) find that the number of independent factors is related to the size of the sample of the number of stocks. This is not surprising. As the number of stocks increases, the number of distinguishable industries within the data also increases. Each industry can have its own set of underlying fundamental factors. While the number of significant independent factors is found to increase as the number of stocks per group increases, the additional percentage of variation explained by more than five factors is marginal.

The use of factor analysis is just a mathematical expedient to determine the values of the b_{ik} when all the f_k are independent but unidentified. Factor analysis is also useful to estimate the true number of independent f_k to look for when trying to discover the fundamental factors in nature that could or should have an impact on the return of investment i.

Results from the use of factor analysis set the stage for the search for specific fundamental factors that should have an impact on the investment returns.

FUNDAMENTAL MACROECONOMIC FACTOR APPROACH

The open question of what the factors are that seem to have an impact on the stock market did not need to wait long for a suggested answer. Roll and Ross (1984) propose four factors that their research indicates were important: unanticipated inflation, changes in the expected level of industrial production, unanticipated shifts in the risk premium,* and unanticipated movements in the shape of the term structure of interest rates. Subsequently Chen, Roll, and Ross (1986) provide the analysis that lead them to employ these four factors. A detailed explanation of the rationale that suggests the use of these factors and factors considered by others to be employed in the return-generation process for the stock market is deferred until Chapter 3.

The significant point is that there is a methodological shift away from the use of factor analysis to determine the values of the unknown variables of equations (2–1) and (2–2). A more direct approach is taken up identifying and evaluating fundamental

---

*The use of the term *risk premium* here refers to the difference between a Baa bond portfolio and a long-term government bond portfolio and not to the $b_{ik}P_k$ risk premium used in (2–2).

economic and financial variables that should have an impact on the stock market.

Another noteworthy alteration to the APT is the definition of the factors in terms of *unanticipated changes* in value. This concept results from the idea that if the value of the factor had been previously anticipated, then the anticipation would have already caused an impact on the investment return. So only unanticipated changes in the factor cause unanticipated changes in the investment return.

PARAMETER ESTIMATION METHODOLOGIES

Chen, Roll, and Ross (1986) use a variation of the two-step process previously described. This procedure ignores any estimation errors contained in the b_{ik} resulting from step 1. This means that any statement of statistical significance of the P_k resulting from step 2 may be questionable for small samples.

What was required was a multivariate nonlinear regression model capable of solving (2–8). McElroy and Burmeister (1988) provide such an approach by applying a procedure called iterated nonlinear seemingly unrelated regression (ITNLSUR). The requirements for solving nonlinear regression problems using ITNLSUR techniques allow the investment return distributions to be nonnormal. Estimates of parameter values and tests on these estimates are robust even for nonnormal distributions of returns. For a set of factors slightly different from those of Chen, Roll, and Ross, they are able to explain 30 to 50 percent of individual stock variance as well as 24 percent of market variance.

TIME-VARYING RISK PREMIUMS

Investigators, including Connor and Korajczyk (1988) and Ferson and Harvey (1991), soon considered that the risk premiums might not be constant over time. For this to occur, from (2–2) either the b_{ik} or the P_k or both need to change with time in response to a set of exogenous variables. Generally, it has been assumed that if the risk premiums are not constant, then the source of variation is in the P_k. For example, the P_k could really be P_{kt} and be linear functions of a set of M zero-mean exogenous variables g_{kmt} such that

$$P_{kt} = P_k + \sum_{m=1}^{M} d_{km} g_{kmt} \qquad (2\text{--}6)$$

where the d_{km} are unknown constants to be determined, and g_{kmt} is a set of exogenous variables changing in time that influence P_{kt}. The expected value of the g_{kmt} are defined to be zero. For simplicity, the variables g_{kmt} do not need to include any of the original factors f_{kt}. This formulation allows the expected value of P_{kt} to be P_k.

Merton (1980), Cox, Ingersoll, and Ross (1985), and Ferson and Harvey (1991) develop theoretical findings that the g_{kmt} are functions of the standard deviations of the original risk factors f_{kt}. Others including Koutoulas and Kryzanowski (1996) use a similar variable risk premium formulation to test for the January effect and the small firm effect.

On the other hand, it is possible that the reason that the risk premiums appear to change in time is a misspecification of the basic model. Having a significant factor missing from the linear factor model (2–1) might make it appear that the expected return E_i needs to vary with time. The question is whether or not having a risk premium be a function of an exogenous time variable is equivalent to having another risk factor in the basic APT linear factor model.

If each factor premium P_k is set to a time function P_{kt}, then substituting (2–6) into equation (2–3) produces

$$R_{it} = R_0 + \sum_{k=1}^{K} b_{ik} P_k + \sum_{k=1}^{K} \sum_{m=1}^{M} b_{ik} d_{km} g_{kmt} + \sum_{k=1}^{K} b_{ik} f_{kt} + e_{it} \qquad (2\text{--}7)$$

where the d_{km} are unknown constants to be determined, and the loading factors b_{ik} are the same unknown constants defined in (2–1). This version of the APT allows for risk premiums that are functions of the zero mean time variables g_{kjt}.

The product $b_{ik} d_{km}$ is just a constant c_{ikm} to be determined. But it is a constrained constant and is not free to take on any independent value. It is true that the b_{ik} can take on any value for each investment i and for each risk factor k, but the d_{km} must be the same for each investment i. If c_{ikm} were completely free to take on any value, then the associated g_{mkt} would behave as another f_{kt}. It is true that the return R_{it} varies as the g_{mkt} change with time, but because the c_{ikm} are constrained and because there is no term in the summation of $b_{ik} P_k$ for a risk factor corresponding to g_{kmt}, then g_{mkt} is not truly missing from the original specification. This means that (2–3) with constant factor risk premiums and (2–7) with varying factor risk premiums are fundamentally different models.

PROBLEMS WITH PARAMETER ESTIMATION

Computational difficulties can result from the potential for multicollinearity among the risk factors f_{kt}. If one or more risk factors are linear functions, or close to being linear functions, of any combination of the other factors, then the factors are not independent. While the APT does not require the f_{kt} to be independent, a practical problem arises in attempting to determine the values of the b_{ik} from a set of historical values of the nonindependent risk factors. A singular or nearly singular matrix of the f_{kt} will be obtained which must be inverted to determine the b_{ik}. Inverting a singular matrix is not possible since this involves a division by zero, and inverting a nearly singular matrix strains the precision characteristics of the inversion process since there are divisions by numbers very close to zero. Multicollinearity can lead to large errors in the estimates for the b_{ik} as well as large serial correlation in the values of the unexplained model-fit errors e_{it}.

Another difficulty can arise from not having sufficient variation in the values of the factors f_{kt}. Assume a particular factor, f_{kt}, truly has an effect on the return R_{it}. If the range of values for f_{kt} over the time t is zero, then it will be impossible to determine the true value of the b_{ik}. If the range of values for f_{kt} over the time t is nonzero but very small, then it will be difficult to determine the true value of the b_{ik}, because the impact on the rate of return, R_{it}, will be small. This is equivalent to a design of experiments problem. For example, if all the values of one particular f_{kt} were within 1 percent of each other, then it would be virtually impossible to determine the true value of any b_{ik} associated with this factor. For instance, when attempting to discover the effect of an agricultural fertilizer on the growth of a plant, researchers might try values of 50, 100, and 150 percent of a standard application rate. They would assume that applications at 99, 100, and 101 percent of the standard application would not produce measurable differences in growth rates.

Unfortunately, in the world of finance, we do not have the option of specifying the range of values for the factors we would like to evaluate. We must accept whatever values happened to occur within the history available. Ideally, we would like to have a sufficient number of historical data points over a wide enough range of market conditions to produce a true diversity of values in each one of the f_{kt}. While the simple number of historical data points is important, it is actually more important to have a wide enough distribution of factor values to be able to accurately measure the impact of each factor. Estimates of the b_{ik} can be highly dependent on the particular historical data set selected, especially if the data set is not rich in a diversity of market conditions. It is recommended that at least 30 years of history be employed to have sufficient history to be reasonably confident in the resulting b_{ik}.

Finally, we must consider model misspecification. If one or more important factors is missing from the model, the factors that are present will be used to try to explain the impact of the factors that are missing, as well as their own impact, on the investment rate of return. Spurious relationships can result, especially when the number of data points is small. If the true model variables that control the investment performance are not known and must be determined empirically, then the only approach to this problem is to have sufficient performance history to encompass a wide range of market conditions. It is hoped that the dispersion of values of the missing factors will then be wide enough to avoid spurious correlations with the factors available. If this is true, then the impact of the missing factors will simply appear as unexplained error in the investment performance, as it should.

MUST RISK PREMIUMS/EXPECTED RETURNS BE DETERMINED?

If one only wished to develop a linear factor model (LFM) in order to establish the relationship between the exogenous factors f_{kt} and the investment return R_{it}, the question arises whether it is necessary to explicitly determine the values of the factor risk premiums P_k at all. For a sufficiently long time period T an estimate of the expected value of the investment return R_i can simply be determined as the value of $\Sigma\ R_{it}/T$. Once this is established, the values of the b_{ik} in (2–1) can be estimated using ordinary least squares regression, setting the regression constant to zero. In fact, if the regression constant is not set to zero, then a simple regression analysis using (2–1) will not only determine the b_{ik} but will also determine the value of R_i as the regression constant.

In the seminal paper by Ross (1976), equation (2–2) is shown to be equivalent to the CAPM when the risk factor used is the return on a market index. Since the CAPM was viewed as the most important theory available at the time to explain the differences in return among similar assets, then it was useful to show this equivalence between the CAPM and the APT in order to validate the basic linear factor model given in (2–1). But that being done, it is certainly possible to use (2–1) on its own as a model for discovering factors that seem to influence the return on investments and for determining the coefficients for the resulting forecasting equations. However, this approach of using (2–1) to determine the impact of a set of factors on the performance of an investment is not the APT. The APT itself requires the set of cross-sectional constraints from equation (2–2) to limit the values that the b_{ik} can take on. But there is nothing prohibiting the use of (2–1) on its own as a model for determining the impact of factors on investment returns.

MISSING FINAL STEP TO ASSET ALLOCATION

Equation (2–1) is useful for estimating expectations for future investment returns. It provides a major point of departure from the MPT mean-variance approach to asset allocation as developed by Markowitz.

The MPT assumes that a constant expected return is available at each point in time at which a portfolio is to be constructed. Predicting an expected return for each investment that is a function of exogenous macroeconomic and financial variables would seem to be a more promising approach than using simple historical averages, which is a quite common procedure for the MPT approach. If we were to use (2–1) to form expectations of returns for use in the MPT model, then we would need to generate expectations of standard deviations and correlation coefficients in some similar manner. The difficulty with this approach is that all these expectations would need to be mutually consistent.

REFERENCES

Chen, Nai-Fu, Richard Roll, and Stephen A. Ross. "Economic Forces and the Stock Market." *Journal of Business* 59 (1986): 383–403.

Connor, Gregory, and Robert A. Korajczyk. "Risk and Return in an Equilibrium APT." *Journal of Financial Economics* 21 (1988): 255–289.

Cox, John C., Jonathan E. Ingersoll, Jr., and Stephen A. Ross. "A Theory of the Term Structure of Interest Rates." *Econometrica* 53 (May 1985): 385–407.

Dhrymes, Phoebus, Irwin Friend, and B. Gultekin. "A Critical Examination of the Empirical Evidence on the Arbitrage Pricing Theory." *Journal of Finance* 39 (1984): 323–346.

Ferson, Wayne E., and Campbell R. Harvey. "The Variation of Economic Risk Premiums." *Journal of Political Economy* 99, no. 2 (1991): 385–415.

Koutoulas, George, and Lawrence Kryzanowski. "Macrofactor Conditional Volatilities, Time-Varying Risk Premia and Stock Return Behavior." *Financial Review* 31, no. 1 (February 1996): 169–195.

Kryzanowski, Lawrence, and Minh Chan To. "General Factor Models and the Structure of Security Returns." *Journal of Financial and Quantitative Analysis* 18 (1983): 31–52.

McElroy, Marjorie B., and Edwin Burmeister. "Arbitrage Pricing Theory as a Restricted Nonlinear Multiple Regression Model: Iterated Nonlinear Seemingly Unrelated Regression Estimates." *Journal of Business and Economic Statistics* 6, no. 1 (1988): 29–42.

Merton, Robert C. "On Estimating the Expected Return of the Market: An Exploratory Investigation." *Journal of Financial Economics* 8 (December 1980): 323–361.

Priestley, Richard. "The Arbitrage Pricing Theory, Macroeconomic and Financial Factors, and Expectations Generating Processes." *Journal of Banking and Finance* 20 (June 1996): 869–890.

Roll, Richard, and Stephen A. Ross. "An Empirical Investigation of the Arbitrage Pricing Theory." *Journal of Finance* 35, no. 5 (December 1980): 1073–1103.

Roll, Richard, and Stephen A. Ross. "The Arbitrage Pricing Theory Approach to Strategic Portfolio Planning." *Financial Analysts Journal* (May/June 1984): 14–26.

Ross, Stephen A. "The Arbitrage Theory of Capital Asset Pricing." *Journal of Economic Theory* 13 (December 1976): 341–360.

CHAPTER 3

Factors Influencing Stock Returns

> The stock market is but a mirror which. . .provides an image of the underlying or *fundamental* situation. Cause and effect run from the economy to the stock market, never the reverse.
>
> *John Kenneth Galbraith*
> *The Great Crash, 1929 (1955)*

The identification of the factors that should influence the changes in the price of stocks can be looked upon as a search for the Holy Grail of market timing. Many academic papers, articles in the popular press, and comments by television financial news analysts give reasons why the stock market moved up or down in a particular time period. Often one factor moving in the same direction is used to explain why the market moves up one time and then down another time. For example, does an increase in reported unemployment mean that the market should move up or down or not have any influence at all?

This chapter evaluates a number of financial and economic factors suggested as having an influence on broad equity market price changes. Both theoretical and empirical viewpoints are evaluated. The ultimate purpose of these evaluations is to try to establish a consensus of which factors can be shown to be the most useful in predicting future changes in the price of stocks.

SEARCHING FOR A FUNDAMENTAL APPROACH

As described in Chen, Roll, and Ross (1986), the conventional starting point for a model of stock prices is the dividend discount model:

$$p = \frac{E(c)}{k} \tag{3-1}$$

where:

  p = expected stock price
  $E(c)$ = expected dividend stream from the stock
  k = discount rate

Thus implies that

$$\frac{dp}{p} + \frac{c}{p} = \frac{d[E(c)]}{E(c)} - \frac{dk}{k} + \frac{c}{p} \tag{3-2}$$

This indicates that anything that influences the discount rate k or the expected dividend stream $E(c)$ should have an impact on the stock returns. Since the dividend stream at each point in the future depends on the discount rate effective for that point in time, the discount rate is not constant but is determined by the term structure of forward interest rates. It has been suggested that the discount rate is also influenced by the risk premium between high-yield and high-quality bonds. Changes in any of these factors could have an effect on the change in stock prices.

Any factor that can be statistically shown to have an influence on the future value of the stock is a possible causative factor for influencing the present price. But correlation does not necessarily imply causality. The use of empirical evaluations of proposed factors is a common approach in establishing a relationship between the performance of the stock market and measures of market and economic conditions. Before we delve into empirical evaluations, let us consider a more detailed theoretical approach.

One of the first theoretical discussions of factors that should influence the equity market was undertaken by John Burr Williams in 1938. He reasoned that the true value of a stock was more than just the present value of a stream of dividend payments. These dividend payments are not known with certainty and are subject to a number of risks. The dividend payments themselves should be influenced by future productivity of the specific firm or the economy in general. Therefore, current dividends plus changes in productivity have an influence on stock prices. The level of the discount rate itself as it changes in time will certainly have an impact on the present value of the dividend stream. So the discount rate is crucial to the value of stocks. The current interest rate may not apply for the entire interval of the dividend stream. This means that anticipated future interest rates as measured by the interest rate term structure should have an impact on stock prices.

As shown by Williams (1938), the influence of a time-varying stream of dividends and time-varying discount rate produces a current stock value, V_0, equal to

$$V_0 = \sum_{t=1}^{t=\infty} \pi_t \prod_{k=1}^{k=t} v_k \qquad (3\text{–}3)$$

where:

π_t = the dividend yield for year t
v_k = the discount factor in year k, $v_k = 1/(1 + i_k)$
i_k = the interest rate for year k

Thus, the expectation of every future dividend payment and the expected interest rate at every future point in time have an impact on the current stock value. A change in the risk premium (sometimes called the default premium), the difference between high-yield corporate bonds and high-quality government bonds, is frequently taken as a proxy for the uncertainty of future interest rates.

Furthermore, the dividend stream received should be discounted not only by the discount interest rate but also by the effect of inflation. If the value of the future dividend payments is eroded by strong inflation, this should have an impact on stock values. Investors will seek a real return after inflation. The timing of the impact of inflation is not intuitively obvious. Williams (1938) holds that stock prices ought not to rise in anticipation of inflation. He further states that stock prices often do not begin to rise during the period of inflation itself because "the actuality of inflation often hurts corporate earnings temporarily." But he argues that the price of stocks will surely rise after inflation. We can then anticipate that there will be a lag between the timing of inflation and the impact on stock prices.

Finally, if investors from outside a given country invest in that country's stocks, changes in the exchange rate will have an impact on the future value of the dividend stream. This occurs because the impact of future changes in the exchange rate will appear as if there were inflation or deflation in the price of the stock to an external investor. Since not all investors in a given country's stocks lie outside the country, exchange rates should only have a partial effect on the prices of stocks.

FACTORS INVESTIGATED FOR AN EQUITY RETURN MODEL

The result of Williams's (1938) view of the valuation of stocks provides a considerable list of fundamental factors that should have an influence on the future value of a stream of dividends: recent dividends, productivity, the discount rate, the term structure of interest rates, the interest risk premium, inflation, and exchange rates.

These factors as well as many others have been considered as indicators of future changes in the rate of return for equity markets. The impact of the factors has variously been said to cause, correlate with, or otherwise influence stock market returns. The overall purpose of seeking such relationships is to establish a forecasting framework. The rationale for suggesting the use of any specific factor can run the gamut from truly fundamental to purely empirical. Whether there is an intention to indicate causality between the factors and movement of equity prices may not actually be important. What does appear to be important is that the factors should seem logical and stand the test of time over many market cycles.

In reviewing a number of investigations that attempt to evaluate the relationship between predictive factors and equity market returns, three key features of the selected factors stand out:

- Factors relating to the general economy and the market itself are useful.
- No single factor controls all market movement.
- There is no strong consensus on the best set of factors.

The purpose of this chapter is to enumerate the factors that have been considered and to evaluate a measured impact on the stock market. Each factor will be judged by the number of researchers who have considered it to be important, by the positive or negative direction of its influence over the stock market, and by the confidence level that the factor truly exhibits a significant impact on market returns. The value of the coefficient calculated will not be displayed, only the sign. The values of the coefficients are not comparable across the studies undertaken because the date ranges evaluated are different, the number of months for the stock market index prediction is not consistent, and the specific definition of each factor is not the same from one investigator to another. The degree of confidence will be rated using a three-star system based on statistical confidence intervals. One of the following entries will be entered in the tables under the heading of "Degree of Significance."

Not   Indicates that the factor is considered but is not found to be significant and is excluded from the equation by the investigator.

N/A   Indicates that the factor coefficient is significant but the level of significance is not provided by the investigator.

Low   Indicates a very low probability of any relationship. This is typically indicated by one-tailed t-statistics below 1.88, indicating more than a 3 percent probability of a zero coefficient.

*   Indicates that a modest relationship is established. This is typically measured by one-tailed t-statistics in the range of 1.88–2.99, indicating a probability of a zero coefficient between 0.15 and 3 percent.

**   Indicates that a strong relationship is established. This is typically measured by one-tailed t-statistics in the range of 3.00–3.99, indicating a probability of a zero coefficient between 0.004 and 0.3 percent.

***   Indicates that an exceptionally strong relationship is established. This is typically measured by one-tailed t-statistics above 4.00, indicating less than a 0.004 percent probability of a zero coefficient.

Each factor is summarized to indicate any apparent consensus for the direction of the influence of the factor and to indicate the overall level of the confidence in the use of that factor. This summary is on the bottom row of each evaluation and is marked "Consensus."

We shall evaluate each of the fundamental factors suggested by the work of Williams (1938) first. And then we shall evaluate a number of other factors that have been evaluated empirically and found, with some regularity, to have a statistical co-movement with stock prices. For each factor k a table is presented based on the work of a fixed list of investigators who have each evaluated a set of assumed factors $f_{k,t-n}$ during various time periods $t - n$ and calculated a set of coefficients b_k for a linear factor model to predict stock returns at time t from factors with a lag of $n > 0$ periods. The value of n must be greater than zero in order to obtain a true forecasting model. The factor model has the form

$$R_t = \alpha + b_1 f_{1,t-n} + b_2 f_{2,t-n} + b_3 f_{3,t-n} + \cdots + b_K f_{K,t-n} + e_t$$

$$= \alpha + \sum_{k=1}^{K} b_k f_{k,t-n} + e_t \tag{3-4}$$

as described in Chapter 2 on arbitrage pricing theory. A number of other investigators have proposed many of the same factors as well as additional factors. Only those investigators who have determined models of a form similar to equation (3–4) will be specifically considered in the accompanying comparison tables.

The full list of investigators considered is shown in Table 3–1. This table also shows the set of common factors considered by this list of investigators. Other factors are considered by these investigators, but only those factors that appear for three or more investigators are presented in the table. Since we are seeking to evaluate the consensus of investigators concerning the selection of a set of factors, any factor mentioned by only one or two of the investigators is not considered a common factor.

The macro factors considered in this chapter consist of economic or market variables that have an influence on the broad market as a whole. They are not intended to evaluate the differences among industries and certainly not meant to reflect the differences among individual stocks. Individual stocks may be influenced by company-specific measures such as size of capitalization, number of outstanding shares, ratings by brokerage firm analysts, the book-to-market value ratio, reported insider trading activity, recent trading volumes, and numerous financial statement measures. While these measures would be of significance in determining the differences among individual stock prices, they would probably not be of much value in estimating future rates of return for a stock market index.

Some of the factors may be considered as surrogates for each other. This can present two types of problems. The first problem occurs when one investigator uses a factor and another investigator uses a surrogate for this factor. In this case, we will make an indication in the tables to follow that a surrogate was evaluated and show the impact on the surrogate along with the factor being evaluated.

Another problem occurs when one investigator includes a factor plus one or more of the surrogates for the same factor. Regression analysis or any other procedure for determining the values of the coefficients b_{ik} will tend to adopt one of the factors as the most important factor and assign the correct sign and significance to the factor. When used in combination, surrogates tend to be assigned coefficients of the opposite sign and are treated as "correction factors." When this occurs, a comment will be made about this possible occurrence.

DIVIDEND YIELD

The dividend yield of an index is calculated by dividing the sum of the annualized dividends paid on all the stocks in an index by the price of the index itself. There are several sources for the dividend yield for U.S. stocks. One source is Standard & Poor's representing the dividend yield on the S&P 500 index. A second source is the

T A B L E 3-1

Stock Market Factors Considered by Various Investigators

Investigators	Dividend Yield	Industrial Production	Interest Rate (T-Bills)	Term Spread	Default Spread Baa-Aaa	Inflation (% Chg CPI)	Exchange Rates	GNP or GDP	Trade or Trade Deficit	Money Supply	Unemployment	Previous Stock Returns	January Effect
Ajayi and Mougoué	A				A	A						A	
Anderson							X						
Beenstock and Chan		BC	BC			BC		BC		BC			
Berry, Burmeister, and McElroy				Be	Be								
Black and Fraser	BF			BF	BF								
Booth and Booth	BB		BB	BB	BB								
Bulmash and Trivoli		B	B			B		B	B	B	B		
Burmeister and McElroy			BM			BM							BM
Burmeister, Roll, and Ross				BR	BR	BR							
Chen	Ch	Ch	Ch					Ch					
Chen, Roll, and Ross		CR		CR	CR	CR							
Cutler, Poterba, and Summers (1989)	CP	CP	CP			CP				CP			

Investigator												
Domian and Reichenstein				DR	DR							
Durell	D		D	D	D						D	
Fama and French	FF			FF	FF							
Hardouvelis		H	H			H		H	H	H		
Hardy	Ha		Ha	Ha								Ha
Hodrick, Ng, and Sengmueller	HN		HN	HN								
Jagannathan and Wang		JW		JW	JW	JW						
Jensen, Mercer, and Johnson	JM		JM	JM	JM							
Keim and Stambaugh					KS						KS	KS
Koutoulas and Kryzanowski		KK		KK	KK		KK	KK				
Lamont	La		La	La	La						La	
Leeb	Le		Le			Le			Le	Le	Le	
Mukherjee and Naka		M	M			M	M		M			
Priestley		P		P	P	P	P					
Number of investigators using this factor out of 26 investigators	12	9	14	15	15	12	4	3	6	3	5	3

Center for Research in Securities Prices. And a third source is
Wilshire Associates.

The dividend yield is the most obvious and most significant of
all the factors influencing the rate of return on stocks. Theoretically,
since the value of a stock is based on the expected stream of
dividends, it is not surprising that the recent level of dividends
should have a major influence on the rate of return of stocks. The
results shown in Table 3–2 are the strongest for any factor
considered in this chapter. Note that Hodrick, Ng, and Sengmueller
(1999) simultaneously employ both a dividends-to-earnings ratio
and a dividends-to-price ratio, with coefficients of opposite sign,
which makes their results difficult to interpret.

All the investigators referenced in Table 3–2 employ dividend
yield as a factor influencing stock returns except for Leeb (1993),
who employs the price-to-earnings (p/e) ratio. The sign on Leeb's
reported result has been reversed in order to account for the fact
that p/e ratios and dividend yields move in opposite direction to
one another. While p/e ratios and dividend yields are related, they

T A B L E 3-2

Investigators	Begin Data	End Data	Years of Data	Sign of Coefficient	Degree of Significance
Anderson	1964	1993	30	+	***
Black and Fraser (U.K.)	1965	1992	28	+	***
Booth and Booth	1954	1992	38	+	*
Chen	1954	1986	33	+	***
Cutler, Poterba, and Summers (1989)	1926	1985	60	+	***
Durell	1987	1994	7	+	***
Fama and French	1927	1987	61	+	***
Hardy (Netherlands)	1974	1988	15	+	Low
Hodrick, Ng, and Sengmueller (U.S.)	1970	1998	29	+	Low
Jensen, Mercer, and Johnson	1954	1992	39	+	*
Lamont	1947	1994	48	+	***
Leeb (P/E ratio)	1953	1992	40	+	N/A
Consensus				+	***

are not perfectly related unless a constant percentage of earnings is paid out as dividends. For the purposes of Table 3–2, the two factors are taken as surrogates for each other.

With regard to the use of the p/e ratio, Williams (1938) is quite adamant that the use of earnings as the determinant of the value of stocks is less useful than dividends. He reasons that earnings need not be paid out at all. They can be retained for corporate use at a later time, potentially circumventing any immediate benefit to the investor. Earnings only impact the rate of return when they are ultimately paid out as a dividend. Retained earnings could be used to shore up a failing company, delaying the inevitable and providing no benefit to the investor in the case of an ultimate bankruptcy.

Every investigator obtains a positive sign for the dividend yield coefficient. Given the extremely strong confidence levels obtained, this factor has an undeniable influence on stock returns.

INDUSTRIAL PRODUCTION

If high industrial activity signals strong future dividends, then an increase in industrial production should indicate an increase in stock returns. Any number of other factors could fill the function of monitoring the level of productive activity. GNP could be such a surrogate factor. As indicated in Table 3–3, Bulmash and Trivoli (1991) and Chen (1991) each employ industrial production as well as GNP in their factor models. The sign of the industrial production factor is negative, and the sign of the GNP factor is positive in both these models. The GNP coefficient has a larger t-statistic than the industrial production coefficient in both cases. This normally indicates that the weaker industrial production factor is being treated as a correction factor to the stronger GNP factor.

While all the investigators who produce a coefficient value for industrial production or its GNP surrogate attain the same positive sign on the coefficient, the overall level of significance is only modest. The degree of significance does not come close to the level attained by the dividend yield. This lack of strong significance could result from the specific list of other factors in the model.

T A B L E   3-3

Investigators	Begin Data	End Data	Years of Data	Sign of Coefficient	Degree of Significance
Beenstock and Chan	1977	1983	7	None	Not
Bulmash and Trivoli	1961	1987	27	− (GNP +)	Low(low)
Chen	1954	1986	33	− (GNP +)	**(***)
Chen, Roll, and Ross	1958	1984	27	+	*
Cutler, Poterba, and Summers (1989)	1926	1985	60	+	**
Hardouvelis	1979	1984	6	+	Low
Jagannathan and Wang	1963	1990	28	+	Low
Koutoulas and Kryzanowski (Canada)	1962	1988	27	+	*
Mukherjee and Naka (Japan)	1971	1990	20	+	**
Priestley (U.K.)–Kalman filter method	1980	1993	14	None	Not
Consensus				+	*

Because of the consistency of the sign, this factor is assumed to be important.

Two surrogates for industrial production are evaluated in later sections of this chapter. These surrogates are the GNP, as already mentioned, and trade balance.

INTEREST RATE

The dividend discount model calls for future dividends to be discounted by an appropriate interest rate. If the interest rate fluctuates, then the stock value obtained by the dividend discount model must also move. Since the current value of future dividends decreases as interest rates increase, one would expect a negative coefficient for the impact of the interest rate on stock market returns. In fact, most investigators did obtain negative coefficients, indicating that stock prices and the interest rate move in opposite directions. Even though three investigators find strongly significant relationships (see Table 3–4), the average degree of significance is surprisingly low. Some investigators employ the level of previous

T A B L E   3-4

Investigators	Begin Data	End Data	Years of Data	Sign of Coefficient	Degree of Significance
Beenstock and Chan	1977	1983	7	−	***
Booth and Booth	1954	1992	38	−	*
Bulmash and Trivoli	1961	1987	27	−	***
Burmeister and McElroy	1972	1982	11	+	*
Chen	1954	1986	33	−	***
Cutler, Poterba, and Summers	1926	1985	60	−	Low
Durell	1987	1994	7	−	Low
Hardouvelis	1979	1984	6	−	*
Hardy (Netherlands)	1974	1988	15	−	**
Hodrick, Ng, and Sengmueller (U.S.)	1970	1998	29	−	Low
Jensen, Mercer, and Johnson	1954	1992	39	−	Low
Lamont	1947	1994	48	−	Low
Leeb	1953	1992	40	−	N/A
Mukherjee and Naka (Japan)	1971	1990	20	+	Low
Consensus				−	*

interest rates as the variable influencing the return on the stock market, and others employ the change in the interest rate as the variable.

It appears that if the term spread or the default spread factors are included in a factor model, then the interest rate factor does not seem significant. See the next two sections for definitions of these two factors. Of the seven investigators who obtain higher than the low rating for significance, only two investigators have the term spread in the factor model. And none of these seven had the default spread factor in the model. Of the six investigators who have low significance for the interest rate, one has the term spread and two others have both spread factors. Placing both bond spread factors in the model seems to make the interest rate factor have low significance. Not having either bond spread factor in the model seems to allow the interest rate to become significant.

A unique approach is undertaken by Booth and Booth (1997) by including two interest rate variables. The first is the annualized federal funds rate. The second is a binary variable taking on the value 1 when the last change in the discount rate is positive and zero if the last change is negative. Both factors are found to be significant.

TERM SPREAD

Most researchers use the difference between long-term government bonds (typically 10 years) and the Treasury bill rate (typically 90 days) as the measure for the term spread of interest rates. In a few cases the short-term rate is taken to be the 1-year Treasury bond.

From the representation of the dividend discount model shown in equation (3–3), there is a need for interest rates to discount each future month of dividend payments. This requires expectations of interest rates for each month in the future. Using a single recent measure of the interest rate for all future-month expectations of a discount rate may be too simplistic. Some method is required for projecting the interest rate into the distant future. Both the term spread of interest rates and inflation expectation are considered significant variables in the prediction of future nominal interest rates.

The term spread might be considered more appropriate for predicting bond returns rather than stock returns. Fama and French (1989) suggest that the term spread can be considered a risk premium for bearing any type of long-term security including stocks.

In the results obtained in Table 3–5, there is some disagreement about the sign of the coefficient. Two-thirds of the researchers obtain positive coefficients, and a third obtains negative coefficients. From the dividend discount model, one would expect that if distant interest rates were to be higher than current rates, this would give rise to smaller discount factors that would lower the value of distant dividends paid. Normally future interest rates are forecasted to become lower as the value of the term spread moves higher. Thus, an increasing term spread should give rise to lower future interest rates, which should result in higher stock market valuations. So the coefficient should be positive.

T A B L E   3-5

Investigators	Begin Data	End Data	Years of Data	Sign of Coefficient	Degree of Significance
Berry, Burmeister, and McElroy	1972	1982	11	+	***
Black and Fraser (U.K.)	1965	1992	28	+	*
Booth and Booth	1954	1992	38	+	*
Burmeister, Roll, and Ross	1986	1992	7	+	N/A
Chen, Roll, and Ross	1958	1984	27	−	Low
Durell	1987	1994	7	+	*
Domian and Reichenstein	1942	1994	53	+	Low
Fama and French	1927	1987	61	+	Low
Hardy (Netherlands)	1974	1988	15	−	*
Hodrick, Ng, and Sengmueller (U.S.)	1970	1998	29	+	**
Jagannathan and Wang	1963	1990	28	−	Low
Jensen, Mercer, and Johnson	1954	1992	39	+	Low
Koutoulas and Kryzanowski (Canada)	1962	1988	27	−	Low
Lamont	1947	1994	48	+	Low
Priestley (U.K.)	1980	1993	14	None	Not
Consensus				+	Low

While there is a positive coefficient consensus, the degree of significance is low, indicating that there is only a small impact of term spread on stock market returns.

DEFAULT SPREAD

The default spread, sometimes called the credit spread, is normally taken as the difference between corporate bonds and government bonds, or it is taken as the difference between lower-quality corporate bonds (typically Baa bonds) and high-quality corporate bonds (typically Aaa bonds). This bond spread can be considered a default premium because it is a measure of the risk premium that must be paid for bonds that are subject to the possibility of default over bonds that are not likely to default.

The rationale for relating the stock market return to the default spread is based on an argument concerning the state of general business conditions. If business conditions are poor, then there is an increase in the likelihood of default in lower-quality corporate bonds. While business conditions are poor, the outlook for the stock market is also poor. The market price would then need to include a higher risk premium on stocks in order to induce investors to accept the added risk due to poor business conditions.

The investigators shown in Table 3–6 unanimously obtain a positive sign on the default spread coefficient. For factors considered by 10 or more investigators, this factor and the dividend yield are the only two that unanimously obtained the same sign on the coefficient. The degree of confidence in this positive coefficient is quite strong, indicating that the default spread must have some relationship to stock market returns.

T A B L E 3–6

Investigators	Begin Data	End Data	Years of Data	Sign of Coefficient	Degree of Significance
Anderson	1964	1993	30	+	*
Berry, Burmeister, and McElroy	1972	1982	11	+	***
Black and Fraser (U.K.)	1965	1992	28	+	**
Booth and Booth	1954	1992	38	+	*
Burmeister, Roll, and Ross	1986	1992	7	+	N/A
Chen, Roll, and Ross	1958	1984	27	+	*
Durell	1987	1994	7	+	Low
Domian and Reichenstein	1942	1994	53	+	***
Fama and French	1927	1987	61	+	*
Jagannathan and Wang	1963	1990	28	+	**
Jensen, Mercer, and Johnson	1954	1992	39	+	Low
Keim and Stambaugh	1928	1978	51	+	*
Koutoulas and Kryzanowski (Canada)	1962	1988	27	None	Not
Lamont	1947	1994	48	+	Low
Priestley (U.K.)	1980	1993	14	+	**
Consensus				+	*

INFLATION

A very wide range of inflation measures is employed by the investigators shown in Table 3–7. The retail price index, the consumer price index, the producer price index, a commodity price index, a manufacturing cost index, and a wage rate index are all utilized by one or more investigators. Furthermore, three main approaches are used: historical measures of actual inflation, calculations of expected inflation, and calculations of changes in expected inflation. Despite the variations in approach, the investigators determine a common sign for the coefficient.

Yet there are two surprising results concerning the estimation of a coefficient for the effect of inflation on stock market returns. The first surprise is that Beenstock and Chan (1988) obtain a positive coefficient for inflation measured by the changes in the U.K. retail price index. But this result is offset by the fact that they also include a manufacturing fuel and materials cost as a second measure of inflation. This second coefficient has a strong negative sign. This could be a case of one variable acting as a *correction*

TABLE 3-7

Investigators	Begin Data	End Data	Years of Data	Sign of Coefficient	Degree of Significance
Anderson	1964	1993	30	−	**
Beenstock and Chan	1977	1983	7	+/−	***
Bulmash and Trivoli	1961	1987	27	−	Low
Burmeister and McElroy	1972	1982	11	−	Low
Burmeister, Roll, and Ross	1986	1992	7	−	N/A
Chen, Roll, and Ross	1958	1984	27	−	*
Cutler, Poterba, and Summers (1989)	1926	1985	60	−	Low
Hardouvelis	1979	1984	6	−	Low
Jagannathan and Wang	1963	1990	28	−	Low
Leeb	1953	1992	40	−	N/A
Mukherjee and Naka (Japan)	1971	1990	20	−	**
Priestley (U.K.)	1980	1993	14	−	*
Consensus				−	*

variable to the other. The consensus on the negative sign is unanimous with this one exception.

The second surprise is that 5 out of the 12 investigators obtain a low degree of significance. The dividend discount model should be subject to the effect of inflation. But it appears that the impact of inflation is difficult to measure empirically. Williams (1938) seems to be correct when he argues that the influence of inflation on the price of stocks occurs much later than the time of actual inflation. The difficulty in establishing a strong link between inflation and the stock market return could just be a problem in establishing the correct lag for the impact of inflation.

EXCHANGE RATES

Only 4 out of the 26 investigators consider the effect of exchange rates (see Table 3–8). The exchange rate is expressed as local currency per currency numeraire, where the currency numeraire is usually taken as the U.S. dollar or special drawing rights (SDRs). The exchange rate variable employed is the log of the exchange rate or the percent change in the exchange rate.

There are two views of the impact of exchange rates on the return of the stock market. The first view is associated with the dividend discount model and an adjustment that must be made on the current value of future dividends due to the impact of future expectations of the exchange rate. Only investors who hold shares of stocks whose price is denominated in a currency other than their

T A B L E 3-8

Investigators	Begin Data	End Data	Years of Data	Sign of Coefficient	Degree of Significance
Ajayi and Mougoué	1985	1991	7	−	***
Koutoulas and Kryzanowski (Canada)	1962	1988	27	−	Low
Mukherjee and Naka (Japan)	1971	1990	20	−	Low
Priestley (U.K.)	1980	1993	14	−	**
Consensus				−	*

home currency need to make this adjustment. According to the U.S. Treasury Department (1997), during 1997 only 6.3 percent of the value of U.S. equities was held by foreign investors. Because this is a fairly small level, from the point of view of the dividend discount model, there should only be a minor impact on U.S. stock market returns. The second view is that exchange rates impact the level of imports and exports, which in turn can have a major impact on the future productivity and earnings of corporations. These factors can then influence the level of stock prices.

Ajayi and Mougoué (1996) evaluate the effect of changes in the exchange rate on subsequent stock market returns for eight separate countries. The currencies for all countries except the United States are found to have a significant negative effect on stock market returns. Perhaps their nonsignificant result for the United States is dependent on smaller external participation in the U.S. stock market than for other countries. Alternatively, it could simply be due to the short time interval of only 7 years employed.

All investigators obtain a negative impact of exchange rates on stock market returns. While there is consensus on the direction of impact, the level of significance is mixed. Surprisingly, the two investigations with the longest range of data both obtain low levels of significance.

GNP OR GDP

Changes in the gross national product or in the gross domestic product could be taken as surrogates for industrial production. The three investigators (see Table 3–9) who included GNP also include

T A B L E   3–9

Investigators	Begin Data	End Data	Years of Data	Sign of Coefficient	Degree of Significance
Beenstock and Chan	1977	1983	7	None	Not
Bulmash and Trivoli	1961	1987	27	+	Low
Chen	1954	1986	33	+	***
Consensus				+	*

industrial production as a factor. In the investigation by Chen
(1991), the GNP appears to be more significant than industrial
production. On the other hand, Beenstock and Chan (1988) find
that neither factor is significant. Since so few investigators include
GNP in their evaluations, it is difficult to say whether GNP or
industrial production is the more useful factor. The signs obtained
for the GNP coefficients are positive, which is in agreement with
the signs found for industrial production.

TRADE OR TRADE DEFICIT

Trade (see Table 3–10) is another possible surrogate for
productivity. But judging from the mixture of signs obtained for
the coefficients and the low degree of significance, trade does not
appear to be as effective a measure of productivity as industrial
production.

T A B L E 3–10

Investigators	Begin Data	End Data	Years of Data	Sign of Coefficient	Degree of Significance
Bulmash and Trivoli	1961	1987	27	−	Low
Hardouvelis	1979	1984	6	+	Low
Koutoulas and Kryzanowski (Canada)	1962	1988	27	−	*
Consensus				+/−	Low

MONEY SUPPLY

Up until this point, all the factors considered fit neatly within the
concept of an extended version of the dividend discount model.
The rationale for the inclusion of the money supply in a factor
model affecting the return on the stock market (see Table 3–11) is
not so clear. Should the impact of increasing money supply have a
positive or negative effect? Leeb (1993) has three factors containing
money supply components. One of them has a positive sign,

T A B L E   3-11

Investigators	Begin Data	End Data	Years of Data	Sign of Coefficient	Degree of Significance
Beenstock and Chan	1977	1983	7	+	***
Bulmash and Trivoli	1961	1987	27	+	***
Cutler, Poterba, and Summers (1989)	1926	1985	60	+	Low
Hardouvelis	1979	1984	6	−	*
Leeb	1953	1992	40	+/−	N/A
Mukherjee and Naka (Japan)	1971	1990	20	+	Low
Consensus				+	*

another has a negative sign, and the final factor has a positive sign on a factor utilizing the difference between the M1 and M2 measures of money supply.

Money supply could be considered as a factor measuring the dilution of the value of money. This might make the money supply be a surrogate for inflation. As such, a negative coefficient would be expected.

UNEMPLOYMENT

Unemployment (see Table 3–12) is another factor that does not fit easily within the dividend discount framework. If high unemployment signals low productivity, the positive coefficients obtained all have the wrong sign. If high production can be maintained while

T A B L E   3-12

Investigators	Begin Data	End Data	Years of Data	Sign of Coefficient	Degree of Significance
Bulmash and Trivoli	1961	1987	27	+	*
Hardouvelis	1979	1984	6	+	Low
Leeb	1953	1992	40	+	N/A
Consensus				+	*

unemployment is allowed to increase, then this should have a positive effect on the corporate bottom line because net earnings should increase. The low significance coupled with the small number of investigators utilizing an unemployment factor does not suggest that this is an important factor.

PREVIOUS STOCK RETURNS

There has been a good deal of investigation into the concept that the return on the stock market is a mean-reverting process. By this we mean that when the returns exceed or underperform their historical average, then within a short period of time, the returns will move back toward the average. This concept is related to the size of the market crash that results after a run-up in prices during a market bubble. For a discussion of the concept of reversion to the mean, see Poterba and Summers (1988), Cutler, Poterba, and Summers (1991), and Fama and French (1988).

Most investigators use the previous 24 months of returns as the factor to relate to subsequent returns. Cutler, Poterba, and Summers (1991) generally find the strongest autocorrelations for a 13–24-month lag across a range of 13 countries. By definition, mean reversion requires a negative coefficient, which all three investigators referred to in Table 3–13 did obtain. On the other hand, the degree of significance is frequently low even though many of these evaluations had more than 30 years of data.

T A B L E   3-13

Investigators	Begin Data	End Data	Years of Data	Sign of Coefficient	Degree of Significance
Anderson	1964	1993	30	−	*
Durell	1987	1994	7	−	**
Keim and Stambaugh	1928	1978	51	−	Low
Lamont	1947	1994	48	+	Low
Leeb	1953	1992	40	−	N/A
Consensus				−	*

JANUARY EFFECT

A much-discussed market phenomenon is the so-called January effect. As seen in Table 3–14, two of the investigators obtain very strong significance levels for this effect. So there must be a measurable difference between the performance in January and the performance in other months. Three possible reasons could explain this phenomenon. First of all, it could simply be a matter of some other fundamental factor tending to have higher or lower values during the month of January. A factor such as industrial production or dividend yields could tend to have larger values during this month than during other months. Keim and Stambaugh (1986) report that the value of the annualized default premium during January months from 1967 to 1984 averaged 1.74 percent while all other months only averaged 1.17 percent. Of course, this sort of explanation for the January effect only trades one problem for another. We are left with the question of why the default premium might be higher in January.

A second, and the most widely held, view is that certain year-end tax strategies give rise to lower prices in December and higher prices in January. It is thought that some investors sell their losing stocks in December in order to realize a loss as a write-off against other gains for the year. They could buy the stocks back later in the next year after waiting the required time, getting the tax benefit, and only suffering one transaction cost for the privilege.

A third possible cause of the January effect could come from the timing of investments in pension accounts. If corporations or individuals wait to determine the amount that they might

T A B L E 3-14

Investigators	Begin Data	End Data	Years of Data	Sign of Coefficient	Degree of Significance
Burmeister and McElroy	1972	1982	11	+	*
Hardy (Netherlands)	1974	1988	15	+	***
Keim and Stambaugh	1928	1978	51	+	***
Consensus				+	**

contribute to pension plans until the end of the calendar year, the first month in the new year might see a fillip in the amount of funds contributed. This sudden increase in demand might easily explain the January effect.

OTHER FACTORS FOUND TO BE SIGNIFICANT

The factors evaluated above reflect the collective thought of a large number of investigators. To be included, a factor needs to be evaluated by at least three investigators. A number of other less frequent, yet worthwhile, factors are considered by these investigators. While these additional factors will not be specifically evaluated in this chapter, the following list of factors is provided to record the fact that they were found to be significant in some evaluations and to stimulate additional research into their usefulness.

Dividend Payout Ratio

Lamont (1998) employs a factor called the dividend payout ratio. This represents the fraction of earnings that are actually paid out as dividends. This factor is found to be more significant than dividend yields when both are included in the factor model.

Real Final Sales

Burmeister and McElroy (1988) incorporate a factor in their model measuring the unexpected growth in real final sales, constructed from data in the *Survey of Current Business*.

Federal Debt

Bulmash and Trivoli (1991) find that increases in federal debt have a short-term positive effect on stock prices but ultimately have a long-term negative impact.

Stock Market Volatility

Merton (1980) describes the use of the variance of market returns as a determinant of the equilibrium expected excess return on purely theoretical grounds. He determines that the expected return should be positively proportional to the variance. Cutler, Poterba, and Summers (1989) specifically evaluate volatility along with other factors in a linear factor model and show that it had been a significant factor between 1926 and 1986, but with a strongly negative coefficient.

Free Reserves

Hardouvelis (1987) evaluates a factor called free reserves, defined to be the difference between excess reserves and borrowed reserves. He finds announcements of increases in this factor to have a significant positive impact on stock market returns.

Personal Income

Hardouvelis (1987) indicates that announcements of increases of personal income have a positive effect on stock market returns.

Per Capita Labor Income

Jagannathan and Wang (1996) find that a factor based on per capita labor income has a positive impact on a value-weighted index of stocks.

Prices of Small Stocks

Keim and Stambaugh (1986) employ a factor based on the previous price level of small stock firms. They find that increases in the level of small stock prices lead to decreases in the S&P 500 stock market return.

Leading Indicators Index

Koutoulas and Kryzanowski (1996) develop a factor model for the return of the Toronto Stock Exchange index. They include two factors based on leading indicators: the Canadian index of 10 leading indicators and the U.S. composite index of 12 leading indicators. They find both factors to have significant positive coefficients in their model. This may be circuitous since both the Canadian and the U.S. leading indicators have a stock market index as one of their components.

Consumer Confidence or Consumer Sentiment

Otoo (1999) and Fisher and Statman (2002) both indicate that a consumer sentiment or consumer confidence index is related to stock market returns. Such indices are tracked by the Survey Research Center at the University of Michigan and the Conference Board. Unfortunately, the direction of cause and effect between these consumer measures and the stock market is not what might be expected. Both these investigations suggest that there is more evidence that stock market returns influence the consumer sentiment index than the reverse relationship. If there is an effect by the consumer indices on the stock market, there is some concern about the sign of the coefficient. Otoo (1999) holds that the coefficient is positive based on the University of Michigan data between June 1980 and June 1999 when evaluating a contemporaneous effect on the Wilshire 5000 stock index. Fisher and Statman (2002) also find a positive coefficient when evaluating a contemporaneous model with the S&P 500, NASDAQ, and small-cap returns. On the other hand, they find a weak negative coefficient when attempting to predict these same three stock indices 1 month ahead. For a description and evaluation of the consumer sentiment index from the University of Michigan versus the consumer confidence index from the Conference Board, see Bram and Ludvigson (1998).

Stock Market Expectations or Investor Sentiment

Using the Conference Board survey of stock price expectations from June 1987 to December 1996, Durell (2001) finds that there is a negative relationship between the stock market expected return and the actual market returns. This study also shows that the stock market expectations are strongly related to past stock market returns. The research on reversion to the mean for the stock market indicates that future market returns are negatively related to past market returns. So it is not surprising that a factor such as stock market expectations, which is strongly related to past market returns, should be negatively related to past market returns as well.

Fisher and Statman (2000) evaluate the expectations of large- and small-cap stock market returns by individual investors, newsletter writers, and Wall Street strategists from July 1987 through July 1998. They find a small but significant negative relationship between future large-cap stock returns and stock market expectations of individual investors and newsletter writers. No one of the three groups demonstrates a significant ability to forecast future small-cap stock market returns. This study also finds a much stronger relationship between stock market returns and the subsequent changes in the stock market sentiment than the reverse relationship of predicting stock returns from market sentiment.

Manufacturing Capacity Utilization

None of the investigators referred to in Table 3–1 specifically considers capacity utilization as a factor to be used to explain stock market returns. Yet there is ample indication from other investigators that capacity utilization is an important factor in the business cycle. It has been proposed that when capacity utilization goes below 73 percent, this signals the end of a recessionary cycle and industry is stimulated to utilize more of its existing capacity. When the capacity utilization exceeds 85 percent, this signals an overstimulated economy in which demand exceeds supply. This gives rise to higher prices and results in increasing inflationary expectations. The effect of capacity utilization on anticipated inflation could produce a significant impact on stock market returns. For discussions of the relationship between capacity utilization and inflation, see Finn (1999) and Garner (1994).

OTHER CONSIDERATIONS

When constructing linear models of the form shown in equation 3–4, there are many considerations to be dealt with. While the selection of the particular explanatory factors may be the most important consideration, there are many other decisions to be made in constructing the form of the model.

Selection of the Variable to Be Forecasted

Leaving aside the selection of the country to evaluate, several decisions concerning the nature of the forecasted variable remain. For the United States many investigators employ the S&P 500 as the predicted variable. The Dow Jones 30 industrial index could be employed. Even though this represents far fewer stocks, they could be viewed as the most important. If having more stocks in the index is important, then the Russell 3000 stock index or the Wilshire 5000 stock index could be employed.

Selecting one industry or market sector could be another choice. A technology index such as the NASDAQ index could be utilized. Or a value stock index or growth stock index might be chosen.

Once a specific index such as the S&P 500 is chosen, there is an additional decision about what performance component should be measured. Is a price-only or a total-return index to be employed?

Historical Time Interval Selection

How much history should be employed in fitting the linear equation model? Do we always choose the widest data set possible dependent on the length of available historical data? Or do we custom-select the date range to fit depending on the nature of market circumstances during that interval? While most researchers would opt for the longest data set possible in order to incorporate the largest number of market conditions, there may be some good reason to believe that a structural change has taken place at a point in history demanding that a new model be implemented from that point forward. Changes in governmental policy could dictate new variables would need to be incorporated.

Choice of Prediction Horizon

The determination of the length of time to be included in a predicted time interval is of critical importance. Deciding to predict a 1-day, 1-month, or 1-year rate of return for the S&P 500 may lead to different sets of variables. This decision could also lead to completely different kinds of model structures as well. Predicting stock market returns for a 12-month horizon is much easier than predicting returns for a 1-month horizon. The longer the horizon, the better the relationship between fit and actual returns. Daily and monthly returns are strongly impacted by news events, human psychology, and technical trading systems. Quarterly and annual returns are less influenced by these factors. Kandel and Stambaugh (1996) point out that it is a well-known effect for the R^2 (percent of variance explained) to increase as the length of the horizon increases.

ANNUAL RETURN FACTOR MODEL FOR STOCKS

In order to demonstrate the usefulness of a factor model based on an expanded dividend discount formulation, a linear factor model utilizing a number of components is evaluated. The market return variable is the 12-month return for the S&P 500 on a price-only basis without the dividends reinvested. This gives rise to an overlapping returns data set, with each month having 11 months in common with the previous month's annual return. An adjustment to the standard error of the coefficients and the standard error of the regression will need to be made to correct for this overlap. All factors include at least a 1-month lag.

The following factors based on an expanded dividend discount model are employed:

The S&P 500 dividend yield for the month prior to the S&P 500 performance year.

The annualized producer price index change over the 5 years prior to the S&P 500 performance year.

The compounded percent return on the S&P 500 for the 36 months prior to the S&P performance year. This is the reversion-to-the-mean variable.

The civilian unemployment rate in the month before the S&P 500 performance year.

The annualized term spread between the 10-year Treasury bond yield and the 1-year government bond yield averaged over the 12 months before the S&P 500 performance year.

The annualized credit spread between the Baa Moody's corporate bond yield and the 10-year government bond yield in the month before the S&P 500 performance year.

A linear regression is conducted based on the time interval of March 1955 through December 1994, consisting of nearly 40 years of monthly data. The results obtained are shown in Table 3–15.

According to Anderson (1997), for overlapping time intervals, special adjustments need to be made to the ordinary standard error of the factor beta coefficients. Ordinary beta coefficient standard errors have been multiplied by the adjustment factor, ADJ_{coef} to produce the results shown in Table 3–15.

Let

$m =$ number of total time periods available
$n =$ number of factors in the model for which coefficients are determined
$p =$ number of time periods in the prediction interval
$w =$ true number of independent time periods $= m/p$
$ADJ_{coef} =$ adjustment factor for the standard error of coefficients
$ADJ_{reg} =$ adjustment factor for the standard error of the regression

Then

$$ADJ_{coef} = \left[\frac{(m - n - 1)}{(w - n - 1)} \right]^{1/2} \qquad (3\text{–}5)$$

T A B L E 3-15

12-Month Horizon Model Based on March 1955–December 1994

Factor	Beta	Std. Error	t-Statistic
Stock index-S&P composite stock: dividend yield	20.8025	2.6820	7.7562***
Producer price index–5-year percent change	−6.2317	0.8658	−7.1977***
Stock S&P 500–Price only–mean reversion	−0.3316	0.0660	−5.0246***
Unemployment rate–civilian labor	3.0588	1.7503	1.7475*
Bonds-government-U.S.–10 year minus 1 year	4.8365	2.0814	2.3237*
Baa Corp–10 year govt.	3.3717	2.9723	1.1344
Alpha = −67.1464			
$R^2 = 0.717$			
Regression standard error = 8.8260			

Significance based on a one-tailed test.
* Significant at 0.05 level.
** Significant at 0.01 level.
*** Significant at 0.001 level.
All standard errors adjusted for overlapping time intervals.

If this correction for overlapping data is not made, the values of the standard errors of the coefficients are strongly underestimated and the resulting t-statistics are strongly overestimated.

Similarly, the regression standard error is corrected by multiplying the ordinary regression standard error by the adjustment factor ADJ_{reg}.

$$ADJ_{reg} = \left[\frac{(m - n - 1)}{p(w - n - 1)} \right]^{1/2} \qquad (3\text{-}6)$$

When the total number of time period m is large compared with the number of factors n in the model, then the value of the coefficient standard error adjustment ADJ_{coef} is approximately equal to the square root of the number of time periods in the prediction interval p. Under these same circumstances, the value of the regression standard error adjustment ADJ_{reg} is approximately equal to 1.

All factors other than the Baa–10-year government bond credit risk variable are significant at the 0.05 level or better. The signs of the coefficients agree with the consensus coefficient signs from other investigators reported in Tables 3–2 to 3–13.

A graphical representation of the actual performance of the 12-month S&P 500 return versus the fit values of the linear factor model described in Table 3–15 is shown in Figure 3–1 for 1955 to 1994. There are at least 11 market cycles represented over this time interval. The degree of fit, both graphically and statistically, seems very encouraging. However, using the model coefficients as a forecasting tool for January 1995 to December 2001 presents a huge challenge. This out-of-sample time interval of 7 years contains what turned out to be the most significant stock market "bubble" since the 1920s. The model developed on the data from 1955 to 1994 severely underforecasts the actual market returns. Many commentators on this era attribute the bubble to an irrational exuberance over the financial promise of technology stocks.

F I G U R E   3-1

Actual versus Fit Values—Stock Market Factor Model Fit to 1994

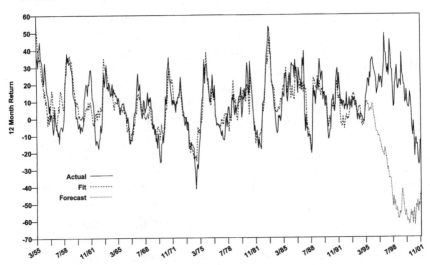

F I G U R E   3-2

NASDAQ Index

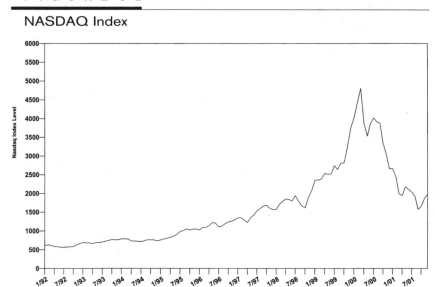

Of course, technology stocks did skyrocket during this interval but then fell back substantially. The strong run-up in the NASDAQ began in 1995 and peaked in early 2000, as shown in Figure 3–2. This presents us with a fundamental problem to explain the difference between the high actual S&P 500 returns and the low forecasted returns from 1995 to 2001. The low forecasts stem from the decrease in the dividend yield to levels not seen in the previous 50 years, as shown in Figure 3–3. Since the dividend yield is the most important component of the dividend discount model, it is not surprising that the model would have forecasted lower returns for the S&P 500 return in order to bring the dividend yield back to a normal level. Pesaran and Timmermann (2002) suggest that the long-standing relationship between dividend yield and stock return simply broke down in the 1990s. Instead of accepting a break in the relationship between dividend yield and stock market returns, let us assume that there were other factors that overcame this extreme excursion in dividend yield.

The challenge is to uncover which economic or financial factors explain the huge deviation between actual and forecasted performance between January 1995 and December 2001. A number

F I G U R E   3-3

S&P 500 Dividend Yield

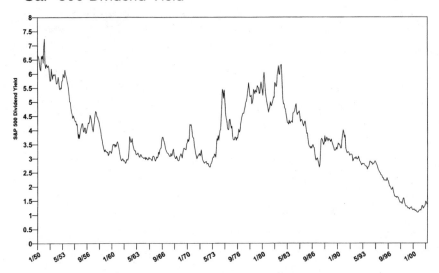

of factors measuring equity-market liquidity were considered. These included the net flows of capital into mutual funds and net flows of capital into the United States from foreign investors. Unfortunately, capital flows seem to lag rather than lead stock market returns. These capital flow liquidity factors were unable to provide increased explanatory power for the 1995–2001 interval while maintaining satisfactory goodness of fit for the 1954–1994 interval. A number of liquidity factors were also considered in research by Martin (1999) and found to be of little value.

Various measures of investor sentiment and consumer confidence were also investigated. Unfortunately, all these measures seem to lag stock prices instead of leading them. So these measures do not appear to be useful predictors of future equity returns.

A number of macroeconomic factors were tested and rejected including exchange rates, retail sales, U.S. debt levels, U.S. budget deficits, and U.S. free reserves, all of which have been suggested by various investigators. Several market-related factors were also evaluated including stock and bond price volatility and stock market margin credit on the New York Stock Exchange. All these provided little help in explaining the 1995–2001 time era.

After considering a wide range of factors, several new factors did appear to help in the fit of the 1995–2001 interval, without destroying the goodness of fit between 1955 and 1994. Most of these additional factors are macroeconomic measures of the economy, and one is a measure of the market itself.

The new macroeconomic variables are the 90-day Treasury bill rate, industrial capacity utilization, and a change in industrial capacity. The measure of the equity market that helps explain the last half of the 1990s is the monthly turnover ratio on the New York Stock Exchange. The monthly turnover ratio is the ratio of the value of the shares traded in a month's time to the total value of all shares listed on the exchange. An increase in the turnover ratio signals an increase in the rate at which shares are traded. Since 1996, the amount of day trading has increased dramatically. This has been especially true since the coming-of-age of the Internet. By the year 2000, 38 percent of all trading on the combined total of the NYSE and NASDAQ was conducted on Internet-based accounts, a large fraction of which must be day-trading accounts. A significant increase in day trading is bound to place bullish pressure on the stock market since virtually all day traders carry long positions. As these buy orders from new traders come into the marketplace, the market is pushed higher.

When these additional factors are added to the model, the unemployment rate, the term premium (10-year government bond yield − 1-year government bond yield), and the risk premium (Baa corporate bond − long government bond) cease to be useful. The unemployment rate and the risk premium are not very strong in the original model in the first place. Taking these additional factors and the dropped factors into account, a new linear regression is performed using the following set of factors:

The S&P 500 dividend yield for the month prior to the S&P 500 performance year.

The annualized producer price index change over the 5 years prior to the S&P 500 performance year.

The compounded percent return on the S&P 500 for the 36 months prior to the S&P 500 performance year. This is the reversion-to-the-mean variable.

The manufacturing capacity utilization yield for the month prior to the S&P 500 performance year.

The percent change in the industrial capacity for manufacturing in the 6 months prior to the S&P 500 performance year.

The 90-day average Treasury bill rate for the 12 months prior to the S&P 500 performance year.

The average monthly NYSE turnover ratio for the 24 months prior to the S&P 500 performance year.

Using these factors, a new linear regression is performed, based on data over the entire date range from March 1955 to December 2001. The results are shown in Table 3–16. Figure 3–4 shows the resulting actual versus fit comparison on a monthly basis. The

T A B L E 3-16

12-Month Horizon Model Based on March 1955–December 2001

Factor	Beta	Std. Error	t-Statistic
Stock index-S&P composite: dividend yield	17.4403	2.8168	6.1916***
Producer price index–5-year percent change	−3.0697	0.9336	−3.2880***
Stock S&P 500–price only–mean reversion	−0.2806	0.0744	−3.7700***
Manufacturing capacity utilization	−1.9838	0.4417	−4.4907***
Industrial capacity for manufacturing– percent change	14.5438	2.9534	4.4944***
Treasury bills–90 days	−2.6208	1.0679	−2.4541**
NYSE average turnover	9.0643	1.7993	5.0376***
Alpha = 89.9054			
$R^2 = 0.607$			
Regression standard error = 10.7191			

Significance based on a one-tailed test.
* Significant at 0.05 level.
** Significant at 0.01 level.
*** Significant at 0.001 level.
All standard errors adjusted for overlapping time intervals.

F I G U R E   3-4

Actual versus Fit Values—Revised Stock Market Factor Model
Fit to 2001

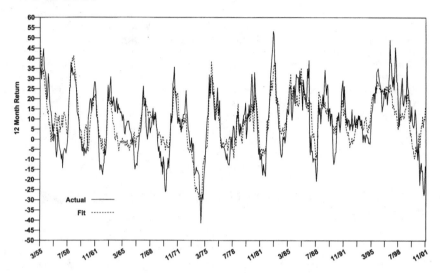

standard errors of the coefficients shown in Table 3–16 have been
adjusted as was done for Table 3–15 to account for overlapping
time intervals.

There must be other factors that could further decrease the
unexplained error of this model. What is required is a better
understanding of the fundamental nature of the marketplace as
well as the psychological reactions of investors to market
circumstances. Further evaluation of the dividend discount
model is likely to introduce additional factors that make logical
sense and are borne out by empirical studies.

To gain some perspective on the degree of the fit ($R^2 = 0.607$)
between the factors shown in Table 3–16 and the 12-month stock
returns, Table 3–17 shows R^2 for similar multifactor 12-month
stock models developed in other investigations. All the original
investigators included in Table 3–1 are considered for this
evaluation. Only those utilizing multifactor models, using
regression analysis based on 12-month forecasted returns, that
are not cross-sectional models across multiple stocks and had a
reported R^2 are included in Table 3–17.

T A B L E 3-17

R^2 for Multifactor 12-Month Stock Return Models

Investigators	Begin Data	End Data	Years of Data	12-Month Bond Model R^2
Cutler, Poterba, and Summers (1991)	1926	1985	60	0.077
Domian and Reichenstein	1942	1994	53	0.200
Durell	1987	1994	7	0.640
Fama and French	1927	1987	61	0.070
Kirby	1927	1987	61	0.084
Average				0.248

MONTHLY RETURN FACTOR MODEL FOR STOCKS

The models developed in the previous section are not actually practical to use as forecasting models. Forecasting 12 months forward on an overlapping (rolling) basis is not a very satisfactory forecasting process. A 12-month horizon is useful for discovering which variables seem to have an impact on the market. The 12-month forecast interval washes out a great deal of noise generated by spurious news events, by technical trading impact, and by seasonal effects. The seasonal effects are eliminated in a 12-month horizon because every forecast includes each month of the year. There are problems using a 12-month forecasting horizon. The first problem is that only factor data from before the beginning of the 12-month interval can be used to predict the 12-month return. This represents a considerable lag. The second problem is that no investor will be willing to wait 12 months to evaluate the forecast before changing the portfolio allocations. And a third problem is that adjustments must be made in estimating the standard errors of the model.

It would be preferable to forecast returns for a 1-month horizon from information available at any time before the beginning of the month. Having to wait 1 month to compare actual versus forecasted performance before adjusting the asset allocations is much more practical. On the other hand, this type of forecast does suffer from spurious news events, from the impact of technical trading, and from seasonality. There are sure to be huge errors in fitting a 1-month-forecast model with macroeconomic and market factors. Yet this monthly model is more natural for a practical environment of making forecasts, comparing forecasts with actual performance, and then adjusting allocations.

Trying to determine the correct factors to use while employing a 1-month horizon is difficult because of the large expected model-fit errors. So we will use the factors that resulted from the 12-month horizons as a starting point for the search for best factors and factor lags. Some of the factors employed at the 12-month horizon may not be effective because they may not undergo sufficient change in a month to produce a measurable impact on returns.

Starting with the same factor types employed in Table 3–16, but allowing different factor lags, we employ the following factor definitions:

> The S&P 500 dividend yield for the 24 months prior to the S&P 500 performance month.

> The annualized producer price index change over the 5 years prior to the S&P 500 performance month.

> The compounded percent return on the S&P 500 for the 24 months prior to the S&P 500 performance month. This is the reversion-to-the-mean variable.

> The manufacturing capacity utilization for the month prior to the S&P 500 performance month.

> The percent change in the industrial capacity for manufacturing in the 6 months prior to the S&P 500 performance month.

> The 90-day average Treasury bill rate for the 12 months prior to the S&P 500 performance month.

> The average monthly NYSE turnover ratio for the 12 months prior to the S&P 500 performance month.

Using this procedure allows us to test the usefulness of the stock market model developed in Table 3–16 to explain 12-month forecasted returns when used to explain 1-month forecasted returns. While the same forecasting factors have been employed, the lags have been empirically adjusted to produce the best results. The results for the 1-month model are shown in Table 3–18 using data from May 1952 to December 2001.

Using the factors incorporated in Table 3–18 as a starting point, empirical investigations lead to three additional useful factors at the 1-month forecasting horizon. The first factor added is the previous 12-month value of the long government bond return. This factor may indicate that when large gains are made in the bond market, additional investment may be made in the stock market, pushing stock prices up. Conversely, when large losses are suffered in the bond market, there can be a disinvestment in the stock market.

The second factor added is the 12-month percentage change in the implicit price deflator based on the gross domestic product. In agreement with Table 3–7, this inflation factor has a very significant negative coefficient.

T A B L E 3-18

1-Month Horizon Model Using the Same Factors as the 12-Month-Horizon Model

Factor	Beta	Std. Error	t-Statistic
Stock index–S&P composite: dividend yield	0.9908	0.2288	4.3308***
Producer price index–5-year percent change	− 0.1683	0.0976	− 1.7248*
Stock S&P 500–price only–mean reversion	− 0.0298	0.0091	− 3.2741***
Manufacturing capacity utilization	− 0.1717	0.0462	− 3.7129***
Industrial capacity for manufacturing–percent change	1.1261	0.3008	3.7435***
Treasury bills–90 days	− 0.1347	0.0996	− 1.3528
NYSE average turnover	0.4410	0.1527	2.8886**
Alpha = 9.5983			
$R^2 = 0.041$			
Regression standard error = 4.0566			

Significance based on a one-tailed test.
* Significant at 0.05 level.
** Significant at 0.01 level.
*** Significant at 0.001 level.

The third factor added is a dummy variable for the month of January to measure the so-called January effect.

When these three new factors are added to the 1-month-forecasting-horizon model, the producer price index factor ceases to be significant. Consequently, the producer price index is dropped from the list of factors. The definitions of the factors incorporated into the revised monthly horizon stock model are:

The S&P 500 dividend yield for the month prior to the S&P 500 performance month.

The compounded percent return on the S&P 500 for the 48 months prior to the S&P 500 performance month. This is the reversion-to-the-mean variable.

The manufacturing capacity utilization for the 12 months prior to the S&P 500 performance month.

The 6-month percent change in the industrial capacity for manufacturing averaged over the 2 months prior to the S&P 500 performance month.

The 90-day average Treasury bill rate for the 16 months prior to the S&P 500 performance month.

The average monthly NYSE turnover ratio for the 53 months prior to the S&P 500 performance month.

The rate of return of the long government bond for the 12 months prior to the S&P 500 performance month.

The 12 annual percentage change in the implicit price deflator based on the gross domestic product averaged over the 48 months prior to the S&P 500 performance month.

A dummy variable that has the value of 1 when predicting January returns and 0 otherwise.

The resulting model coefficients are shown in Table 3–19 based on data from February 1954 to December 2001. All the factors except the January effect are significant, and the coefficient signs agree with the consensus of other investigators. We will employ the model shown in Table 3–19 as a starting point for research into factors affecting dynamic asset allocation when U.S. stocks are a component of the investment portfolio.

T A B L E   3-19

1-Month-Horizon Stock Model Using a Revised Set of Factors

Factor	Beta	Std. Error	t-Statistic
Stock index—S&P composite: dividend yield	2.1832	0.3226	6.7674***
Stock S&P 500—price only—mean reversion	−0.0282	0.0068	−4.1683***
Manufacturing capacity utilization	−0.3008	0.0660	−4.6693***
Industrial capacity for manufacturing—percent change	1.9889	0.3661	5.4328***
Treasury bills—90 days	−0.2639	0.1222	−2.1595*
NYSE average turnover	1.0332	0.2135	4.8388***
Long government bond return	0.5228	0.2401	2.1771*
Gross domestic product—implicit price deflator	−0.6329	0.1751	−3.6153***
January effect	0.7706	0.6081	1.2672
Alpha = 16.3649			
$R^2 = 0.094$			
Regression standard error = 3.9948			

Significance based on a one-tailed test.
* Significant at 0.05 level.
** Significant at 0.01 level.
*** Significant at 0.001 level.

It is instructive to note that both dividend yield and inflation (represented by the GDP implicit price deflator) are strongly significant in this model, with signs agreeing with those found by other investigators. In contrast, the most frequent result found for inflation by other investigators, as shown in Table 3–7, is a low, nonsignificant, coefficient for inflation when mixed with other factors. In addition, the manufacturing capacity utilization is considered to be related to future inflation, and it has a strong negative coefficient in the 1-month model. Manufacturing capacity utilization also seems to have a modest impact on bond returns at the 1-month horizon, as will be shown in Chapter 4.

Two other factors are conspicuous by their absence because they play major roles in the results of other investigations. These are the term spread and the default spread. Adding these factors to the model in Table 3–19 generates nonsignificant coefficients. It is possible that their role has been picked up by the Treasury bill and the long government bond return factors already present.

The dummy variable for the January effect is not as significant as what Keim and Stambaugh (1986) found. This might indicate that one or more of the other factors in the model shown in Table 3–19 may regularly take on higher or lower values than normal during January. Nonetheless, this dummy variable adds a little over 0.7 percent of additional return when the performance month is January.

To gain some perspective on the degree of the fit ($R^2 = 0.094$) between the factors shown in Table 3–19 and the 1-month stock returns, Table 3–20 shows R^2 for similar multifactor 1-month stock regression models from other investigators that report values for R^2. An R^2 of 0.094 represents a very small fraction of the monthly stock return variance explained. It may be difficult to accept that a model with such small explanatory power is capable of helping to produce a useful market timing methodology. Yet according to Clarke, FitzGerald, Berent, and Statman (1989), a monthly regression model with an R^2 as small as 0.090 can help a stock market timer add up to a 5.5 percent annual return over a buy-and-hold strategy. This is obtained with a simple one-factor model to control switching between stocks and cash. Their method even

T A B L E 3-20

R^2 for Multifactor 1-Month Stock Return Models

Investigators	Begin Data	End Data	Years of Data	Monthly Stock Model R^2
Booth and Booth	1954	1992	38	0.050
Cutler, Poterba, and Summers (1991)	1926	1985	60	0.003
Fama and French	1927	1987	61	0.010
Hardy (Netherlands)	1974	1988	15	0.064
Hodrick, Ng, and Sengmueller (U.S.)	1970	1998	29	0.033
Jensen, Mercer, and Johnson	1954	1992	39	0.030
Kirby	1927	1987	61	0.012
Average				0.029

includes transaction costs associated with using futures markets as the investment vehicle. So a model with an R^2 of 0.094 does hold out promise for building a successful dynamic asset allocation strategy.

REFERENCES

Ajayi, Richard A., and Mbodja Mougoué. "On the Dynamic Relation between Stock Prices and Exchange Rates." *Journal of Financial Research* 19, no. 2 (Summer 1996): 193–207.

Anderson, Richard. *Market Timing Models.* Chicago: Irwin Professional Publishing, 1997.

Beenstock, Michael, and Kam-Fai Chan. "Economic Forces in the London Stock Market." *Oxford Bulletin of Economics and Statistics* 50, no. 1 (1988): 27–39.

Berry, Michael A., Edwin Burmeister, and Marjory B. McElroy. "Sorting Out Risks Using Known APT Factors." *Financial Analysts Journal* (March/April 1988): 29–42.

Black, Angela, and Patricia Fraser. "U.K. Stock Returns: Predictability and Business Conditions." *Manchester School of Economics and Social Studies* 63, Supplement (1995): 85–102.

Booth, James R., and Lena Chua Booth. "Economic Factors, Monetary Policy, and Expected Returns on Stocks and Bonds." *Federal Reserve Bank of San Francisco Economic Review*, no. 2 (1997): 32–42.

Bram, Jason, and Sydney Ludvigson. "Does Consumer Confidence Forecast Household Expenditure? A Sentiment Index Horserace." *Federal Reserve Bank of New York Economic Policy Review* (June 1998): 59–78.

Bulmash, Samuel B., and George W. Trivoli. "Time-Lagged Interactions between Stock Prices and Selected Economic Variables." *Journal of Portfolio Management* (Summer 1991): 61–66.

Burmeister, Edwin, and Marjorie B. McElroy. "Joint Estimation of Factor Sensitivities and Risk Premia for Arbitrage Pricing Theory." *Journal of Finance* 43 (July 1988): 721–735.

Burmeister, Edwin, Richard Roll, and Stephen A. Ross. "Using Macroeconomic Factors to Control Portfolio Risk." *BIRR Portfolio Analysis, Inc.*, available http://www.birr.com/documen2.htm, revised March 1997. Paper based on an earlier version of "A Practitioner's Guide to Arbitrage Pricing Theory," a contribution to *A Practitioner's Guide to Factor Models* for the Research Foundation of the Institute of Chartered Financial Analysts, 1994.

Chen, Nai-Fu. "Financial Investment Opportunities and the Macroeconomy." *Journal of Finance* 46, no. 2 (June 1991): 529–554.

Chen, Nai-Fu, Richard Roll, and Stephen A. Ross. "Economic Forces and the Stock Market." *Journal of Business* 59 (1986): 383–403.

Clarke, Roger G., Michael T. FitzGerald, Philip Berent, and Meir Statman. "Market Timing with Imperfect Information." *Financial Analysts Journal* (November–December 1989): 27–36.

Cutler, David M., James M. Poterba, and Lawrence H. Summers. "What Moves Stock Prices?" *Journal of Portfolio Management* 58 (Spring 1989): 4–12.

Cutler, David M., James M. Poterba, and Lawrence H. Summers. "Speculative Dynamics." *Review of Economic Studies* 58 (1991) 529–546.

Domian, Dale L., and William Reichenstein. "Term Spreads and Predictions of Bond and Stock Excess Returns." *Financial Services Review* 7, no. 1 (1998): 25–44.

Durell, Alan. "Stock Market Expectations and Stock Market Returns." Working paper, Dartmouth College, Department of Economics, Hanover, N.H. (August 2001).

Fama, Eugene F., and Kenneth R. French. "Permanent and Temporary Components of Stock Prices." *Journal of Political Economy* 96, no. 2 (1988): 246–274.

Fama, Eugene F., and Kenneth R. French. "Business Conditions and Expected Returns on Stocks and Bonds." *Journal of Financial Economics* 25 (1989): 23–50.

Finn, Mary G. "Is 'High' Capacity Utilization Inflationary?" *Federal Reserve Bank of Richmond Economic Quarterly* 81 (Winter 1999): 1–16.

Fisher, Kenneth L., and Meir Statman. "Investor Sentiment and Stock Returns." *Financial Analysts Journal* 56, no. 2 (March/April 2000): 16–23.

Fisher, Kenneth L., and Meir Statman. "Consumer Confidence and Stock Returns." Working paper, Department of Finance, Leavy School of Business, Santa Clara, Calif. (2002).

Garner, C. Alan. "Capacity Utilization and U.S. Inflation." *Federal Reserve Bank of Kansas City Economic Review* (Fourth Quarter 1994): 5–21.

Hardouvelis, Gikas A., "Macroeconomic Information and Stock Prices." *Journal of Economics and Business* 39 (1987): 131–140.

Hardy, Daniel C. "Market Timing and International Diversification." *Journal of Portfolio Management* (Summer 1990): 23–27.

Hodrick, Robert J., David Tat-Chee Ng, and Paul Sengmueller. "An International Dynamic Asset Pricing Model." *International Tax and Public Finance* 6 (November 1999): 597–620.

Jagannathan, Ravi, and Zhenyu Wang. "The Conditional CAPM and the Cross-Section of Expected Returns." *Journal of Finance* 51 (March 1996): 3–53.

Jensen, Gerald R., Jeffrey M. Mercer, and Robert R. Johnson. "Business Conditions, Monetary Policy, and Expected Security Returns." *Journal of Financial Economics* 40, no. 2 (1996): 213–237.

Kandel, S., and Roger F. Stambaugh. "On the Predictability of Stock Returns: An Asset Allocation Perspective." *Journal of Finance* 51 (1996): 385–424.

Keim, Donald B., and Robert F. Stambaugh. "Predicting Returns in the Stock and Bond Markets." *Journal of Financial Economics* 17 (1986): 357–390.

Kirby, C. "Measuring the Predictable Variation in Stock and Bond Returns." *Review of Financial Studies* 10 (1997): 579–630.

Koutoulas, George, and Lawrence Kryzanowski. "Macrofactor Conditional Volatilities, Time-Varying Risk Premia and Stock Return Behavior." *Financial Review* 31 (February 1996): 169–195.

Lamont, Owen. "Earnings and Expected Return." *Journal of Finance* 53, no. 5 (1998): 1563–1587.

Leeb, Stephen. *Market Timing for the Nineties: The Five Key Signals for When to Buy, Hold and Sell.* New York: HarperBusiness, 1993.

Martin, Bill. "Does Liquidity Matter?" *Phillips & Drew Research Group Occasional Paper* 6 (August 1999).

Merton, Robert C. "On Estimating the Expected Return of the Market: An Exploratory Investigation." *Journal of Financial Economics* 8 (December 1980): 323–361.

Mukherjee, Tarun K., and Atsuyuki Naka. "Dynamic Relations between Macroeconomic Variables and the Japanese Stock Market: An Application of a Vector Error Correction Model." *Journal of Financial Research* 18 (Summer 1995): 223–237.

Otoo, Maria Ward. "Consumer Sentiment and the Stock Market." Working paper, Board of Governors of the Federal Reserve System (November 1999).

Pesaran, M. Hachem, and Allan Timmermann. "Market Timing and Return Prediction under Model Instability." *Journal of Empirical Finance* 9 (2002): 495–510.

Poterba, James M., and Lawrence H. Summers. "Mean Reversion in Stock Prices: Evidence and Implications." *Journal of Financial Economics* 22, no. 1 (March 1988): 27–59.

Priestley, Richard. "The Arbitrage Pricing Theory, Macroeconomic and Financial Factors, and Expectations Generating Processes." *Journal of Banking and Finance* 20 (June 1996): 869–890.

U.S. Treasury Department. *Summary of Report on Foreign Portfolio Investment in the United States* (December 31, 1997).

Williams, John Burr. *The Theory of Investment Value.* Cambridge, Mass.: Harvard University Press, 1938.

CHAPTER 4

Factors Influencing Bond Returns

If you loved me ever so little,
I could bear the bonds that gall...
Algernon Charles Swinburne
Satia Te Sanguine (1866)

In an investment world that tends to concentrate on the performance advantages of the equity market, the need to determine the
factors influencing bond returns might seem unimportant. In recent
times, institutional as well as private investors have generally
concentrated the majority of their asset allocation in the equity
market. Yet there are special circumstances for which bonds are the
investment of choice. Those required to live off the proceeds of a
portfolio may find that the ultimate security of a guaranteed fixed
income is worth giving up the larger long-term expected returns
associated with equities. Many investors simply cannot tolerate the
year-to-year risk that equity portfolios exhibit. There is an even
more important reason for considering the intrinsic value of bonds
in an investment portfolio. If investors who normally have large
equity allocations believe that the stock market will perform poorly,
then many would consider the bond market the safe haven of
choice. This is a frequently accepted view despite the fact that
bonds being held to maturity can suffer considerable month-to-
month valuation risk.

    If an investor with a portfolio risk tolerance allowing a large
stock allocation forecasts the stock market to be down for a
substantial length of time, there is an unavoidable decision to

make. Either decrease the allocation to stocks, or suffer an expected loss. If the allocation to stocks must decrease, then the allocation to some other investment must increase. As long as the expected return in the bond market is greater than the expected return in the stock market, an asset allocation shift to bonds would be rational. To form an expectation of bond returns, a model of the factors influencing the bond market must be constructed. Thus, each of the factors associated with changes in bond market returns will be investigated in the same way that factors influencing the stock market are studied in Chapter 3.

A FUNDAMENTAL APPROACH

The same general concept that was applied to the valuation of stocks can be applied to the valuation of bonds. The value of a bond paying dividends can be considered to be the present value of all future dividends plus the repayment of the principal at maturity. Following John Burr Williams (1938), we can state that the price of a bond, which is assumed to be the value of the bond when it is purchased, should be

$$P_0 = \sum_{t=1}^{t=n} \pi_t v^t + C v^n \qquad (4\text{-}1)$$

where:

$C =$ principal of the bond
$\pi_t =$ dividend paid at the end of year t
$v =$ constant discount factor $= 1/(1 + i)$
$i =$ declared constant interest rate over the term of the bond
$n =$ number of years in the term of the bond

This bond price is based on the stream of dividend payments and a declared interest rate. A purchaser of the bond will only acquire the bond if the declared interest rate is thought to be a favorable rate at the time of purchase. After a bond is purchased, the value of the bond may no longer be the same as the price originally paid. If the market interest rate drops for a bond maturing at the same time as the purchased bond, then the held bond becomes more valuable because it pays a higher rate than the current market rate. Of course, the converse is true in that a previously purchased bond value will go down if current interest rates increase. Once purchased, a bond's value fluctuates with the level of interest rates. The value of a bond paying a stream of dividends, originally determined by the initial fixed rate, becomes subject to an uncertain discount value influenced by expectations of future interest rates.

For stock valuations the problem is even more difficult since the dividends to be paid are random variables subject to the uncertainty of future corporate financial performance. In the case of bonds, the dividends to be paid are constants established at the time of bond purchase. Only the time value of these dividends is subject to uncertainty.

Taking the known dividend stream and the uncertain future discount rates into account gives an expression for the residual value of a bond. This expression ignores the value of any dividends already received. The residual value of a bond is

$$V_0 = \sum_{t=1}^{n} \left\{ \pi_t \prod_{k=1}^{t} v_k \right\} + C \prod_{t=1}^{n} v_t \qquad (4\text{-}2)$$

where:

C = principal of the bond
π_t = dividend paid at the end of year t
v_k = expected discount factor for year $k = 1/(1 + i_k)$
i_k = expected interest rate for year k
n = residual number of years in the term of the bond

If a bond is not subject to default or to being called, then the current residual value of a bond is dependent on the stream of expected interest rates until maturity. The bond value represented in (4–2) is an intrinsic value unaffected by any supply-demand relationship not directly influencing the expected discount factor. The price that someone is willing to pay to purchase a bond and the intrinsic value of the bond based on a dividend discount model are two different concepts. The price paid for a bond is a function of the bond value as well as supply and demand for the bond. If the supply-demand relationship for bonds gets out of kilter, then any factor influencing the supply-demand ratio could have an effect on the current price of the bond beyond the factors affecting the intrinsic value of the bond.

It could be argued that certain factors having a direct impact on interest rates, such as inflationary expectations, need not be present in a bond factor model if an interest rate expectation is already included. Since these factors have a direct impact on the expected future stream of interest rates, their inclusion in a factor model might be redundant. On the other hand, factors that have an influence on the relative demand for other investments competing for the same investment capital, such as stocks, could have an indirect impact on bonds. For example, if the dividend yield for stocks increases dramatically, the expected return for stocks would increase. This would likely result in a large asset allocation shift to stocks and a concurrent decrease in the asset allocation to bonds. This supply-demand effect has nothing directly to do with interest rate expectations, but it could cause the price of bonds to change. Therefore, to build a factor model for bond returns, we must be willing to consider any rational factor that directly influences bond values as well as other factors that leak in from the relative demand for other investments.

FACTORS INVESTIGATED FOR A BOND RETURN MODEL

We shall review the investigations conducted by researchers looking for factors influencing the bond market in the same way that we evaluated investigations of stock market factors. We include only those investigations that propose a list of bond market factors and then calculate coefficients for those factors over a significant time range. Each factor will be judged by the number of researchers who have considered it to be important, by the positive or negative direction of its influence over the bond market, and by the degree of confidence that the factor exhibits a significant impact on bond returns. The values of the calculated coefficients will not be displayed, only the sign. The values of the coefficients are not comparable among the studies undertaken because the date ranges evaluated are different, the number of months for the bond market index prediction is not consistent, and the specific definition of each factor is not the same from one investigation to another. The degree of confidence will be rated using a three-star system based on statistical confidence intervals. One of the following entries is entered in the tables under the heading of "Degree of Significance."

Low   Indicates a very low probability of any relationship. This is typically indicated by one-tailed t-statistics below 1.88, indicating more than a 3 percent probability of a zero coefficient.

*   Indicates that a modest relationship is established. This is typically measured by one-tailed t-statistics in the range of 1.88–2.99, indicating less than a 3 percent probability of a zero coefficient.

**   Indicates that a strong relationship is established. This is typically measured by one-tailed t-statistics in the range of 3.00–3.99, indicating less than a 0.15 percent probability of a zero coefficient.

***   Indicates that an exceptionally strong relationship is established. This is typically measured by t-statistics above 4.00, indicating less than a 0.004 percent probability of a zero coefficient.

Each factor is summarized to indicate any apparent consensus for the direction of the influence of the factor and to indicate the overall level of the confidence in the use of that factor. This summary is on the bottom row of each evaluation and is marked "Consensus."

While a considerable amount of research has been devoted to the factors influencing the stock market, the number of investigations into factors influencing the bond market is not quite as voluminous. Specifically, only research into factors influencing bond market *returns* is relevant. The return is the percentage change in price during one time period. Investigations into factors influencing bond yields (the implied interest rate that a bond pays) or into factors influencing the term structure of interest rates are not directly useful.

Several factors can be thought of as fundamental to the intrinsic value of bonds. These factors include interest rate measures, interest rate forecasts, and the term structure of interest rates. Yet there are other factors that seem to be proposed with some regularity. These factors, some of which may be related to the supply-demand ratio for bonds, include the stock dividend yield and the level of stock prices. For each factor k a table is presented based on the work of a fixed list of investigators who have each evaluated a set of assumed factors $f_{k,t-n}$ during various time periods $t - n$ and calculated a set of coefficients b_k for a linear factor model to predict bond returns at time t from factors with a lag of $n > 0$ periods. The factor model has the form

$$R_t = \alpha + b_1 f_{1,t-n} + b_2 f_{2,t-n} + b_3 f_{3,t-n} + \cdots + b_K f_{K,t-n} + e_t$$

$$= \alpha + \sum_{k=1}^{K} b_k f_{k,t-n} + e_t \tag{4-3}$$

Only investigations evaluating linear models with lagged factors will be included in the comparison tables.

The list of investigators evaluated is shown in Table 4–1 along with the factors considered. Note that several factors are only employed by one investigator. Although these one-investigator factors may not be used for further comment in this chapter, they are left in the table for reference purposes.

TERM SPREAD

The term spread is the most frequently proposed factor for predicting future bond returns. The term spread is normally defined as the difference between a long-term bond yield and a short-term interest-bearing instrument yield, although other maturity differences are sometime employed. Most of the researchers shown in Table 4–2 use the yield difference between long-term (10 or 20 years) government bonds and the 30-day Treasury bill rate as the measure for the term spread of interest rates. In several instances, the long-term yield is based on the Moody's Aaa bond portfolio. In a few cases, the short-term yield is based on the 1-year Treasury bond.

It is possible that the term spread measures nothing more than a tendency for interest rates to return to their long-term average as pointed out by Fama and Bliss (1987). For example, if the long-term yield is exceptionally high and begins to drop, the owner of a long-term bond will find that the price of this bond will increase because

T A B L E   4-1

Bond Market Factors Considered by Various Investigators

Investigators \ Factors	Previous Stock Returns	Previous Bond Returns	Dividend Yield	Oil and Gold Stocks	Discount Rate Change	Real Interest Rate	Inflation (% Chg CPI or PPI)	Bond Yield Volatility	Interest Rate Volatility	Interest Rate	Default Spread	Term Spread Volatility	Term Spread
Anderson	A			A		A	A			A			
Balduzzi, Elton, and Green							BE						
Becker, Finnerty, and Kopecky							BF						
Booth and Booth			BB		BB					BB	BB		BB
Borio and McCauley		BM						BM					
Cutler, Poterba, and Summers		C											C
Domian and Reichenstein											D		D
Elder									E	E		E	E
Fama and Bliss		FB											FB
Fama and French			FF								FF		FF
Fama and Schwert							FS						
Ilmanen (June 1995)	I					I							I
Ilmanen (August 1995)	I2	I2				I2	I2						I2
Jensen, Mercer, and Johnson			J		J						J		J
Keim and Stambaugh	KS										KS		
Kirby			K										K
Lamont		L	L							L	L		L
Number of investigators using this factor out of 17 investigators	4	5	5	1	2	3	5	1	1	4	6	1	11

T A B L E   4-2

Investigators	Begin Data	End Data	Years of Data	Sign of Coefficient	Degree of Significance
Booth and Booth	1954	1992	39	+	*
Cutler, Poterba, and Summers (U.S.)	1926	1988	63	+	**
Domian and Reichenstein	1942	1994	53	+	*
Elder	1966	1991	24	+	***
Fama and Bliss	1964	1985	22	+	**
Fama and French	1927	1987	61	+	**
Ilmanen (June 1995)	1978	1993	16	+	Low
Ilmanen (August 1995)	1965	1995	31	+	*
Jensen, Mercer, and Johnson	1954	1992	39	+	*
Kirby	1927	1987	61	+	***
Lamont	1947	1994	48	+	**
Consensus				+	**

it carries a higher yield than similar bonds currently available. Conversely, if the long-term yield is exceptionally low, then the owner of a bond purchased at the previous low yield will find that the price of this bond will drop as interest rates rise. The existing low-yield bond will not be as valuable since new bonds will obtain higher yields. Therefore, the simple process of interest rates returning to their long-term mean could explain the apparent impact of a term spread on bond returns.

Fama and French (1989) suggest another explanation for the importance of terms spreads. The term spread can be considered as the risk premium associated with bearing the duration risk of an investment held for an extended period. This duration risk could have an impact on the return of stocks or bonds.

The empirical evidence seems overwhelming in support of the concept that bond returns can be expected to increase at high levels of a single term spread. Yet it also appears that more information about expected bond returns can be obtained from the entire structure of the yield curve. Cochrane and Piazzesi (2002) show that forecasts of the 1-year bond returns using several term spreads up to 5 years of maturity doubles the predictive power of the bond return regression. In their analysis, the short-term spread

(1 year − spot) provides the same positive effect on bond returns as shown by all researchers in Table 4–2. However, a more distant spread (4 years − 2 years) provides a significant negative coefficient when used in conjunction with the shorter spread. A very symmetric tent-shaped function of yields at different terms is shown to have a superior capability of forecasting 1-year returns.

DEFAULT SPREAD

The default spread, sometimes called the credit spread, represents the difference between a low-quality bond and a high-quality bond, generally at similar term levels. It is frequently taken as the difference between corporate bonds and government bonds. Other times it is taken as the difference between lower-quality (higher-yield) corporate bonds and high-quality (lower-yield) corporate bonds. The default spread represents a premium differential between bonds that are more likely to default and bonds that are less likely to default.

Just as in the case for the stock market, the rationale for relating bond returns to the default spread is based on the state of general business conditions. If business conditions are poor, then there is an increase in the likelihood of default in lower-quality corporate bonds. In addition, when business conditions are poor, the Federal Reserve Board is likely to lower interest rates in order to stimulate the economy. The drop in interest rates would generate higher returns on previously purchased bonds that carry a higher stated yield.

Table 4–3 shows those investigators who specifically considered default spreads in their linear factor models for bond returns. The consensus is unanimous that the impact of the default spread on bond returns has a positive coefficient. However, the degree of significance is modest. Only the Keim and Stambaugh (1986) results seem highly significant. This could be explained by the fact that their measure of the default spread is the difference between long-term Baa corporate bonds and a 30-day T-bill rate. This factor would seem to mix the term spread and the default spread into one factor since the terms of the two instruments are quite different. As such, this factor might be more representative of a term spread than a default spread. Ignoring the Keim and

T A B L E   4-3

Investigators	Begin Data	End Data	Years of Data	Sign of Coefficient	Degree of Significance
Booth and Booth	1954	1992	39	+	Low
Domian and Reichenstein	1942	1994	53	+	Low
Fama and French	1927	1987	61	+	Low
Jensen, Mercer, and Johnson	1954	1992	39	+	Low
Keim and Stambaugh	1928	1978	51	+	***
Lamont	1947	1994	48	+	*
Consensus				+	Low

Stambaugh results, Table 4–3 confirms the average significance of the results at a low level. With this one investigation removed, it would appear that the default spread may not exhibit much predictability, even in combination with other factors.

It seems somewhat counterintuitive that the default spread has a positive effect on bond returns as well as a positive effect on stock returns. This could indicate that weak business conditions require a higher premium be paid to induce investors to take funds out of cash and invest in either stocks or bonds.

INTEREST RATE

Bond returns might be expected to go down as the interest rate goes up, resulting in a negative coefficient. The empirical results presented in Table 4–4 do not unanimously confirm this expectation. One source of confusion stems from the fact that Anderson (1997) and Booth and Booth (1997) employ two measures of interest rates in their linear factor models. For these two instances, the more significant of the two factors did have a negative coefficient. The other factor might then be considered a correction factor. This leaves the Lamont (1998) results indicating the lone clearly positive coefficient.

An overall evaluation of Table 4–4 suggests a minor negative relationship between the interest rate and bond returns. A similar low-level relationship was found between the interest rate and stock returns. The fact that the interest rate has such a modest effect

T A B L E   4-4

Investigators	Begin Data	End Data	Years of Data	Sign of Coefficient	Degree of Significance
Anderson (6-month T-bill return)	1964	1993	30	−	***
Anderson (real interest rate)	1964	1993	30	+	**
Booth and Booth (change in discount rate)	1954	1992	39	−	*
Booth and Booth (federal funds rate)	1954	1992	39	+	Low
Elder (change in federal funds rate)	1966	1991	24	−	***
Lamont (T-bill−12-month average T-bill)	1947	1994	48	+	*
Consensus				−	*

on both stocks and bonds is somewhat unexpected. This probably indicates that the interest rate term is subordinate to some other term in the linear factor model. This appears to be the case. The correlation between the 90-day U.S. T-bill rate and the term spread (10-year government bonds minus 1-year government bonds) is greater than 0.96 using monthly data from April 1953 to June 2001. The information content in the term structure subsumes the expected logical relationship between the interest rate and bond returns. If the interest rate and the term spread are both in the model, then one of them is redundant due to collinearity.

INFLATION

Actual inflation and unanticipated inflation are both considered to have a major influence on bond market returns. The limited empirical evidence shown in Table 4–5 suggests that this is true. The impact of inflation on the stock market was found to be negative and to have a strong significance. With the exception of Fama and Schwert (1977), the influence of inflation on the bond market returns is also negative and very significant. The results obtained by Fama and Schwert were based on the inflation rate alone without any other factors. A univariate model employing the

T A B L E   4-5

Investigators	Begin Data	End Data	Years of Data	Sign of Coefficient	Degree of Significance
Anderson (lagged change in the CPI)	1964	1993	30	−	***
Balduzzi, Elton, and Green (CPI and PPI)	1991	1995	4	−	**
Becker, Finnerty, and Kopecky (CPI surprise)	1988	1990	2	−	***
Fama and Schwert	1953	1971	19	+	***
Ilmanen (August 1995)	1965	1995	31	−	*
Consensus				−	***

inflation rate results in a seemingly strong positive relationship with bond returns. When other factors are included in a linear factor model, it seems that the incremental impact of inflation does indeed have a negative coefficient.

DIVIDEND YIELD

As reflected in Table 4–6, there appears to be a low-level relationship between equity dividend yields and bond returns. The cause of any relationship between dividend yields on stocks and bond market returns is not obvious. Fama and French (1989) suggest that the level of dividend yields is an indication of general

T A B L E   4-6

Investigators	Begin Data	End Data	Years of Data	Sign of Coefficient	Degree of Significance
Booth and Booth	1954	1992	39	−	Low
Fama and French	1927	1987	61	+	Low
Jensen, Mercer, and Johnson	1954	1992	39	+	*
Kirby	1927	1987	61	+	Low
Lamont	1947	1994	48	+	*
Consensus				+	Low

business conditions. They take comfort in the result that the term spread, the default spread, and the dividend yield all have measurable impacts on both the stock and bond markets. They show no surprise that the dividend yield has the same directional effect on bonds and stocks with nearly the same value for the coefficient.

On the other hand, it is somewhat perplexing that Booth and Booth (1997) and Jensen, Mercer, and Johnson (1996) obtain opposite signs for the effect of dividend yields on bond returns using the same historical performance data from 1954 to 1992. This is probably caused by interactions with the other factors in their models.

PREVIOUS BOND RETURNS

Since reversion to the mean was identified as a significant factor for stocks, it is not surprising that a similar factor should be significant for bonds. Cutler, Poterba, and Summers (1991) and Fama and Bliss (1987) calculate that bond returns exhibit significant negative serial correlation although they do not include previous bond returns in their own linear factor models. Ilmanen (August 1995) employs a momentum factor, equivalent to a factor measuring the reversion of bond yield to the mean. A dummy variable is defined as $+1$ if the 20-year bond yield is more than 5 basis points below its 6-month average, -1 if the yield is more than 5 basis points above its 6-month average, and zero otherwise. These approaches may only indirectly indicate that there is a negative relationship between bond returns and previous bond return levels. They are displayed here, in Table 4–7, because further research in this chapter indicates

T A B L E 4–7

Investigators	Begin Data	End Data	Years of Data	Sign of Coefficient	Degree of Significance
Cutler, Poterba, and Summers (U.S.)	1926	1988	63	−	N/A
Fama and Bliss	1964	1985	22	−	N/A
Ilmanen (August 1995)	1965	1995	31	−	*
Lamont	1947	1994	48	−	Low
Consensus				−	*

that previous levels of bond returns do seem to have an influence
on subsequent returns.

PREVIOUS STOCK RETURNS

As can be seen from Table 4–8, there seems to be a small negative
impact of lagged stock returns on bond returns. While the
consensus is not unanimous in this regard, it does agree with a
similar conclusion regarding the impact of general economic
growth as applied to the stock market. Anderson (1997) argues that
a positive 24-month change in stock prices is a measure of future
economic strength. This strength is translated into an increased
demand for borrowing, resulting in higher interest rates and lower
bond returns.

Another explanation of the negative impact of stock returns on
bonds could come from the asset allocation shifts triggered when
the stock market undergoes a major move. When the stock market
moves up strongly, then the resulting anticipation of continued
stock market strength could encourage some liquidation of bonds
in order to increase the allocation to stocks. When the stock market
moves down strongly, then there could be a large subsequent
allocation shift from stocks to bonds for safety.

T A B L E 4–8

Investigators	Begin Data	End Data	Years of Data	Sign of Coefficient	Degree of Significance
Anderson	1964	1993	30	−	*
Ilmanen (June 1995)	1978	1993	16	−	**
Ilmanen (August 1995)	1965	1995	31	−	***
Keim and Stambaugh	1928	1978	51	+	**
Consensus				−	*

OTHER FACTORS FOUND TO BE SIGNIFICANT

The factors evaluated above reflect the collective thoughts of a large
number of investigators. To be included, a factor needs to be

evaluated by at least three investigators. A number of other less frequent, yet worthwhile, factors are considered by these investigators. While these additional factors will not be specifically evaluated in this chapter, the following list of factors is provided to record the fact that they were found to be significant in some evaluations and to stimulate additional research into their usefulness.

Volatility of Yield Changes

Borio and McCauley (1996) propose that the volatility of the daily changes in 10-year bond yields might offer some benefit in explaining the large negative bond returns experienced in 1994. This could prove quite useful because the extremely deep bond losses of 1994 prove vexing to justify.

Manufacturing Capacity Utilization

None of the investigators referred to in Table 4–1 specifically consider capacity utilization as a factor to be used to explain bond returns. Yet it is easy to demonstrate that manufacturing utilization has a demonstrable impact on both bond returns and stock returns. The linkage to bond returns could be through the relationship between capacity utilization and anticipated inflation. For discussions of this relationship, see Finn (1999) and Garner (1994).

Small-Stock Price Levels

Keim and Stambaugh (1986) find that the price level of small stocks has a significant impact on all classes of bond returns. While the impact on government bonds is measurable and significant, the impact on low-rated corporate bonds is the strongest. No theoretical basis for utilizing small-stock returns to predict subsequent bond returns is proposed. These results were obtained using in-sample evaluations. When attempting to use the small-stock variable to predict 1-month-ahead bond returns on an out-of-sample basis, the relationship ceases to be significant.

ANNUAL RETURN FACTOR MODEL FOR BONDS

An annual linear factor model for bonds is developed based on an expanded dividend discount formulation. The market return variable is the 12-month compounded return for a long-term government bond index consisting of bonds with terms 10 years or longer. Using a 12-month return for each of the 12 months in all available calendar years gives rise to an overlapping returns data series. Each month's annual return has 11 months in common with the previous month's annual return. The same adjustment to the standard error of the coefficients and the standard error of the regression is made to correct for this overlap as was done for the annual stock model.

Many factors were considered to explain the performance of bond returns. Following the lead of Cochrane and Piazzesi (2002) who employ bond yields for maturities of 1, 2, 3, 4, and 5 years, we also employ bond yields for bonds of multiple maturities. When incorporated with the other factors shown in the following model, bond yields at 1-, 5-, and 10-year terms appear to produce better results than Cochrane and Piazzesi's 1, 2, 3, 4, and 5 years.

The other factors in the model were determined by evaluating a host of interest rate variables and scanning empirically for the best lags. All the factors found to influence the stock market for a 12-month horizon were evaluated as well. Of these, the S&P 500 dividend yield and the manufacturing capacity utilization proved to be significant.

It is worth noting at this point that a large number of additional factors were evaluated and rejected purely on empirical grounds. Those factors that were eliminated included bond return volatility, consumer sentiment, U.S./non-U.S. bond yield differentials, industrial capacity growth, NYSE turnover, PPI and CPI inflation rates, U.S. budget deficit, changes in U.S. debt, and seasonal dummy variables. After evaluating all these factors, it is surprising that no measure of inflation proved beneficial in forecasting bond returns. This concern is somewhat offset by the inclusion of the manufacturing capacity utilization, which is considered to be a measure of inflationary expectation.

The following list of factors is employed in the annual bond return model:

The 1-year Treasury bond yield averaged over months 2–13 before the long-term government bond performance year.

The 5-year Treasury bond yield averaged over months 2–13 before the long-term government bond performance year.

The 10-year Treasury bond yield averaged over months 2–13 before the long-term government bond performance year.

The S&P 500 dividend yield averaged over months 2–13 before the long-term government bond performance year.

The 90-day Treasury bill yield averaged over months 2–13 before the long-term government bond performance year.

The 90-day Treasury bill yield averaged over months 14–43 before the long-term government bond performance year.

The long-term government bond return averaged over months 1–6 prior to the long-term government bond performance year. This is a reversion-to-the-mean variable.

The long-term government bond return averaged over months 7–12 prior to the long-term government bond performance year. This is another reversion-to-the-mean variable.

The average of all positive changes in the discount rate over months 1–10 before the long-term government bond performance year.

The manufacturing capacity utilization averaged over months 1–12 before the long-term government bond performance year.

The annualized default spread between the Baa Moody's corporate bond rate and the 10-year government bond rate averaged over months 2–13 before the long-term government bond performance year.

A linear regression was conducted based on the time interval of April 1955 through December 2001, consisting of more than 46 years of monthly data. The results obtained are shown in Table 4–9. Figure 4–1 shows the resulting actual versus fit comparison on a monthly basis for the 12-month bond factor model. The signs of the coefficients all agree with the consensus signs shown in Tables 4–2 to 4–8 except for the default spread and the dividend yield. More than likely, they are acting as correction variables for other factors in the model. Furthermore, the signficance of these two factors may be somewhat questionable because of their low *t*-statistics. Results of other research generally show that these factors have low significance, as shown in Tables 4–3 and 4–6.

Note the difficulty experienced by the model in fitting the 1994 era. This large negative performance has escaped explanation in several research efforts. Borio and McCauley (1996) proposed that high bond yield volatility or bond return volatility might be used to explain the 1994 low returns. They investigate both actual volatility

T A B L E 4-9

12-Month Horizon Bond Model Based on April 1955–December 2001

Factor	Beta	Std. Error	*t*-Statistic
Bond yield–U.S. Treasury–1 year	−34.8683	8.1585	−4.2739***
Bond yield–U.S. Treasury–5 year	59.1219	13.9293	4.2444***
Bond yield–U.S. Treasury–10 year	−28.3120	9.6103	−2.9460**
Stock index-S&P composite stock: dividend yield	−2.3254	1.1779	−1.9742*
Treasury bill yield–90 days–months 2–13	13.4850	4.7663	2.8292**
Treasury bill yield–90 days–months 14–43	−5.2664	1.3384	−3.9350***
Bond return–long term–months 1–6	−4.3974	0.9937	−4.4254***
Bond return–long term–months 7–12	−2.2490	0.9684	−2.3223*
Discount rate–percent increase	−38.7162	17.1787	−2.2537*
Manufacturing capacity utilization	−0.9448	0.4000	−2.3622**
Baa corp–long Govt. default spread	−5.7403	3.4835	−1.6478*

Alpha = 73.8052

$R^2 = 0.759$

Regression standard error = 6.1937

Significance based on a one-tailed test.
*Significant at 0.05 level.
**Significant at 0.01 level.
***Significant at 0.001 level. All standard errors adjusted for overlapping time intervals.

F I G U R E   4-1

Actual versus Fit Values—Bond Market Factor Model Fit to 2001

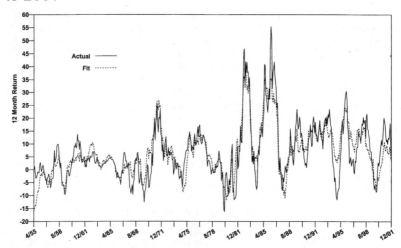

and implied volatility through options. While it is clear that this era did have high bond volatility, other intervals have similar high bond return volatility without generating such low returns. An attempt to employ bond return volatility as an additional factor in the model shown in Table 4–9 failed to produce a significant coefficient when using the entire 46-year time interval.

To gain some perspective on the degree of the fit ($R^2 = 0.759$) between the factors shown in Table 4–9 and the 12-month bond returns, Table 4–10 shows R^2 for similar multifactor 12-month bond regression models by investigators that report values for R^2.

MONTHLY RETURN FACTOR MODEL FOR BONDS

The model developed in the previous section is not practical to use as a forecasting model for all the same reasons that were pointed out for 12-month stock market models. The 12-month bond model smoothes out a great deal of noise due to investor reactions to news events and due to technical trading activities. But the 12-month model is not suitable for a continuing process of revising portfolio allocations. We can use the results of the 12-month horizon to

T A B L E 4-10

R^2 for Multifactor 12-Month Bond Return Models

Investigators	Begin Data	End Data	Years of Data	12-Month Bond Model R^2
Cochrane and Piazzesi	1964	1991	28	0.450
Cutler, Poterba, and Summers (U.S.)	1926	1988	63	0.055
Domian and Reichenstein	1942	1994	53	0.250
Fama and Bliss	1964	1985	22	0.140
Fama and French	1927	1987	61	0.150
Kirby	1927	1987	61	0.099
Average				0.191

discover those factors that have an impact on the bond market. Then we will attempt to apply these factors to a 1-month forecasting horizon. We anticipate that a 1-month model will not have the same goodness of fit as a 12-month model, but will be more suitable for a forecasting and model revision process.

Using the same factors that were employed for the 12-month factor model for bonds, it was found that a number of the original factors proved not to be significant at the 1-month horizon. Only one of the three government bond yield factors remained significant, the one at the 5-year term. This is likely due to a strong correlation among the 1-, 5-, and 10-year bond yields. For example, the correlation coefficient between the 1- and 5-year government bond yields is 0.9678 for the months from April 1953 to December 2001. For the same interval, there is a 0.9949 correlation between the 5- and 10-year government bonds. This could mean that the 1- and 10-year bond yields in the 12-month model could be correction variables to the 5-year bond yield, as evidenced in the opposite sign as the 5-year yield shown in Table 4–9.

Similarly, only one of the two Treasury bill factors remained significant in the 1-month-horizon model. Since the Treasury bill factors had opposite signs in the 12-month regression, this could mean that one of the factors was a correction variable for the other.

Two additional factors appear in the 1-month model. These factors are the average return of the S&P 500 in the previous 2 months and the unemployment rate.

After the above additions and deletions in factors are made, the following list of factors is employed in the 1-month bond return model:

The 5-year Treasury bond yield averaged for the 13 months before the long-term government bond performance month.

The S&P 500 dividend yield average for the 21 months before the long-term government bond performance month.

The 90-day Treasury bill yield average for the 13 months before the long-term government bond performance month.

The long-term government bond return average for the 3 months prior to the long-term government bond performance month.

The long-term government bond return averaged over months 14–38 prior to the long-term government bond performance month. This is a reversion-to-the-mean variable.

The manufacturing capacity utilization in the month before the long-term government bond performance month.

The annualized default spread between the Baa Moody's corporate bond rate and the 10-year government bond rate average for the 24 months before the long-term government bond performance month.

The rate of return for the S&P 500 without dividends for the 3 months before the long-term government bond performance month.

The civilian labor unemployment rate for the 14 months before the long-term government bond performance month.

With the use of these factors, the regression results shown in Table 4–11 are obtained.

We will employ the factors shown in Table 4–11 for bonds along with the factors in Table 3–19 for stocks to conduct research into factors affecting dynamic asset allocation when U.S. bonds and U.S. stocks are a component of the investment portfolio.

Again the dividend yield and the default spread are found to have coefficients opposite in sign to what we might expect. It is assumed that they are acting as correction variables for other

T A B L E 4-11

1-Month Horizon Model Based on April 1955 – December 2001

Factor	Beta	Std. Error	t-Statistic
Bond yield–U.S. Treasury–5 year	1.7428	0.2431	7.1680***
Stock index-S&P composite stock: dividend yield	− 0.4494	0.1808	− 2.4851**
Treasury bill yield–90 days–months 1–13	− 1.3080	0.2083	− 6.2795***
Bond return–long term–months 1–3	− 0.1894	0.0734	− 2.5802**
Bond return–long term–months 14–38	− 0.4687	0.2538	− 1.8467*
Manufacturing capacity utilization	− 0.0772	0.0356	− 2.1700*
Baa corp–long Govt. default spread–months 1–24	− 1.3047	0.3929	− 3.3211***
Stock S&P 500–price only–months 1–3	− 0.1942	0.0451	− 4.3071***
Unemployment rate–civilian labor–months 1–14	− 0.2756	0.1654	− 1.6670*

Alpha = 8.2658

$R^2 = 0.119$

Regression standard error = 2.4344

Significance based on a one-tailed test.
*Significant at 0.05 level.
**Significant at 0.01 level.
***Significant at 0.001 level.

factors in the model. They will both be retained for research into the factors influencing optimal asset allocations.

Both the recent bond returns and the recent stock market returns have negative coefficients in the 1-month-horizon bond model. This is the opposite direction for similar factors in the 1-month-horizon stock market model. The 1-month stock market model has positive coefficients for both the recent stock and bond returns. This indicates that when both the stock and bond markets are up in a given month, the stock market is expected to be up in the next month and the bond market is expected to be down. This pair of reactions could simply mean that the stock market behaves as the investment of choice after large investment profits and that the bond market behaves as the investment of choice after times of large investment losses. This would be a rational response for

T A B L E 4–12

R^2 for Multifactor 1-Month Bond Return Models

Investigators	Begin Data	End Data	Years of Data	12-Month Bond Model R^2
Booth and Booth	1954	1992	39	0.010
Cutler, Poterba, and Summers (U.S.)	1926	1988	63	0.004
Fama and French	1927	1987	61	0.010
Ilmanen (June 1995)	1978	1993	16	0.123
Ilmanen (August 1995)	1965	1995	31	0.103
Jensen, Mercer, and Johnson	1954	1992	39	0.030
Kirby	1927	1987	61	0.012
Consensus				0.042

investors anticipating that only stocks will continue moving in the same direction.

To gain some perspective on the degree of the fit ($R^2 = 0.119$) between the factors shown in Table 4–11 and the 1-month bond returns, Table 4–12 shows R^2 for similar 1-month multifactor bond regression models from other investigations that report values for R^2. Note that the high Ilmanen (June 1995) result, $R^2 = 0.123$, does not include data for the 1994 bond returns, which have proved so elusive to explain. The follow-up research presented in Ilmanen (August 1995) covers an extended date range including the enigmatic 1994 era, resulting in a lower R^2 of 0.103.

As with the monthly stock model, the level of the R^2 at 0.119 may not seem to explain very much of the month-to-month variation in bond prices. But even this low level turns out to be enough to present an advantage in a market timing model controlled by multiple factors.

REFERENCES

Anderson, Richard. *Market Timing Models*. Chicago: Irwin Professional Publishing, 1997.

Balduzzi, Pierluigi, Edwin J. Elton, and T. Clifton Green. "Economic News and Bond Prices: Evidence from the U.S. Treasury Market." *Journal of Financial and Quantitative Analysis* (February 2001).

Becker, Kent G., Joseph E. Finnerty, and Kenneth J. Kopecky. "Macroeconomic News and the Efficiency of International Bond Futures Markets." *Journal of Futures Markets* 16 (1996): 131–145.

Booth, James R., and Lena Chua Booth. "Economic Factors, Monetary Policy, and Expected Returns on Stocks and Bonds." *Federal Reserve Bank of San Francisco Economic Review,* no. 2 (1997): 32–42.

Borio, Claudio E. V., and Robert N. McCauley. "The Anatomy of the Bond Market Turbulence of 1994." Working paper no. 159. Presented at a Symposium on Global Capital Flows in Economic Development, sponsored by the Jerome Levy Economics Institute of Bard College, United Nations Conference on Trade and Development Global Interdependence Division and Intergovernmental Group of Twenty-Four on International Monetary Affairs, March 8–9, 1996.

Cochrane, John H., and Monika Piazzesi. "Bond Risk Premia." Working paper, Graduate School of Business, University of Chicago and Anderson School, UCLA, Los Angeles (August 2002).

Cutler, David M., James M. Poterba, and Lawrence H. Summers. "Speculative Dynamics." *Review of Economic Studies* 58 (1991): 529–546.

Domian, Dale L., and William Reichenstein. "Term Spreads and Predictions of Bond and Stock Excess Returns." *Financial Services Review* 7, no. 1 (1998): 25–44.

Elder, John. "Sources of Time-Varying Risk Premia in the Term Structure." *Advances in Investment and Portfolio Management* 9 (2002): 85–108.

Fama, Eugene F., and Robert R. Bliss. "The Information in Long-Maturity Forward Rates." *American Economic Review* 77, no. 4 (1987): 680–692.

Fama, Eugene F., and Kenneth R. French. "Business Conditions and Expected Returns on Stocks and Bonds." *Journal of Financial Economics* 25 (1989): 23–50.

Fama, Eugene F., and G. William Schwert. "Asset Returns and Inflation." *Journal of Financial Economics* 5 (1977): 115–146.

Finn, Mary G. "Is 'High' Capacity Utilization Inflationary?" *Federal Reserve Bank of Richmond Economic Quarterly* 81 (Winter 1999): 1–16.

Garner, C. Alan. "Capacity Utilization and U.S. Inflation." *Federal Reserve Bank of Kansas City Economic Review* (Fourth Quarter 1994): 5–21.

Ilmanen, Antti. "Time-Varying Expected Returns in International Bond Markets." *Journal of Finance* 50, no. 2 (June 1995): 481–506.

Ilmanen, Antti. "Forecasting US Bond Returns: Understanding the Yield Curve, Part 4." *Salomon Brothers United States Fixed Income Research* (August 1995): 1–20.

Jensen, Gerald R., Jeffrey M. Mercer, and Robert R. Johnson. "Business Conditions, Monetary Policy, and Expected Security Returns." *Journal of Financial Economics* 40, no. 2 (1996): 213–237.

Keim, Donald B., and Robert F. Stambaugh. "Predicting Returns in the Stock and Bond Markets." *Journal of Financial Economics* 17 (1986): 357–390.

Kirby, C. "Measuring the Predictable Variation in Stock and Bond Returns." *Review of Financial Studies* 10 (1997): 579–630.

Lamont, Owen. "Earnings and Expected Return." *Journal of Finance* 53, no. 5 (1998): 1563–1587.

Williams, John Burr. *The Theory of Investment Value.* Cambridge, Mass.: Harvard University Press, 1938.

Factors Influencing Interest Rates

> Every man, as long as he does not violate the laws
> of justice, is left perfectly free to pursue his own
> interest his own way, and to bring both his
> industry and capital into competition with those
> of any other man or order of men.
>
> *Adam Smith*
> *Wealth of Nations (1776)*

Of the three traditional investments categories of stocks, bonds, and interest rates, the role of interest rates provides the least impact on an investment portfolio over the long horizon. The level of interest rate returns is simply much lower than the average return for stocks or bonds. While there is some uncertainty concerning the level of future interest rates, the range of uncertainty is much smaller than that of the other two assets. On the risk side, the probability of losing significant capital in a short-term interest instrument is zero for all practical purposes. Although interest rates represent low returns, they do have a legitimate place in an investment portfolio. Essentially, the use of interest-bearing instruments is useful in two situations. The first situation is a reserve to provide a source of ready cash in case of an emergency. The second situation is to provide a safe haven for the portfolio during times when both stocks and bonds are expected to have low returns or high risk.

Compared with forecasting future stock and bond returns, estimating the future return on short-term interest-paying instruments is a much easier problem. It is easier to arrive at good accuracy levels on interest rate forecasts because the returns just do not vary as much as they do for stocks and bonds. As we shall see in the remainder of this chapter, the simple model that forecasts future interest rates from past interest rates is hard to improve on. For the purpose of mixing an interest-bearing instrument with stocks and bonds, this naive forecast of future interest rates from past interest rates may be accurate enough. Using such a procedure would likely yield interest rate forecasting errors much smaller than the errors on the stock and bond forecasts using much more complex models. On the other hand, a great deal is known about mechanisms that influence interest rates, and we may want to take advantage of this knowledge.

Before investigating these mechanisms, we need to define which investment instrument is to be used to represent interest rates. Long-term, and even medium-term, bonds are not suitable instruments to use as interest rate instruments. These instruments suffer at the hands of factors that influence the difference between the bond's declared yield and its actual periodic return. As a matter of principle, the shortest-term instrument that is readily available to investors is the one to use. While the discount rate or U.S. federal funds rate or an overnight repurchase agreement may have very short terms, they are not available to individual investors. So it is sensible to consider short-term Treasury instruments such as 30-day or 90-day T-bills. These are readily available to any investor and do not suffer significant differences between the declared rate and the market rate during their term. In the end, we shall employ the 90-day T-bill rate because of the long history available for this instrument.

FUNDAMENTAL APPROACHES

A number of interest rate forecasting methodologies have been investigated extensively in the literature. For an account of some of the methodologies that have been applied, see the survey by Fauvel, Paquet, and Zimmermann (1999). Rather than considering every available method, we shall restrict ourselves to the following three approaches:

Future interest rates are determined solely by past rates.

Future rates are functions of past influential factors.

Future rates are functions of past rates as well as influential factors.

Each of these approaches is discussed in turn.

Interest Rates Are Determined Solely by Past Rates

Much research has been conducted using a continuous-time short-term rate model specification such as

$$dr = (\alpha + \beta r)dt + \sigma r^{\gamma}dz_t \qquad (5\text{--}1)$$

where:

r = short-term interest rate
α, β, γ = model coefficients to be determined
σ = standard deviation of the short-term rates
z = Brownian motion

This formulation assumes that movements in interest rate are strictly a function of interest rate levels and volatility. For investigations of such formulations, see Brenner, Harjes, and Kroner (1996), Chan, Karolyi, Longstaff, and Sanders (1992), and Sanders and Unal (1988).

From (5–1) a discrete time model can be obtained:

$$r_t = \alpha + \beta r_{t-1} + \varepsilon_t \qquad (5\text{--}2)$$

where:

r_t = short-term interest rate at time t
r_{t-1} = short-term interest rate at time $t - 1$
ε_t = model error term at time
Expected value $(\varepsilon_t) = 0$
α, β = model coefficients to be determined

Depending on the date range evaluated, the value of β is normally found to be very significant and close to 1. This indicates that interest rates have high serial correlation. Such a result is to be expected since, on average, interest rates are only changed every 4 or 5 months by the Fed. In the sections that follow, the model described in (5–2) will be used as a kind of base model on which to evaluate the effectiveness of other models.

Interest Rates Are Functions of Past Influential Factors

In the United States, there is one governmental authority that has the power to actually influence interest rates: the Federal Reserve Board. The Fed is charged with conducting monetary policy. By various mechanisms, the Fed can establish targets for variables it can influence called monetary policy instruments. These targeted instruments are short-term interest rates such as the federal funds rate, monetary aggregates such as M1, or some combination of the two. The Humphrey-Hawkins Act of 1978 mandates that the federal government is responsible to promote "full employment and production ... and reasonable price stability." Unfortunately, setting a policy to achieve all three of these objectives simultaneously is good politics but unrealistic science. A widely accepted economic theory presented in Phillips (1958) called the Phillips curve is violated by establishing such a trinary objective. The Phillips curve holds that there is an inverse relationship between the inflation rate and the unemployment rate. That is, when unemployment goes down, then inflation should go up. And conversely, when inflation goes down, then unemployment should go up. Based on the Phillips curve, it should not be possible to maintain low inflation and low unemployment for an indefinite period.

Deciding how to achieve these goals is the responsibility of the Federal Reserve Board's Federal Open Market Committee (FOMC). The policies are then executed by the FOMC trading desk in New York that purchases and sells government securities. The volume of such transactions can be used to control the level of monetary aggregates or the interest rate.

Many investigators have attempted to deduce whether the Fed, in the implementation of its policies, is following formalized policy rules that might be expressed in equation form. These rules are termed monetary policy reaction functions. Investigators have sought to determine if the Fed policy is a function of a range of actual as well as anticipated macroeconomic factors.

Unfortunately, no single consistent monetary policy reaction function can describe the course of interest rates or monetary aggregates over the interval from 1951 to 2002. Monetary policy reaction functions seem to change with the chairmanship of the Federal Reserve Board and, to some extent, with the economic conditions occurring within a chairman's tenure. To make matters more complex, according to Sheehan (1985) and Bordo and Schwartz (1998), the policy instrument was not constant over the last half of the twentieth century. Table 5–1 indicates the shifting policy instruments targeted. Since the target policy instrument is shifting in time, the factor coefficients that influence each particular policy instrument may have one set of values when that policy instrument is being targeted and then take on another set of values when another policy instrument is targeted. Therefore, the effect of any factor that influences monetary policy may change with time. Nonetheless, there seems to be a limited number of macroeconomic factors that are suggested to influence the decision process of the FOMC in its deliberations. Any policy reaction function that characterizes the way that the Fed sets interest rates can be used as a reasonable forecasting tool for interest rates.

The most noted policy reaction function is the Taylor rule described by Taylor (1993). The factors incorporated in this model are two of the objectives that the Fed is charged by Congress to

T A B L E　5–1

History of Federal Reserve Targeted Policy Instruments

Chairman	Date Range	Basic Policy Instrument
William Martin	1951–1970	Interest rate
Arthur Burns	1970/Q1–1978/Q1	Mixed target
G. William Miller	1978/Q2–1979/Q2	Mixed target
Early Paul Volcker	1979/Q3–1982/Q2	Monetary aggregate
Later Paul Volcker	1982/Q3–1987/Q2	Mixed target
Alan Greenspan	1987/Q3–Forward	Mixed target

control: inflation and output. The coefficients of this equation are not determined empirically. They are hypothesized based on rational values that should tend to stabilize the mandated objectives.

$$r_t = p_{t-1} + 0.5y_{t-1} + 0.5(p_{t-1} - 2) + 2 \qquad (5\text{--}3)$$

where:

   r_t = federal funds rate
   p_{t-1} = rate of inflation over the previous four quarters
   y_{t-1} = previous quarter percent deviation of real GDP from a
        target

Note that this equation indicates that the federal funds rate should be changed 1.5 percent for each 1 percent change in inflation. It is felt that such a forceful reaction to inflation tends to drive future inflation to a lower value. Judd and Rudebusch (1998) show that when interest rates are not adjusted strongly in reaction to past inflation, the result can be rampant future inflation similar to the inflation exhibited during the era of 1970–1978.

   The Taylor rule has become the basis for comparison and development of other policy reaction functions. Modifications to the Taylor rule include the addition of other variables such as unemployment and money growth, as exemplified by Fair (2001) and Clarida, Galí, and Gertler (1998). Other considerations include the addition of expectations of future values of inflation and output, as shown in Mehra (1999) and Orphanides (2001b).

Interest Rates Are Functions of Past Rates as Well as Influential Factors

The third approach combines the factors of the Taylor rule with previous interest rates. By combining equations (5–2) and (5–3), we obtain the following using slightly different coefficient symbols:

$$r_t = \alpha + \beta p_{t-1} + \lambda y_{t-1} + \rho r_{t-1} + \varepsilon_t \qquad (5\text{--}4)$$

where:

      r_t = short-term interest rate at time t
   p_{t-1} = inflation rate at time $t - 1$

y_{t-1} = output gap at time $t - 1$, equal to GDP less potential GDP

ε_t = model error term at time t

Expected value $(\varepsilon_t) = 0$

$\alpha, \beta, \lambda, \rho$ = model coefficients to be determined

Numerous investigators have evaluated equations of this form using past values of inflation and the output gap for various time intervals and various countries including Fair and Howrey (1996), Judd and Rudebusch (1998), and Clarida, Galí, and Gertler (1998).

FACTORS INVESTIGATED FOR AN INTEREST RATE RETURN MODEL

We have the benefit of a defined monetary policy rule, the Taylor rule. Taylor (1993) shows that this rule fits the changes in the federal funds rate with reasonable accuracy. Using the Taylor rule as a starting point, a number of additional factors have also been considered in other investigations.

We include only those investigations that propose a list of interest rate factors and empirically calculate coefficients for those factors based on a significant time range. Only those factors considered by two or more investigators will be evaluated. The coefficient value is displayed along with its confidence level. Although the investigators employ different date ranges to determine the coefficients, it is useful to see the range of coefficient values. Many of the investigators obtain multiple sets of results under different assumptions and combinations of variables. The one set of results thought to be the most meaningful was selected for inclusion in the tables below. In some investigations, separate results were obtained for multiple historic date ranges. In this case, the most recent range is the one evaluated. The degree of confidence will be rated using a three-star system based on statistical confidence intervals. One of the following entries is entered in the tables under the heading of "Degree of Significance."

Low   Indicates a very low probability of any relationship. This is typically indicated by one-tailed t-statistics below 1.88, indicating more than a 3 percent probability of a zero coefficient.

*   Indicates that a modest relationship is established. This is typically measured by one-tailed t-statistics in the range of 1.88–2.99, indicating less than a 3 percent probability of a zero coefficient.

**   Indicates that a strong relationship is established. This is typically measured by one-tailed t-statistics in the range of 3.00–3.99, indicating less than a 0.15 percent probability of a zero coefficient.

***   Indicates that an exceptionally strong relationship is established. This is typically measured by t-statistics above 4.00, indicating less than a 0.004 percent probability of a zero coefficient.

Each factor is summarized to indicate any apparent consensus for the direction of the influence of the factor and to indicate the overall level of the confidence in the use of that factor. This summary is on the bottom row of each evaluation and is marked "Consensus." Only models that attempt to predict the federal funds rate or Treasury bills are evaluated. Investigations into the factors affecting longer-term instrument returns are excluded.

We have seen that past levels of inflation and the output gap are suggested as the most important fundamental factors considered by the Fed when setting interest rate levels. Since several investigators believe it important to consider expectations of future values of these two factors, these too are included. The past level of interest rates is also found useful. Finally, other factors such as unemployment and money supply are frequently considered. For each factor k, a table is presented based on the work of a fixed list of investigators who have each evaluated a set of assumed factors $f_{k,t-n}$ during various time periods $t-n$ and calculated a set of coefficients b_k for a linear factor model to predict interest rates at time t from factors with a lag of $n > 0$ periods. The factor model has the form

$$R_t = \alpha + b_1 f_{1,t-n} + b_2 f_{2,t-n} + b_3 f_{3,t-n} + \cdots + b_K f_{K,t-n} + e_t$$

$$= \alpha + \sum_{k=1}^{K} b_k f_{k,t-n} + e_t \tag{5-5}$$

T A B L E 5-2

Federal Funds Rate Factors Considered by Various Investigators

Investigators	Actual Inflation	Expected Inflation	Actual Output Gap	Expected Output Gap	Previous Federal Funds Rate	Money Supply	Unemployment Rate or Change	Bond Yield	Exchange Rates
Clarida, Gali, and Gertler (1998)	C8		C8		C8	C8			C8
Clarida, Gali, and Gertler (2000)	CO		CO		CO				
Fair	F				F	F	F		
Fair and Howrey	FH		FH		FH		FH		
Judd and Rudebusch	JR		JR						
McNees	Mc	Mc	Mc		Mc	Mc	Mc		Mc
Mehra (1997)	M7		M7		M7	M7	M7	M7	
Mehra (1999)	M9	M9	M9	M9	M9	M9		M9	
Nelson	N	N	N		N				
Orphanides (2001a)	OA	OA	OA	OA	OA				
Orphanides (2001b)		OB		OB	OB				
Taylor (1998)	T		T						
Williams	W		W		W				
Number of investigators using this factor out of 13 investigators	12	5	11	3	11	5	4	2	2

Only investigations evaluating linear models employing time lags such as equation (5–5) will be included in the comparison tables.

The list of investigators evaluated is shown in Table 5–2 along with the factors considered. Note that several factors are only employed by two investigators. Although these two-investigator factors may not be used for further comment in this chapter, they are left in the table for reference purposes.

There is a remarkable consistency in the model factors employed. All 13 investigations but one contain both inflation and the output gap as actual past or expected values. All but one of these investigations employ the previous interest rate level. Approximately half the investigations evaluate unemployment or money supply. The other factors evaluated are considered by only two investigators. This indicates that only a handful of factors is considered to influence the Fed in its deliberations concerning interest rates.

ACTUAL INFLATION

Almost all investigators evaluated actual inflation as a factor in the Fed's policy reaction function. It is found to be a very significant factor. Of the two investigators who do not include actual inflation, McNees (1986) ultimately substitutes unemployment for inflation, and Orphanides (2001b) only considers forward-looking factors including expected inflation. Substituting unemployment for inflation is an understandable approach because of the relationship between the two under the terms of the Phillips curve.

The specific measure of inflation employed is variously calculated from changes in the consumer price index, the producer price index, the raw materials price index, and the personal consumption expenditures price index. But the inflation measure most often employed is the same one used by Taylor (1993), the implicit GDP deflator.

As shown in Table 5–3, the average coefficient for inflation rates is near 0.90, with a range from 0.14 to 1.53. Taylor (1993) suggests that changing interest rates by 1.5 times the change in inflation is a sensible rule for controlling future inflation. Raising interest rates by more than the change in inflation increases the real interest rate. Assuming that such a change in real interest rates would propagate its way through the yield curve to affect other interest-bearing instruments, this would encourage more investment in fixed-income investments. Coupled with the effect of an increased cost of borrowing, these reactions should reduce the demand for goods and thereby lower future inflation.

T A B L E 5-3

Investigators	Begin Data	End Data	Years of Data	Coefficient	Degree of Significance
Clarida, Galí, and Gertler (1998)	1982	1994	12	+1.26	***
Clarida, Galí, and Gertler (2000)	1982	1996	14	+1.46	*
Fair	1982	1999	17	+0.145	**
Fair and Howrey	1962	1993	31	+0.389	N/A
Judd and Rudebusch	1987	1997	10	+0.54	*
Mehra (1997)	1970	1992	22	+0.60	***
Mehra (1999)	1979	1998	19	+1.2	***
Nelson (U.K.)	1992	1997	5	+1.267	*
Orphanides (2001a)	1987	1992	5	+1.13	***
Taylor (1998)	1987	1997	11	+1.533	***
Williams	1980	1997	18	+0.38	**
Consensus				0.9004	**

EXPECTED INFLATION

Those investigators who evaluate expected inflation conclude that the Fed is likely to put a heavier weight on expectations of future inflation than on past levels of inflation. Three sources of inflation expectation are available. This first is the inflation forecast from the Survey Research Center at the University of Michigan, and the second is the inflation expectations contained in the Greenbook prepared by Federal Reserve staff for the FOMC before each of its meetings. Unfortunately, the Greenbook is not made public until 5 years after the fact. The information contained therein is only available for research purposes and not available for real-time forecasting. The third source of inflation expectations is available from commercial forecasting services. Most of the investigations shown in Table 5–4 utilize the FOMC Greenbook forecasts.

On this small sample, it appears that the degree of significance may be slightly higher for expected inflation than it is for actual inflation. It is noteworthy that the average policy reaction function coefficients for actual and expected inflation are nearly the same.

T A B L E 5-4

Investigators	Begin Data	End Data	Years of Data	Coefficient	Degree of Significance
McNees	1970	1986	16	+0.24	***
Mehra (1999)	1979	1998	19	+0.40	***
Orphanides (2001a)	1987	1992	5	+1.29	***
Orphanides (2001b)	1979	1995	16	+1.80	**
Consensus				0.9325	***

ACTUAL OUTPUT GAP

The output gap is defined as the percentage difference between the actual GDP and a target or potential GDP. Potential GDP is defined by the Congressional Budget Office as a measure of maximum sustainable output—the level of real GDP in a given year that is consistent with a stable rate of inflation. Potential GDP is calculated in various ways. Mehra (1997) estimates potential GDP based on a linear trend of past GDP values. Another frequently used estimator is the structural definition of potential GDP developed by the Congressional Budget Office (2001). According to this CBO publication:

> If actual output rises above its potential level, then constraints on capacity begin to bind and inflationary pressures build; if output falls below potential, then resources are lying idle and inflationary pressures abate.

Using this model, the CBO regularly publishes estimates of potential GDP.

Table 5–5 indicates that the actual output gap must be a significant component of the Federal Reserve's policy reaction function. Most of the coefficients are strongly significant. The average value of the output gap coefficient of 0.512 is very close to the original theoretical estimate of 0.50 in Taylor (1993). For the low-valued coefficients developed by Fair and Howrey (1996) and Williams (1999), the values of the coefficients and their degree of significance depend strongly on other factors in the model. For example, Fair and Howrey (1996) utilize several lagged values of unemployment. Okun's law holds that there is a relationship

TABLE 5-5

Investigators	Begin Data	End Data	Years of Data	Coefficient	Degree of Significance
Clarida, Gali, and Gertler (1998)	1982	1994	12	+0.52	***
Clarida, Gali, and Gertler (2000)	1982	1996	14	+0.74	*
Fair and Howrey	1962	1993	31	+0.077	N/A
Judd and Rudebusch	1987	1997	10	+0.99	***
Mehra (1997)	1970	1992	22	+0.19	**
Nelson (U.K.)	1992	1997	5	+0.470	**
Orphanides (2001a)	1987	1992	5	+0.74	***
Taylor (1998)	1987	1997	11	+0.762	***
Williams	1980	1997	18	+0.12	*
Consensus				+0.512	**

between the output gap and unemployment. Including unemployment and the output gap in the same model could give rise to a multicollinearity problem influencing the estimates of all the coefficients. Williams (1999) includes both the output gap and a change in the output gap in the policy reaction function. Including both factors alters the significance of the level of the output gap itself.

EXPECTED OUTPUT GAP

Table 5–6 shows the expected output gap. Mehra (1999) calculates the expected output gap using two methods based on past values of the GDP: a smoothing function and a quadratic time trend. Orphanides (2001a, 2001b) employs Federal Reserve Board staff estimates of future values of the output gap. In Orphanides (2001b), two historical date ranges are employed, 1966/Q1–1979/Q2 and 1979/Q3–1995/Q4. Both expected inflation and the expected output gap are significant in the earlier interval, and only expected inflation is significant in the later interval. Because both factors are staff estimates, this result could mean the FOMC placed less emphasis on the expected output gap in the most recent interval. Or it could mean that the staff estimates of the future output gap do

T A B L E 5-6

Investigators	Begin Data	End Data	Years of Data	Coefficient	Degree of Significance
Mehra (1999)	1979	1998	19	+0.26	***
Orphanides (2001a)	1987	1992	5	+1.00	***
Orphanides (2001b)	1979	1995	16	+0.27	Low
Consensus				+0.510	**

not carry as much influence as actual past measures of the output gap in the Fed's policy reaction function.

Nonetheless, it appears from Table 5-6 that there is some value in forward-looking output gap measures. The average significance level is quite high, and the average value of the coefficient is strikingly similar to the average found for the actual output gap.

PREVIOUS FEDERAL FUNDS RATE

As Table 5-7 shows, all evidence points to the fact that previous interest rates are very good predictors of subsequent interest rates. The reason for this is simple. If the Fed does not act to change the

T A B L E 5-7

Investigators	Begin Data	End Data	Years of Data	Coefficient	Degree of Significance
Clarida, Gali, and Gertler (1998)	1982	1994	12	+0.96	***
Clarida, Gali, and Gertler (2000)	1982	1996	14	+0.87	***
Fair	1982	1999	17	+0.939	***
Fair and Howrey	1962	1993	31	+0.651	N/A
McNees	1970	1986	16	+0.94	***
Mehra (1999)	1979	1998	19	+0.59	***
Nelson (U.K.)	1992	1997	5	+0.288	*
Orphanides (2001a)	1987	1992	5	+0.49	***
Orphanides (2001b)	1979	1995	16	+0.79	***
Williams	1980	1997	18	+0.83	***
Consensus				+0.735	***

discount rate, then the discount rate stays the same. Since 1960 the Fed only has acted to change the discount rate every 4 to 5 months on average. As a result, the last value of the discount rate perfectly predicts the next monthly value at least 75 percent of the time. Other short-term interest rates such as the federal funds rate or T-bill rates would tend to follow very closely.

MONEY SUPPLY

The supply of money is one of the policy instruments that the Fed can choose as its target. As Table 5–1 indicates, in the last half of the twentieth century, only during mid-1979 to mid-1982 did the Fed choose to specifically target monetary aggregates. Since 1960, the correlation between the level of the discount rate and changes in M3 has only been 0.29. This means that the two policy instruments are reasonably independent. Since it is impossible to control two independent policy instruments, the interest rate would appear to be the true policy instrument, and the Fed could be treating the growth in the monetary aggregate as a constraint to be kept within bounds. That is, if the money supply begins to grow faster than a preselected rate, the Fed might increase the discount rate by an extra amount in order to keep money growth within bounds.

Nonetheless, as shown in Table 5–8, those investigators who choose to include the money supply in the Federal Reserve's policy reaction function find a significant relationship when other variables are also included. Only Fair (2001) finds the money supply offers no significant contribution to the policy reaction

T A B L E 5-8

Investigators	Begin Data	End Data	Years of Data	Coefficient	Degree of Significance
Clarida, Gali, and Gertler (1998)	1982	1994	12	+0.21	***
Fair	1982	1999	17	+0.001	Low
McNees	1970	1986	16	+0.16	***
Mehra (1997)	1970	1992	22	0.12	***
Mehra (1999)	1979	1998	19	0.26	***
Consensus				+0.15	**

function when evaluating 1982/Q4–1999/Q3. On the other hand, Fair does find that the money supply has a significant influence during the time interval of 1954/Q1–1979/Q3, a time when the Fed is considered to have targeted money aggregates on a regular basis.

UNEMPLOYMENT RATE

Table 5–9 indicates a modestly strong reaction on interest rates from the unemployment rate. McNees (1986) and Fair (2001) find that the effect of the unemployment rate is so strong in the Fed's policy reaction function that it makes the use of the output gap unnecessary. Fair holds that the unemployment rate dominates the output gap in terms of explanatory power. The Humphrey-Hawkins Act of 1978 requires the federal government to promote full employment as a part of its monetary policies. Unemployment may be viewed in the same light as monetary aggregates and be targeted when its value falls outside certain bounds, and not specifically targeted when it is within bounds. Alternatively, the Phillips curve holds that there is a natural relationship between inflation and the unemployment rate. When unemployment levels go outside the historical range suggested by the Phillips curve, the Fed may take this as a signal to keep the relationship within bounds. Either the unemployment rate or the inflation rate could react to put their combined values back on the Phillips curve.

T A B L E 5-9

Investigators	Begin Data	End Data	Years of Data	Coefficient	Degree of Significance
Fair	1982	1999	17	−0.085	*
Fair and Howrey	1962	1993	31	−0.858	N/A
McNees	1970	1986	16	−0.39	***
Consensus				−0.444	**

UNEMPLOYMENT CHANGE

All three investigations identified in Table 5–10 simultaneously use both the level of the employment rate and the change in the

T A B L E 5-10

Investigators	Begin Data	End Data	Years of Data	Coefficient	Degree of Significance
Fair	1982	1999	17	− 0.901	***
Fair and Howrey	1962	1993	31	− 0.747	N/A
McNees	1970	1986	16	− 1.93	***
Consensus				− 1.193	***

unemployment rate in their policy reaction functions. It appears that the change in unemployment is the more significant of the two. The Fed may be somewhat accommodative of high or low levels of unemployment in certain circumstances but reacts to keep down any new changes in the unemployment rate. This would place a stronger emphasis on unemployment rate changes rather than levels.

OTHER FACTORS INVESTIGATED

All the factors described above are employed by three or more of the investigators listed in Table 5–2. Three other factors are noted by one or two investigators. They are mentioned here briefly as background for additional research.

Capacity Utilization

Taylor (1998) indicates that capacity utilization can be used to explain *mistakes* in the implementation of a pure policy rule only involving inflation and real output. He suggests that simple monetary theory could be used to justify some deviations from a pure inflation/output policy rule during times of low capacity utilization.

High capacity utilization is considered a forecaster of future inflation. As a result, capacity utilization might be a substitute variable for expected inflation in a policy reaction function. Capacity utilization could also be a substitute for another factor. Capacity utilization is highly correlated with the output gap. From 1950 to 2001, the correlation between these two factors is greater than 0.87, indicating that one could easily be a substitute for the other.

Bond Yield

Mehra (1997, 1999) indicates that the level of bond yields has an impact on the Federal Reserve policy reaction function. The rationale for including the bond yield could be as a surrogate either for future interest rates or for future inflation rates. Mehra (1999) suggests that the bond yield influences the Fed's expectations of future inflation.

Exchange Rates

If the exchange rate has any influence on the Fed's policy reaction function, it must be due to the impact of the exchange rate on output by way of imports and exports. Clarida, Galí, and Gertler (1998) evaluate the impact of exchange rates on the policy reaction functions for a number of major industrialized countries. They find that exchange rates have a very significant influence on the policy reaction functions for Japan, the United Kingdom, Germany, France, and Italy. They also find that exchange rates and foreign interest rates have no influence on the U.S. Federal Reserve policy reaction function. McNees (1986) also finds that the exchange rate is not significant in determining the Fed's policy reaction function.

MONTHLY RETURN FACTOR MODEL FOR INTEREST RATES

We are interested in predicting the shortest-term interest rate instrument available to individual investors. Most of the research conducted on the Federal Reserve's policy reaction function utilizes the federal funds rate as the policy instrument. Since the federal funds rate is the interest rate for loans made between banks, this instrument is not suitable for our purposes. We shall use the annualized return of 90-day T-bills. This instrument is available to any investor and has a long history of yield values for research purposes. Although the 90-day T-bill rate is technically a yield rate, we shall treat it as a rate of return. The monthly market return of

90-day T-bills is very close to the implied return from the yield rate because the 90-day term is so short.

In the remainder of this section, we shall evaluate each of the fundamental methodologies previously defined for forecasting interest rates: from past interest rates alone, from influential factors, and from a combination of the two. Each methodology is evaluated empirically using the tenure date ranges of Fed chairmen shown in Table 5–1.

Interest Rates Are Determined Solely by Past Rates

In the first model, we assume that T-bill rates are only affected by previous T-bill rates. The specific form of the model projects a continuation of the most recent trend in T-bill changes. To accomplish this the most recent change is added to the last T-bill level. The use of such an autoregressive model may not seem to conform to the fundamental factor approach we have taken for stocks and bonds. But our objective is to be able to predict future T-bill rates using any logical factor. Given the infrequent changes in the discount rate that drives major changes in the T-bill rate, then this model may actually be the most logical. It indicates that the T-bill rate should stay the same unless there has been a recent change in the rate. On the other hand, if there has been no recent change in the T-bill rate, this model has no way to anticipate an upcoming change. If we can accept a model that can only predict a prolongation of a recent change in the T-bill rate, then we can easily accept this structural form. The autoregressive model is expressed as

$$r_t = \alpha + \beta_1 r_{t-1} + \beta_2 \Delta r_{t-1} + \varepsilon_t \qquad (5\text{–}6)$$

where:

r_t = 90-day T-bill rate at time t
r_{t-1} = 90-day T-bill rate at time $t - 1$
Δr_{t-1} = change in the 90-day T-bill rate between time $t - 1$ and $t - 2$
ε_t = model error term at time t
Expected value $(\varepsilon_t) = 0$
α, β_1, β_2 = model coefficients to be determined

T A B L E   5-11

T-Bill Monthly Returns Based on Previous Returns Only

Chairman	Martin	Burns and Miller	Early Volcker	Later Volcker and Greenspan	Entire Date Range
Date Range	1951/01 to 1969/12	1970/01 to 1979/06	1979/07 to 1982/06	1982/07 to 2001/12	1951/01 to 2001/12
α	0.0180	0.2393	3.6786	0.1445	0.0944
β_1 Prev. T-bill (t_1)	1.0002	0.9614	0.7058	0.9713	0.9820
	(109.01)***	(37.84)***	(7.57)***	(106.07)***	(158.21)***
β_2 Prev. T-bill (t_2)	0.3781	0.2260	0.4430	0.4833	0.3409
	(5.92)***	(2.40)**	(2.94)**	(8.61)***	(8.95)***
σ_ε	0.1963	0.4154	1.2562	0.2669	0.4309
Adj R^2	0.9822	0.9317	0.7038	0.9798	0.9766
% months with low consecutive changes	64.0%	18.5%	0.00%	50.0%	46.4%

Significance based on a one-tailed test.
*Significant at 0.05 level.
**Significant at 0.01 level.
***Significant at 0.001 level.

Using ordinary least squares estimates, the values of α, β_1, and β_2 are displayed in Table 5–11 employing data from each of the date ranges associated with the tenure of Fed chairmen.

The coefficient for the previous T-bill rate, β_1, is very significant for each date range and quite close to 1.0 in value in most cases. The coefficient for the previous change in the T-bill rate, β_2, is also quite significant and reasonably consistent across date ranges. The model fit for the early Volcker interval is not as good as for the other intervals. The reason for this poor fit has to do with the fact that the T-bill rate changed too often during this interval for consecutive months. The model expressed in (5–6) works the best when there are few changes in the T-bill rate last month, $t - 1$, and the previous month, $t - 2$. The last row of Table 5–11 shows the percentage of months during the interval that had small changes for the last 2 months. Since a typical smallest change in the federal funds rate is 0.25 percent, small changes for this calculation were taken as anything less than 0.20 percent up or down. The early Volcker interval has no month for which the two most recent absolute changes in the T-bill rate were both less than 0.20 percent.

But even this early Volcker interval has an R^2 larger than the models for stocks and bonds shown in previous chapters. The best stock and bond monthly models have R^2 values less than 0.15. This means that the T-bill model based on past values of the T-bill rate is a very successful model, even under the most difficult circumstances. It is not surprising that it has received so much attention.

Interest Rates Are Functions of Past Influential Factors

Since the Taylor rule is the basis for so many investigations of changes in interest rates, we will specifically evaluate the Taylor rule for each of the Fed chairman eras. In Taylor (1998), the quarterly federal funds rate is empirically evaluated using the GDP implicit price deflator for the last four quarters for inflation and a real GDP output gap using a Hodrick-Prescott filter to estimate the GDP potential. Our results will differ somewhat from Taylor's because we will predict the monthly 90-day T-bill rate using the GDP implicit price deflator. We will also employ a GDP real output gap based on quarterly GDP values but use the real GDP potential time series calculated by the CBO in accordance with its publication, the *CBO Memorandum* (2001). The GDP implicit price deflator and the CBO-based real output gap have quarterly frequencies that are converted to monthly by the simple expedient of employing the quarterly value for each month in the quarter. The model is converted to monthly in order to make it comparable to the other two models.

$$r_t = \alpha + \beta_1 p_{t-1} + \beta_2 y_{t-1} + \varepsilon_t \qquad (5-7)$$

where:

r_t = 90-day T-bill rate during month t

p_{t-1} = change in the GDP deflator over the previous 12 months

y_{t-1} = previous percent deviation of real GDP from the potential

ε_t = model error term at time t

Expected value $(\varepsilon_t) = 0$

α, β_1, β_2 = model coefficients to be determined

Table 5–12 shows the calculated coefficients for the Taylor rule model as expressed in equation (5–7).

T A B L E 5-12

T-Bill Monthly Returns Based on Taylor Rule Variables

Chairman	Martin	Burns and Miller	Early Volcker	Later Volcker and Greenspan	Entire Date Range
Date Range	1951/01 to 1969/12	1970/01 to 1979/06	1979/07 to 1982/06	1982/07 to 2001/12	1951/01 to 2001/12
α	2.4708	1.2512	2.0804	1.3623	2.6314
β_1 ΔGDP defl.	0.1408	0.7622	1.0944	1.7092	0.7116
(t_1)	(2.32)*	(14.85)***	(2.27)*	(17.53)***	(19.78)***
β_2 output gap	0.1648	0.5409	−0.2860	0.2946	−0.1528
(t_2)	(4.72)***	(13.26)***	(−1.41)	(6.63)***	(−4.67)***
σ_ε	1.3648	0.8644	2.2087	1.2145	2.1164
Adj. R^2	0.1419	0.7044	0.0843	0.5828	0.4354

Significance based on a one-tailed test.
* Significant at 0.05 level.
** Significant at 0.01 level.
*** Significant at 0.001 level.

The values of these coefficients do not agree with those found in Taylor (1998) for all date ranges. The reasons for any such disagreement include the fact that (5–7) is a monthly model, that it forecasts T-bills and not the federal funds rate, and that it uses CBO estimates of the potential GDP instead of a Hodrick-Prescott filter. The later Volcker and Greenspan era produces coefficients quite close to the original Taylor (1993) estimates of 1.5 for inflation and 0.5 for the output gap. The coefficients determined for the entire 1951–2001 interval produces a negative coefficient for the output gap. The individual eras all produce positive coefficients for the output gap except for the early Volcker era, which has a coefficient that is negative but not significant at the 0.05 level. The poor fit during the early Volcker era must indicate that interest rates were not being targeted with a consistent policy reaction function based on recent inflation and the output gap. The negative coefficient for the entire interval is probably an indication that it is a poor idea to try to fit all the Fed chairman eras to a Taylor rule with a single set of coefficients.

Note that the residual standard deviations of the Taylor rule model, σ_ε, are much larger than for the autoregressive model for each date range. Models based on past rates appear to be better predictors than the Taylor rule model.

Interest Rates Are Functions of Past Rates as Well as Influential Factors

The Taylor rule is intended as a policy reaction function for the Fed to target the federal funds rate. It is not intended to be a model of T-bill rates. Judging by the modest fit of the Taylor rule to T-bill rates, other explanatory factors beyond those used in the Taylor rule must be required to explain changes in the 90-day T-bill rate from the 1950s to 2001. Part of the reason for the need for other factors stems from the fact that the 90-day T-bill rate is not an overnight rate and is 3 months into the yield curve. Fundamental factors that influence the yield curve could have an influence on even such a short-term instrument.

In addition to these fundamental factors, previous T-bill rates can be included to increase the forecasting accuracy of the model. When the fundamental factors are blended with the past T-bill rates, a superior model results in terms of model fit to history. The specific factors employed are changed somewhat from previous factors to obtain a better fit. The GDP deflator from the Taylor rule is replaced with the consumer price index as a measure of inflation. In addition, the output gap from the Taylor rule is replaced with capacity utilization as a measure of productivity. It is well known that capacity utilization is also related to inflationary expectations. For further information about capacity utilization and inflation, see the discussion in Chapter 3 concerning its influence on equity returns.

The definitions of all the factors incorporated into an expanded model to fit the annual 90-day T-bill rate are:

A 1-month rate of return from 90-day T-bills calculated from the annualized return for the month before the T-bill performance month.

An average 1-month rate of return from 90-day T-bills calculated from the annualized return from 2 to 3 months before the T-bill performance month.

An average 1-month rate of return from 90-day T-bills calculated from the annualized return from 4 to 9 months before the T-bill performance month.

The long-term government bond return for the month before the T-bill performance month.

The difference between the 1-year Treasury bond yield and the 90-day T-bill rate for the month before the T-bill performance month. This represents a term spread.

The manufacturing capacity utilization for the month before the T-bill performance month.

The average rate of return for the S&P 500 without dividends for the 2 months before the T-bill performance month.

The 12-month change in the consumer price index in the month before the T-bill performance month.

The interest rate forecast is the same 90-day T-bill rate used in the previous two models. This allows a direct comparison of the performance characteristics of all three models. A model of the form of equation (5–5) is evaluated to fit the level of 90-day T-bill returns. The results for each of the Fed Chairman tenure date ranges are shown in Table 5–13.

The model for each of the date ranges in Table 5–13 has a better fit to the data than the two previous models. This is not surprising since the expanded model combines the concepts from the first two models with additional factors. The most important factor is the previous level of T-bill rates. The signs on the other two T-bill rate factors indicate that there is both a trend term and an acceleration term at work affecting T-bill rates. The very negative government bond return term signals that when government bond returns are higher than normal, T-bill rates will drop in subsequent months. And when government bond returns are lower than normal, T-bill rates will increase in subsequent months. T-bill rates also seem to respond to the stock market. Since 1979, it appears that T-bill rates react significantly to the recent 2 months of stock market returns. This could indicate a slight reaction by the Fed to increase

T A B L E 5-13

T-Bill Monthly Returns Based on an Expanded Model

Chairman	Martin	Burns and Miller	Early Volcker	Later Volcker and Greenspan	Entire Date Range
Date Range	1951/02 to 1969/12	1970/01 to 1979/06	1979/07 to 1982/06	1982/07 to 2001/12	1951/01 to 2001/12
α	−0.5540	−4.3713	3.2452	−2.1341	−1.5726
β_1 T-bill (1)	14.8942	11.4445	14.0054	15.2797	14.2716
(t_1)	(22.99)***	(10.14)***	(9.71)***	(25.65)***	(37.38)***
β_2 T-bill (2–3)	−2.9046	−0.9408	−1.7757	−3.7765	−2.6436
(t_2)	(−3.52)	(−0.72)	(−1.31)	(−4.99)***	(−5.66)***
β_3 T-bill (4–9)	0.2555	0.2427	−0.6374	0.8555	0.8236
(t_3)	(0.66)	(0.28)	(−0.32)	(2.09)*	(2.99)**
β_4 Long govt. (1)	−0.0340	−0.0469	−0.1788	−0.0269	−0.0661
(t_4)	(−3.94)***	(−2.54)**	(−5.52)***	(−4.37)***	(−9.90)***
β_5 Treas. T-bill	0.2006	0.2767	0.2670	0.1399	0.1842
(t_5)	(3.33)***	(2.79)**	(0.74)	(3.34)***	(4.40)***
β_6 Capacity Util.	0.0057	0.0563	−0.0073	0.0259	0.0168
(t_6)	(1.59)	(4.70)***	(−0.11)	(3.30)***	(3.83)***
β_7 Stocks (1–2)	0.0073	0.0189	0.2445	0.0187	0.0324
(t_7)	(1.36)	(1.60)	(4.06)***	(3.40)***	(5.88)***
β_8 ΔCPI	0.0041	0.0598	−0.1621	−0.0205	0.0166
(t_8)	(0.60)	(2.10)*	(1.93)*	(−1.08)	(2.27)*
σ_ε	0.1897	0.3613	0.8553	0.2504	0.3381
Adj. R^2	0.9834	0.9483	0.8627	0.9823	0.9810

Significance based on a one-tailed test.
* Significant at 0.05 level.
** Significant at 0.01 level.
*** Significant at 0.001 level.

interest rates when the stock market is strongly bullish and decrease interest rates when the market is strongly bearish. For a discussion of the impact of the stock market on central bank policy reaction functions, see Durré (2001).

The original Taylor rule factors were evaluated and do not seem to work very well when combined with the other factors in the model. The measured reaction to capacity utilization is much stronger than using the GDP output gap. The use of the consumer price index is also much stronger than using the growth in the GDP implicit price deflator. A number of other factors were tested for inclusion in the model. The unemployment rate and the M3 money supply were evaluated for their contribution to the models in Table 5–13 and were not found to be significant.

T A B L E 5-14

R^2 for Multifactor 1-Quarter Federal Funds Rate Models

Investigators	Begin Data	End Data	Years of Data	Fed Funds Rate Model R^2
Fair	1982	1999	17	0.97
Fair and Howrey	1962	1993	31	0.99
Judd and Rudebusch	1987	1997	10	0.67
Mehra (1997)	1970	1992	22	0.68
Orphanides (2001a)	1987	1992	5	0.98
Orphanides (2001b)	1979	1995	16	0.90
Taylor	1987	1997	11	0.83
Consensus				0.86

The final model shown in Table 5–13 has a much higher accuracy at fitting the historical performance of T-bills than either the stock or bond models have. Fitting T-bills is easier because T-bills have such a strong serial correlation of returns, a feature that is not present in stocks and bonds.

To gain some perspective on the degree of the fit ($R^2 = 0.9810$ for 1951 to 2001) using the factor model shown in Table 5–13, the comparison in Table 5–14 shows R^2 for federal funds rate regression models using quarterly data that report values for R^2. These other models should have higher R^2 than those shown in Table 5–13 because quarterly data should have less volatility than monthly data and because the federal funds rate should be more predictable than T-bill rates. Nonetheless, the R^2 shown in Table 5–13 compare favorably to these other studies.

REFERENCES

Bordo, Michael D., and Anna J. Schwartz. "Monetary Policy Regimes and Economic Performance: The Historical Record." *Handbook of Macroeconomics*, edited by John B. Taylor and Michael Woodford. Amsterdam: Elsevier/North Holland, 1998.

Brenner, Robin J., Richard H. Harjes, and Kenneth F. Kroner. "Another Look at Models of the Short-Term Interest Rate." *Journal of Financial and Quantitative Analysis* 31 (1996): 85–107.

Chan, K. C., G. Andrew Karolyi, Francis A. Longstaff, and Anthony B. Sanders. "An Empirical Comparison of Alternative Models of the Short-Term Interest Rate." *Journal of Finance* 47, no. 3 (July 1992): 1209–1227.

Clarida, Richard, Jordi Galí, and Mark Gertler. "Monetary Policy Rules in Practice: Some International Evidence." *European Economic Review* 42 (1998): 1033–1067.

Clarida, Richard, Jordi Galí, and Mark Gertler. "Monetary Policy Rules and Macroeconomic Stability: Evidence and Some Theory." *Quarterly Journal of Economics* 115 (2000): 147–180.

Congressional Budget Office. "CBO's Method for Estimating Potential Output: An Update." *CBO Memorandum* (August 2001).

Durré, Alain. "Would It Be Optimal for Central Banks to Include Asset Prices in Their Loss Function?" Discussion paper no. 2001013, Université Catholique de Louvain, Institut de Recherches Économiques et Sociales (IRES) (June 2001): 1–26.

Fair, Ray C. "Actual Federal Reserve Policy Behavior and Interest Rate Rules." *Federal Reserve Bank of New York, Economic Policy Review* (March 2001): 61–72.

Fair, Ray C., and E. Philip Howrey. "Evaluating Alternative Monetary Policy Rules." *Journal of Monetary Economics* 38 (1996): 173–193.

Fauvel, Yvon, Alain Paquet, and Christian Zimmermann. "A Survey on Interest Rate Forecasting." Working paper number 87, Center for Research on Economic Fluctuations and Employment, Université du Québec à Montréal, Montreal (June 1999): 1–38.

Judd, John P., and Glenn D. Rudebusch. "Taylor's Rule and the Fed: 1970–1997." *Federal Reserve Bank of San Francisco Economic Review* 3 (1998): 3–16.

McNees, Stephen K. "Modeling the Fed: A Forward-Looking Monetary Policy Reaction Function." *New England Economic Review* (November/December 1986): 3–8.

Mehra, Yash P. "A Federal Funds Rate Equation." *Economic Inquiry* 35 (July 1997): 621–630.

Mehra, Yash P. "A Forward-Looking Monetary Policy Reaction Function." *Federal Reserve Bank of Richmond Economic Quarterly* 85, no. 2 (Spring 1999): 33–53.

Nelson, Edward. "UK Monetary Policy 1972–97: A Guide Using Taylor Rules." Working paper no. 120, Bank of England (August 2001): 1–44.

Orphanides, Athanasios. "Monetary Policy Rules Based on Real-Time Data." *American Economic Review* 91, no. 4 (2001a): 964–985.

Orphanides, Athanasios. "Monetary Policy Rules, Macroeconomic Stability and Inflation: A View from the Trenches." Working paper no. 115, European Central Bank (December 2001b): 1–43.

Phillips, A. W. H. "The Relation between Unemployment and the Rate of Change of Money Wage Rates in the United Kingdom, 1861–1957." *Economica NS* 25, no. 2 (1958): 283–299.

Sanders, Anthony B., and Haluk Unal. "On the Intertemporal Behavior of the Short-Term Interest Rate." *Journal of Financial and Quantitative Analysis* 23, no. 4 (1988): 417–423.

Sheehan, Richard G. "The Federal Reserve Reaction Function: Does Debt Growth Influence Monetary Policy?" *Federal Reserve Bank of St. Louis Review* 67, no. 3 (1985): 24–33.

Taylor, John B. "Discretion versus Policy Rules in Practice." *Carnegie-Rochester Conference Series on Public Policy* 39 (1993): 195–214.

Taylor, John B. "An Historical Analysis of Monetary Policy Rules." Working paper no. 6768, National Bureau of Economic Research (October 1998): 1–53.

Williams, John C. "Simple Rules for Monetary Policy." *Board of Governors of the Federal Reserve System* (February 1999): 1–34.

Factors Influencing Hedge Fund Returns

> My peculiarity is that I don't have a particular style of investing or, more exactly, I try to change my style to fit the conditions.
>
> *George Soros*
> *Soros on Soros (1995)*

Hedge funds represent an alternative investment class having performance characteristics generally unrelated to the traditional investment classes of stocks, bonds, and interest rates. Hedge funds themselves are not a homogeneous asset class. The specific underlying investments utilized and the nature of the investment procedures employed lead to a wide range of defined hedge fund categories. These hedge fund categories are fundamentally and statistically uncorrelated with each other. Each fund within a given hedge fund class depends on the skills of the investment manager concerning the selection of particular investments and the timing of those investments. Because of this, hedge funds within the same category tend to have low correlations with each other. Thus, individual hedge funds have three levels of independence. They are uncorrelated with other asset classes. They are uncorrelated with other funds in different hedge fund categories. And they are uncorrelated with other funds in their own hedge fund category. These advantageous properties make hedge funds efficient components for building truly diversified portfolios.

As an investment class, hedge funds exhibit a number of common operational characteristics that distinguish them from other asset classes. Hedge funds are normally structured as limited partnerships that may make shares available on an irregular basis. They are generally available as a private offering unaided by any advertising. Since they are not publicly offered securities, they are currently unregulated in the United States by any investment authority. Purchasing shares in a fund may be difficult because none may be currently available. Once in a fund, it may be difficult to sell shares because of fund lock-up provisions that may be as long as 2 years, although there are many funds with 30-day or 90-day exit provisions. Unlike mutual funds, hedge funds do not provide a daily withdrawal provision. Most funds require at least $100,000 as a minimum investment, with many funds requiring $1 million and more. Because of these characteristics, hedge funds are typically only available to high-net-worth investors. For their efforts hedge funds charge a management fee that is on the order of 1 to 2 percent per year irrespective of any profits. They also charge a performance fee that is normally 10 to 20 percent of net new profits. Once a performance fee is paid, no portion is ever given back irrespective of the size of any future losses.

Hedge funds are not restricted in the range of their investment activities. They can buy or sell any type of instrument including stocks, bonds, interest rates, options, futures, and real estate from any country. They can be net short of any instrument, and they frequently make use of leveraging methodologies. Hedge funds can borrow money to leverage up their holdings, limited only by the credit lines they can establish with banks or brokerage firms.

There are no requirements for hedge funds to report their performance to any regulatory body. In the United States their activities are only restricted by certain nonadvertising provisions of the Investment Company Act and general legal provisions regarding fraud and embezzlement. Thus, we can see that hedge funds are the free spirits of the investment world. They are currently free to invest in any instrument, using any methodology available, without worrying about certain short sales or leveraging restrictions imposed on mutual funds.

HEDGE FUND CATEGORIES SELECTED

Identifying factors that influence hedge fund performance should not be attempted for hedge funds as a whole. We must identify factors influencing a category or influencing an individual fund. The very fact that hedge funds within one category have a low performance relationship to one another presents a challenge for identifying the factors that influence that category. While it might make better statistical sense to build factor models for individual funds, we might learn too much about what influences a particular fund and not enough about what influences the category it belongs to. Therefore, this chapter is devoted to predicting performance for hedge fund categories and not individual funds.

There is some disagreement about how to classify hedge funds. This stems from the fact that hedge funds can be classified by the underlying investment instruments employed and can also be classified by the nature of the investment methodologies applied. For the purposes of this chapter, we shall use several of the hedge fund indices defined by Hedge Fund Research (HFR). Since we will be employing HFR indices, we are accepting HFR's category definitions. Because every fund tracked by HFR is classified to belong to one hedge fund category, we are accepting the assignment of each fund to a particular category by HFR. The funds assigned to one category are used to construct the hedge fund index for that category. Other organizations tracking the performance of hedge funds use different overall classification schemes. The assignment of individual funds to hedge fund categories can lead to different hedge fund index performance for similarly named categories between two creators of hedge fund indices. This problem is aggravated by the fact that funds meeting the same category definition can have low correlation with each other. Missing one or more funds from a category index can result in noticeable differences in the performance characteristics of indices created by different organizations. It is hoped that having a large number of funds in each category will tend to overcome part of this difficulty.

In the interest of simplicity, we will not deal with all 97 of the hedge fund categories currently defined by Hedge Fund Research. We will restrict ourselves to five popular categories whose investment methodologies are substantially different. This will give us ample opportunity for learning which macroeconomic factors seem to have an influence on hedge fund performance. In order to understand the differences among these categories, each category is described in terms of its overall goal, the instruments employed, the investment procedures applied, and the risks resulting from the use of the procedure.

Convertible arbitrage attempts to identify companies issuing convertible securities that have a pricing discrepancy relative to the company's stock. The value of a convertible bond is influenced by fluctuations in the price of the associated stock and by fluctuations in similar-term corporate bond yields. By simultaneously purchasing the convertible bond and selling short the related stock, a hedge fund can hedge away the systematic market risk associated with the company's stock and capitalize on the embedded option contained within the convertible bond.

By concurrently selling corporate bonds, the transaction can be immunized from bond yield risks. The determination of the amount of stock and corporate bonds to sell in order to match the risks associated with purchasing a given amount of convertible bonds is a key feature of this methodology. Mismatching these three quantities creates a hedge ratio risk for the investor. Furthermore, misgauging the assumed pricing discrepancy between the convertible bond and the stock could also lead to a loss on the transaction. The convertible arbitrage strategy is far less risky than purchasing naked convertible bonds. But the strategy also carries a lower expected return than the convertible bond itself. Therefore leveraging is frequently employed to amplify the performance of the strategy. Individual hedge funds applying this strategy do not necessarily obtain similar returns because they could be applying the strategy to a different set of companies. Even if two hedge funds were to apply the procedure to the same set of companies, differences in hedge ratios and transaction timing could lead to dissimilar results. The average correlation among convertible arbitrage funds from the Hedge Fund Research database having full data between January 1996 and December 2001 is 0.317.

Fixed-income arbitrage is based on the assumption that one particular interest-bearing instrument will go up more, or down less, than another interest-bearing instrument. It makes no specific assumption about the general direction of interest rates overall— only about the change in the spread between two instruments. The instruments involved can be government bonds, corporate bonds, municipal bonds, options on bonds, bond futures, plus any number of other bond derivatives. The term of the instrument is another factor in selecting the instruments used. Almost any combination of differences in these instruments is a named fixed-income arbitrage substrategy. For example, buying a long-term government bond and selling a short-term government bond is a *term spread*. Buying a corporate bond and selling a government bond of the same term is a *default spread*. Buying a government bond and selling a futures contract on the same bond is a *basis spread*. Because the market risk of the direction of interest rates has been removed, the risks and returns associated with these spreads are much lower than those associated with a simple long position in either one of the instruments. Consequently, leverage is frequently applied to gear up the performance of the strategy. The risks associated with fixed-income arbitrage include the risk that the spread moves in the direction opposite to the one assumed and the risk of default or recall on one of the bonds. Two fixed-income arbitrage funds can easily have uncorrelated performance records because they could be long or short any combination of substrategies at any point in time. The average correlation among fixed-income funds operating continuously between January 1996 and December 2001 is very low at 0.076.

Event-driven strategies fall into two subcategories: reorganization strategies and distressed situations. Reorganization strategies include mergers, spin-offs, acquisitions, recapitalizations, and share buy-backs. The most common reorganization strategy is the acquisition strategy of buying shares of a target company and selling shares of an acquirer predicated on the assumption that the deal will be completed. The opposite strategy is applied if there is an expectation that the acquisition will fail. Distressed situation strategies include backruptcies and restructurings. Distressed strategies frequently involve taking positions in the corporate debt or the shares of the company which may be mispriced due to illiquidity or forced sales. Some hedge funds may specialize in particular types of event-driven strategies such as acquisitions, and other funds may spread their risk across multiple strategies. The main risks for event-driven strategies involve unconsummated deals and unpredicted bankruptcies. While it is possible to hedge away certain risks of event-driven strategies by simultaneously buying and selling two company instruments, usually these strategies are implemented with no hedge at all. The average correlation among event-driven funds operating between January 1996 and December 2001 is relatively high at 0.438. This probably indicates that at any point in time there are relatively few opportunities available and many funds act on them simultaneously.

Global macro is the most liberal of all hedge fund strategies. A macroeconomic view is taken regarding an anticipated situation or event for a country, a region, or the world in general. These anticipations could concern economic situations, political events, regulatory changes, threats of war, or unusual supply-demand situations for commodities. Positions in stocks, bonds, currencies, commodities, or any other liquid investment are initiated to take advantage of the perceived situation. Derivatives and leverage are frequently employed. Global macro funds move freely from one investment concept to the next as opportunities present themselves. The main risks of a global macro position are the possibility that the situation or event will not materialize as expected or, if it does materialize, that it will not have the anticipated effect on the positions taken. The determination of opportunities, the method of implementation, the timing of the position, and the fraction of assets committed to a given concept will vary widely among global macro funds. So it is not surprising that there is a low correlation among these funds between January 1996 and December 2001 of only 0.283.

Market-neutral strategies are the progenitor of all other hedge fund approaches. This kind of strategy is the long-short strategy originated by A. W. Jones to remove the influence of the stock market from a portfolio of equities. In its purest form, the market-neutral strategy consists of buying a basket of undervalued stocks and selling a basket of overvalued stocks. The amount of short sales to use is determined by a risk analysis of the long position. A variant known as pairs-trading matches each stock in the long portfolio with a stock in the short portfolio from the same industry. This removes the possibility of industry risk from overall holdings. The value of the market-neutral approach stems from its ability to make money in both up and down markets. In a bear market, if the long basket goes down less than the short basket, then the strategy still makes money. The success of this strategy depends on the skill of the hedge fund manager in being able to determine undervalued and overvalued companies. If the manager chooses stocks unwisely, does an inefficient job of dollar risk management, or has too few stocks in the two baskets, it is possible to lose money with the approach. Since the market return has been hedged away along with the market risk, some amount of leverage is nearly always used to gear up the returns for this strategy. Despite the leverage, it is still one of the safest hedge fund concepts. When properly applied, the performance is guaranteed to be uncorrelated with stock market movements. Furthermore, since no two funds are likely to hold the same long and short baskets, the average correlation among market-neutral hedge funds is extremely low between January 1996 and December 2001 at 0.108.

Many other hedge fund strategies are available, but these five hedge fund categories should be sufficient to represent the available range. We have seen that the average correlation among funds within each hedge fund strategy tends to be low. This means that hedge funds applying the same method generally have independent performance. Using hedge fund indices prepared by Hedge Fund Research for January 1990 to December 2001, Table 6–1 shows that each of the five hedge fund categories is substantially

T A B L E   6-1

Hedge Fund Index Correlation Coefficients (January 1990 – December 2001)

Investment	Convert Arb. Correl.	Fixed-Income Arb. Correl.	Event-Driven Correl.	Global Macro Correl.	Market-Neutral Correl.	S&P 500 Stock Correl.	Govt. Bond Correl.
Convertible arbitrage funds	1.00	0.13	0.62	0.40	0.14	0.33	0.14
Fixed-income arbitrage funds	0.13	1.00	0.20	0.12	0.06	−0.04	−0.28
Event-driven funds	0.62	0.20	1.00	0.57	0.17	0.60	0.06
Global macro funds	0.40	0.12	0.57	1.00	0.21	0.43	0.33
Market-neutral funds	0.14	0.06	0.17	0.21	1.00	0.11	0.23
S&P 500 stock index	0.33	−0.04	0.60	0.43	0.11	1.00	0.21
U.S. government bond index	0.14	−0.28	0.06	0.33	0.23	0.21	1.00

independent of the others. They are also observed to be generally independent of the stock and bond markets. Only event-driven funds and global macro funds have a modest correlation with the stock market. At the 95 percent confidence level, correlations based on 144 months are indistinguishable from zero for absolute correlation values less than 0.18. This indicates that the fixed-income arbitrage fund index and the market-neutral fund index are uncorrelated with most of the other investments shown.

Other performance statistics for hedge fund indices and stocks and bonds are shown in Table 6–2 for 1990 to 2001. Over this time interval, the event-driven and the global macro fund indices dominate the stock market index based on return and standard deviation values. The Sharpe ratios of all the hedge fund indices are substantially higher than the 0.5287 value for the stock market. The maximum drawdown (peak-to-valley loss) for each hedge fund category is lower than the stock market loss as well. The convertible arbitrage, fixed-income arbitrage, and event-driven hedge fund categories all have significantly negative coefficients of skewness.

T A B L E 6-2

Hedge Fund Index Return Statistics (January 1990 – December 2001)

Investment	Average Annual Return	Annual Standard Deviation	Sharpe Ratio	Maximum Drawdown	Coefficient of Skewness	1-Month Serial Correlation
Convertible arbitrage funds	11.87	3.42	1.9637	4.84	−1.3862	0.5443
Fixed-income arbitrage funds	8.57	4.78	0.7119	14.42	−1.6211	0.3983
Event-driven funds	15.95	6.68	1.6152	10.78	−1.4750	0.2529
Global macro funds	17.66	8.98	1.3925	10.70	0.2343	0.1731
Market-neutral funds	11.12	3.28	1.8150	2.72	−0.0693	−0.0149
S&P 500 stock index	12.86	14.55	0.5287	30.49	0.4743	−0.0719
U.S. government bond index	7.89	4.24	0.6454	5.33	−0.1916	0.2204

Coefficients of skewness with absolute values greater than 0.400 are significantly nonzero at the 95 percent confidence level for the 144-month date range used.

The statistics for the hedge fund indices shown in Tables 6–1 and 6–2 represent the performance of a portfolio of all funds constituting each index. The performance of individual hedge funds within each index could deviate considerably from these statistics. Investing in one hedge fund in each category will not give the same results. An investor wishing to obtain these results exactly would be required to construct similar hedge fund portfolios for each strategy. The question of whether it is worthwhile to evaluate hedge fund indices as potential portfolio building blocks could be raised at this point. Are these indices investable? The answer is yes. Recently, several investment firms have begun offering products that mirror hedge fund indices by constructing portfolios of smaller sets of hedge funds designed to track selected strategies.

SEARCHING FOR A FUNDAMENTAL APPROACH

The low correlations observed among funds using the same hedge fund strategy might indicate that there is not much strength to be expected in a model relating macroeconomic factors to the performance of a hedge fund index. This is indicative of an idiosyncratic variation among individual funds for short intervals of time unexplained by the movements in the stock market or any set of factors related to changes in performance across time. If the idiosyncratic variation across funds is too large, then the influence of a set of factors on the category performance across time may be too difficult to distinguish.

We need to be clear at this point that we are discussing models that *predict* hedge fund performance and *not* models that *explain* hedge fund performance. Prediction models require a time lag between the explanatory variables and the resulting hedge fund index return. Explanatory models in the spirit of Sharpe (1992) style analysis are meant to indicate what instruments are generating the investment performance. For example, style analysis might be capable of determining that the performance of a market-neutral index is composed of:

30 percent long positions in high-value, high-cap stocks

20 percent long positions in high-value, low-cap stocks

35 percent short positions in low-value, high-cap stocks

15 percent short positions in low-value, low-cap stocks

This would tell us the composition of the average portfolio of all funds in the index and would indicate how the returns were being generated. It would only be useful for prediction purpose if we could determine the factors that predict each one of these four components. For example, a useful model for market-neutral funds might involve dividend yields for each of these four stock categories. A standard style analysis breakdown is only valid for the time interval investigated. Suppose the funds in the market-neutral index were shifting their portfolio compositions among these four stock categories as time passed. We would need to know the factors that caused them to shift their allocations. This would require a time-varying style analysis.

It is evident that style analysis for each hedge fund category would require different factor weights, and perhaps even a separate set of factors, to be able to determine the portfolio composition. The determination of factors and weights for a prediction model is sure to require additional factors. Furthermore, hedge fund categories such as global macro allow the hedge fund to switch from one investment to another and to change the investment allocations as opportunities arise. Since the allocation and timing decisions are based on manager discretion, it may be impossible to devise a fundamental model structure for global macro funds that will predict a large portion of the variation in returns. Such a model would require a fundamental component for each investment that the typical manager is evaluating at every point in time.

The closest approach to a fundamental theory of the performance of hedge funds is the suggestion by Fung and Hsieh (1997, 2001) that hedge funds deliver optionlike returns. They hold that the performance of trend followers is equivalent to a look-back options straddle on the underlying investments. But this concept may not apply to funds that are not trend followers or funds that frequently change allocations from one investment to another.

FACTORS INVESTIGATED FOR HEDGE FUND RETURN MODELS

A number of evaluations of hedge funds have been undertaken to discover factors relating to hedge fund returns. Three types of models have been employed. The first is the pure style analysis model that explains returns based on the concurrent performance of multiple traditional investment indices. Sharpe (1992) sets two constraints on style analysis. Each coefficient must be nonnegative, and the sum of the coefficients must equal 1. These constraints are relaxed for the generalized style analysis presented in this chapter. Regression analysis is applied throughout each study. Examples of this generalized style analysis include Schneeweis and Spurgin (1998), Agarwal and Naik (2000b), Gregoriou, Rouah, and Sedzro (2002), and Fung and Hsieh (2002). The second approach is a mixed model that uses concurrent traditional investment return indices plus concurrent macroeconomic factors. Examples of this mixed approach include Agarwal and Naik (2000a, 2002), Capocci (2001), Schneeweis, Kazemi, and Martin (2001), Bürki and Larqué (2001), Edwards and Caglayan (2001), and Kat and Miffre (2002). The third approach is a lagged-factor model as exemplified by Amenc, El Bied, and Martellini (2003).

Since only one study has been identified using a true forecasting model, we will need to utilize the generalized style analysis and mixed concurrent models to help establish factors that might be useful in a forecasting framework. Among the factors most frequently mentioned are market performance indices for stocks, bonds, interest rates, commodities, and currencies. Other market-oriented factors include two suggested by Fama and French (1993): the difference between small- and big-cap stock performance (small minus big, or SMB) and the difference in performance between high-value stocks and low-value stocks (high minus low, or HML). Another market-oriented factor considered is stock exchange trading volume. Several technical factors are employed including return momentum (trend persistence) and an up-minus-down (UMD) factor representing the difference in the 12-month return on positive-return stocks and the 12-month return on negative-return stocks. Macroeconomic factors suggested include inflation, the default spread between corporate bonds and government bonds, and the term spread between long-term government bonds and short-term government bonds. Finally, studies by Agarwal and Naik (2000a) and Fung and Hsieh (2001) show that hedge fund performance can be related to options on the underlying investments. Thus, option returns or the determinants of option prices may be useful in predicting hedge fund index returns.

The remainder of this chapter is devoted to evaluating these factors, either singly or in combination, to determine their impact on the performance of various classes of hedge funds. First, we shall look at a survey of the factors proposed as important in hedge fund studies. The list of investigators and the factors considered are shown in Table 6–3. The bottom row indicates the number of investigators utilizing each of these factors.

The frequent use of the performance of the stock and bond markets is a reflection of the fact that most of the models involved are structured as a concurrent generalized style analysis. In a forecasting framework, previous returns of various asset classes may not be as significant as they are in a contemporaneous model.

Each of the factors with three or more mentions in Table 6–3 is evaluated for the consensus of its sign and the significance of the value of the coefficient obtained. One of the following entries is entered in Tables 6–4 to 6–12 under the heading of each hedge fund category:

Low   Indicates a low probability of any relationship. This is typically shown by one-tailed t-statistics below 1.96, indicating more than a 5 percent probability of a zero coefficient. The sign of the nonsignificant coefficient is unreported.

+Low   The same as low except that the sign of the nonsignificant coefficient is known to be positive.

−Low   The same as low except that the sign of the nonsignificant coefficient is known to be negative.

T A B L E   6-3

Hedge Fund Factors Considered by Various Investigators

Investigators	Currency Options or Volatility	Bond Mkt. Options or Volatility	Stock Mkt. Options or Volatility	Currencies	Inflation	Commodity Prices	Term Spread	Default Spread	Return Momentum	Up Minus Down (UMD)	High-Minus-Low (HML) Stocks	Small-Minus-Big (SMB) Stocks	Interest Rate Index	Bond Market Indices	Stock Market Indices
Agarwal and Naik (2000a, 2002)	AN	AN	AN	AN		AN		AN	AN		AN	AN		AN	AN
Agarwal and Naik (2000b)				A2		A2								A2	A2
Amenc, El Bied, and Martellini			AB			AB			AB				AB		AB
Bürki and Larqué		BL	BL	BL	BL	BL	BL	BL		BL	BL	BL		BL	BL
Capocci						C		C	C		C	C		C	C
Edwards and Caglayan							EC	EC		EC	EC	EC			EC
Fung and Hsieh (2002)														FH	FH
Gregoriou, Rouah, and Sedzro														GR	GR
Kat and Miffre				KM	KM		KM	KM			KM	KM			KM
Schneeweis, Kazemi, and Martin			SK				SK	SK							SK
Schneeweis and Spurgin	SS	SS	SS	SS		SS								SS	SS
Number of investigators using this factor out of 11 investigators	2	3	5	5	2	6	4	6	3	2	5	5	1	7	11

+   Indicates that a significant positive relationship is
                established. This is typically measured by one-tailed
                t-statistics above 1.96, indicating a probability of a
                zero coefficient less than 5 percent.
−   Indicates that a significant negative relationship is
                established. This is typically measured by one-tailed
                t-statistics above 1.96, indicating a probability of a
                zero coefficient less than 5 percent.

Each factor is summarized to indicate the sign and level of the
confidence in the use of that factor. This summary is on the bottom
row of each evaluation and is marked "Consensus."

For each factor k a table is presented based on the work of a
fixed list of investigators who have each evaluated a set of assumed
factors $f_{k,t-n}$ during various time periods $t - n$ and calculated a set
of coefficients b_k for a linear factor model to predict stock returns at
time t from factors with a lag of $n \geq 0$ periods. The value of n must
be greater than zero in order to obtain true forecasting models. The
factor model has the form

$$R_t = \alpha + b_1 f_{1,t-n} + b_2 f_{2,t-n} + b_3 f_{3,t-n} + \cdots + b_K f_{K,t-n} + e_t$$

$$= \alpha + \sum_{k=1}^{K} b_k f_{k,t-n} + e_t \qquad (6\text{-}1)$$

Only the investigation by Amenc, El Bied, and Martellini
(2003) applies a true lagged-factor forecasting model with $n = 1$.
All other investigations utilize $n = 0$ and are essentially generalized
style analysis models.

The factors considered in this chapter consist of economic or
market variables that could have an influence on hedge fund
indices. They are not meant to differentiate the performance among
individual hedge funds. Differences in performance by individual
hedge funds might be influenced by fund size, fees charged, the
selection of specific underlying investments, and the timing of
investments. While these measures would be of significance in
determining the differences among individual hedge funds, they
would probably not be of much value in estimating future rates of

return for hedge fund indices unless these measures change substantially with time.

STOCK MARKET INDICES

Any fund that is truly hedged against the impact of the stock market should not have a relationship with a stock market index. Of the five hedge fund categories, convertible arbitrage, fixed-income arbitrage, and market-neutral funds are defined as *hedged* funds. Event-driven and global macro funds might not be hedged at any point in time and still meet their mandates. Therefore, it is not surprising that these two have a significant positive relationship with a stock index. The significant positive relationship between market-neutral funds and a stock index must indicate that not all market-neutral funds are perfectly hedged. Being partly hedged with a residual long component against stocks could explain the market-neutral fund results in Table 6–4.

T A B L E   6-4

Investigators Factors	Date Range of Available Data	Convertible Arbitrage Hedge Fund Index	Fixed-Income Arbitrage Hedge Fund Index	Event-Driven Hedge Fund Index	Global Macro Hedge Fund Index	Market-Neutral Hedge Fund Index
Agarwal and Naik (2000a)	1990–1998	Low	Low	Low	Low	Low
Agarwal and Naik (2000b)	1994–1998	+Low		+	+Low	+
Amenc, El Bied, and Martellini	1994–2000	+	+	+Low	+	+
Bürki and Larqué	1998–2000					+
Capocci	1984–2000	+	+	+	+	+
Fung and Hsieh (2002)	1994–2001	+Low	+	+	+	+
Gregoriou, Rouah, and Sedzro	1990–2000			+	+	+
Schneeweis, Kazemi, and Martin	1990–2000	+	−Low	+	+	+
Schneeweis and Spurgin	1990–1995	−Low	+Low	+	+	+
Consensus		Low	Low	+	+	+

While the relationship between hedge fund performance and a stock market index is quite significant for concurrent style analysis models, we may find that the relationship is not as strong for forecasting models. The stock market coefficients determined by the forecasting model of Amenc, El Bied, and Martellini (2003) are mostly in the range of 0.20 to 0.30 for significant regressions. This means that for each 1 percent change in the previous S&P 500 index return, there is approximately a 0.25 percent change in the next hedge fund index return.

BOND MARKET INDICES

Table 6–5 shows that there is virtually no impact on hedge fund returns resulting from changes in bond returns. This is especially unexpected for fixed-income arbitrage funds. This must mean that fixed-income arbitrage funds carry no net exposure to bond performance. The fixed-income strategies employed must be perfectly hedged, with no residual bond market exposure.

Another surprising result is that global macro funds have no measurable bond return component. Since global macro funds are

T A B L E   6-5

Investigators	Factors Date Range of Available Data	Convertible Arbitrage Hedge Fund Index	Fixed-Income Arbitrage Hedge Fund Index	Event-Driven Hedge Fund Index	Global Macro Hedge Fund Index	Market-Neutral Hedge Fund Index
Agarwal and Naik (2000a)	1990–1998	Low	Low	Low	Low	Low
Agarwal and Naik (2000b)	1994–1998	−Low		−Low	+Low	−Low
Bürki and Larqué	1998–2000					−Low
Capocci	1984–2000	+	−Low	−Low	−Low	−Low
Fung and Hsieh (2002)	1994–2001	+	+	+	+Low	+Low
Gregoriou, Rouah, and Sedzro	1990–2000			−Low	Low	+Low
Schneeweis and Spurgin	1990–1995	+Low	+Low	+Low	−Low	+Low
Consensus		Low	Low	Low	Low	Low

free to take unhedged positions in bonds, this must indicate that they seldom take advantage of this investment opportunity. Perhaps the expected returns from bond strategies are simply too picayune to compete with other alternative strategies for global macro managers. Since global macro funds are likely to give the largest allocations to investment opportunities with the highest risk-adjusted returns, unleveraged bond strategies must not be comparatively attractive.

All the investigations shown in Table 6–5 are based on concurrent style analysis. Since there is no significant consensus about hedge fund indices being affected by concurrent bond returns, it would be unusual to discover that the return on bonds has any predictive power on the future performance of hedge fund indices.

SMALL-MINUS-BIG STOCKS

A cross-sectional explanation of the returns on stocks is proposed by Fama and French (1992, 1993). One of the variables proposed in these studies is the firm-size variable characterized by the difference in returns between small-capitalization stocks and big-capitalization stocks (SMB). As shown in Table 6–6, for models of concurrent style analysis, this factor seems to have a strong relationship to the returns of most hedge fund categories. This variable is not included in the forecasting model of Amenc, El Bied, and Martellini (2003).

T A B L E   6-6

Investigators	Date Range of Available Data	Convertible Arbitrage Hedge Fund Index	Fixed-Income Arbitrage Hedge Fund Index	Event-Driven Hedge Fund Index	Global Macro Hedge Fund Index	Market-Neutral Hedge Fund Index
Agarwal and Naik (2000a)	1990–1998	+	Low	+	+	+
Bürki and Larqué	1998–2000					+
Capocci	1984–2000	+	+	+	+	+
Consensus		+	Low	+	+	+

HIGH-MINUS-LOW STOCKS

The cross-sectional evaluation of stock returns by Fama and French (1992, 1993) also considers the difference between high- and low-value stocks (HML). Value refers to the book-to-market valuation of individual stocks. Table 6–7 indicates that HML only seems to have a strong bearing on the event-driven and market-neutral hedge fund categories for concurrent models. This variable is also not included in the forecasting model of Amenc, El Bied, and Martellini (2003).

T A B L E   6–7

Investigators	Factors Date Range of Available Data	Convertible Arbitrage Hedge Fund Index	Fixed- Income Arbitrage Hedge Fund Index	Event- Driven Hedge Fund Index	Global Macro Hedge Fund Index	Market- Neutral Hedge Fund Index
Agarwal and Naik (2000a)	1990–1998	Low	Low	+	Low	−
Bürki and Larqué	1998–2000					+
Capocci	1984–2000	+	−Low	+	+Low	+
Consensus		Low	Low	+	Low	+

UP MINUS DOWN OR RETURN MOMENTUM

The momentum or persistence in returns as shown for each hedge fund category in Table 6–8 does not appear to explain any large portion of hedge fund performance. This must be related to the fact that there is only modest serial correlation between the returns of sequential months for hedge fund indices.

DEFAULT SPREAD

The default spread is frequently measured as the difference in yield between a corporate bond index and a government bond index. As discussed in Chapters 3 and 4, changes in the default spread are related to changes in general business conditions. The default spread is frequently considered to have an impact on the

T A B L E 6-8

Factors Investigators	Date Range of Available Data	Convertible Arbitrage Hedge Fund Index	Fixed-Income Arbitrage Hedge Fund Index	Event-Driven Hedge Fund Index	Global Macro Hedge Fund Index	Market-Neutral Hedge Fund Index
Agarwal and Naik (2000a)	1990–1998	Low	Low	Low	Low	+
Amenc, El Bied, and Martellini	1994–2000	+Low	Low	+	−Low	Low
Bürki and Larqué	1998–2000					+
Capocci	1984–2000	−	+Low	−Low	+	Low
Consensus		Low	Low	Low	Low	Low

performance of stock and bond returns. But as shown in Table 6–9, it seems to have very limited impact on the return of hedge fund categories.

T A B L E 6-9

Factors Investigators	Date Range of Available Data	Convertible Arbitrage Hedge Fund Index	Fixed-Income Arbitrage Hedge Fund Index	Event-Driven Hedge Fund Index	Global Macro Hedge Fund Index	Market-Neutral Hedge Fund Index
Agarwal and Naik (2000a)	1990–1998	Low	+	Low	Low	Low
Bürki and Larqué	1998–2000					+Low
Capocci	1984–2000	+	+Low	+Low	+Low	+Low
Schneeweis, Kazemi, and Martin	1990–2000	+Low	−Low	−	−Low	−Low
Consensus		Low	Low	Low	Low	Low

COMMODITY PRICES

Various commodity price indices are employed, including the price of oil and the Goldman Sachs Commodity Index. Except for the Amenc, El Bied, and Martellini (2003) study that uses the price of

T A B L E 6-10

Investigators	Date Range of Available Data	Convertible Arbitrage Hedge Fund Index	Fixed-Income Arbitrage Hedge Fund Index	Event-Driven Hedge Fund Index	Global Macro Hedge Fund Index	Market-Neutral Hedge Fund Index
Agarwal and Naik (2000a)	1990-1998	Low	Low	—	Low	Low
Agarwal and Naik (2000b)	1994-1998	- Low		- Low	+ Low	- Low
Amenc, El Bied, and Martellini	1994-2000	+	+	+	+	+
Bürki and Larqué	1998-2000					Low
Capocci	1984-2000	- Low	- Low	- Low	- Low	+ Low
Schneeweis and Spurgin	1990-1995	+ Low	Low	+ Low	- Low	+ Low
Consensus		Low	Low	Low	Low	Low

oil in a lagged model, there appears to be a low relationship with commodity prices, as shown in Table 6-10. Some hedge funds could trade in commodities for investment purposes. But that may not be the underlying cause for these commodity price variables affecting the returns on hedge fund indices. The Goldman Sachs Commodity Index is strongly weighted toward the price of oil. During the 1990s, the price of oil was highly related to war activities or threats of war. These circumstances can have a significant impact on stock market price movements and are the likely cause.

CURRENCIES

Despite the fact that many hedge funds trade currencies, there appears to be very little impact on hedge fund index returns based on changes in currency markets. As shown in Table 6-11, only the convertible arbitrage and global macro hedge fund indices seem to have some reaction to currency movement. Major changes in the British pound and Far East currencies during the 1990s were considered significant investment opportunities by many of the global macro funds.

T A B L E 6–11

Investigators	Date Range of Available Data	Convertible Arbitrage Hedge Fund Index	Fixed-Income Arbitrage Hedge Fund Index	Event-Driven Hedge Fund Index	Global Macro Hedge Fund Index	Market-Neutral Hedge Fund Index
Agarwal and Naik (2000a)	1990–1998	Low	Low	Low	Low	Low
Agarwal and Naik (2000b)	1990–1998	+		+Low	+	−Low
Bürki and Larqué	1998–2000					−Low
Schneeweis and Spurgin	1990–1995	+Low	−Low	−Low	+Low	+Low
Consensus		Low	Low	Low	Low	Low

STOCK MARKET OPTIONS OR STOCK RETURN VOLATILITY

Research by Agarwal and Naik (2000a) and Fung and Hsieh (1997, 2001) suggests that hedge fund returns may be equivalent to an option on the investments used by the fund. Instead of using options prices directly, it is also possible to relate fund performance to the underlying investment volatility. This is rational since investment price volatility is a major determinant for option prices. The Agarwal and Naik (2000a) and Fung and Hsieh (1997, 2001) studies show strong relationships between options prices and hedge fund returns. Unfortunately, the Fung and Hsieh studies do not utilize any of the five hedge fund categories employed in this chapter. So they cannot be shown in Table 6–12 along with the results of other option price impacts on hedge fund performance for our five categories. The one use of options in a forecasting framework by Amenc, El Bied, and Martellini (2003) shows very little relationship to options prices on stocks.

Options prices on bonds and currencies are also evaluated by Agarwal and Naik (2000a) and Schneeweis and Spurgin (1998). Generally, coefficients with low significance are obtained except for the impact of bond options on fixed-income arbitrage and the impact of currency options on global macro funds.

T A B L E 6-12

Investigators	Date Range of Available Data	Convertible Arbitrage Hedge Fund Index	Fixed-Income Arbitrage Hedge Fund Index	Event-Driven Hedge Fund Index	Global Macro Hedge Fund Index	Market-Neutral Hedge Fund Index
Factors						
Agarwal and Naik (2000a)	1990–1998	–	–	–	+	–
Amenc, El Bied, and Martellini	1994–2000	Low	–	Low	Low	Low
Bürki and Larqué	1998–2000					+
Schneeweis, Kazemi, and Martin	1990–2000	–	–Low	–	–	+Low
Schneeweis and Spurgin	1990–1995	–Low	–Low	–Low	–Low	–Low
Consensus		–	–	–	Low	Low

SUMMARY OF FACTORS INFLUENCING HEDGE FUNDS

Among all the factors evaluated, only the stock market returns, the small-minus-big (SMB) stock returns, and the options on stocks seem to have a demonstrable influence on the performance of the five hedge fund categories. This lack of evidence for identifying factors that correlate with hedge fund returns is due to a number of sources. First, many of the hedge funds themselves are conducting timing strategies. In doing so, they are moving in and out of different investments searching for the highest returns. If each underlying investment is controlled by its own set of factors, this makes it difficult to discover a constant set of factors influencing the fund's performance. When a fund holds no position in a particular investment, the factors influencing that investment cease to be important for the fund.

Another source of difficulty is the short history available for evaluating the five hedge fund categories. The determination of factor effects would be more robust if 20 or 25 years of data were available. In a matter related to this problem of length of history, the number of funds available for the determination of each index may have been several hundred after 2001. But in 1990, there may have only been 10 or 20 funds available for constructing the index. This means that the index may be less representative of the category in the early years and more representative in later years.

Finally, the funds contained within one category are not really a homogeneous set. While they are nominally following the same strategy, they may not have track records strongly related to each other. For example, two global macro funds could be interested in two different sets of investment opportunities at the same time. Just because they are both called global macro funds does not mean that their performance histories need to be related to each other. This essentially questions the usefulness of the creation of an index composed of funds applying similar tactics but actually employing different investments at a point in time. This might mean that two indices based on different sets of global macro managers might not relate to each other. If this were true, then each index might appear to have different factors influencing its performance.

Despite the possibility of a great deal of idiosyncratic variation among hedge funds of the same category, there could still be a legitimate use of hedge funds in a dynamic investment portfolio. Even if no portion of the historical performance of a category could be explained by macroeconomic factors and its performance were just an unconditional random variable, that hedge fund category could still be used as a building block in an investment portfolio. As long as the performance of an individual hedge fund category has a sufficiently high expected return and is uncorrelated with other investments, then it could be used as a random-return safe haven during times of difficulty for traditional investments.

Most of the research evaluated in Tables 6–4 to 6–12 is based on concurrent style analysis models. The factors identified as important may or may not be useful for lagged-performance relationships. We shall proceed under the assumption that one or more factors can be identified for each of our five hedge fund categories that will be useful in a forecasting framework.

MONTHLY RETURN FACTOR MODEL FOR HEDGE FUND CATEGORIES

The factors identified in Table 6–3 plus a number of additional factors are evaluated in a 1-month forecasting framework. A subset of these factors proves useful in predicting the performance of hedge fund indices. All five hedge fund categories are evaluated employing the same set of factors. Using the same factors allows us to compare the impact of a common factor on each hedge fund category. Because we are interested in a forecasting model, the factors utilized have at least a 1-month lag.

The factors used to model returns for each hedge fund index are:

The return for the same hedge fund index in the previous month.

The average return for the S&P 500 price index for the 3 previous months.

The average refiner acquisition cost of crude oil for the 3 previous months.

The average change in the 90-day Treasury bill rate for the 2 previous months.

The standard deviation of the monthly S&P 500 price returns for the previous 24 months.

Fama and French's small-minus-big-size stock return differential averaged over the previous 12 months.

Fama and French's high-minus-low-value stock return differential averaged over the previous 7 months.

The New York Stock Exchange volume in trillions of shares for the previous month.

The average 90-day Treasury bill rate for the previous 2 months.

The average default yield spread between Baa corporate bonds and 10-year U.S. government bonds for the previous 3 months.

The New York Stock Exchange turnover ratio for the previous month.

The intramonth daily standard deviation of the S&P 500 price index for the previous month.

The intramonth daily standard deviation of 10-year U.S. government bond yields for the previous month.

The intramonth daily standard deviation of 90-day Treasury bill rates for the previous month.

The S&P 500 dividend yield for the previous month.

The S&P finance stocks dividend yield for the previous month.

The Federal Reserve Board trade-weighted dollar-denominated currency index for the previous month.

A linear factor model of the form of equation (6–1) is constructed for each hedge fund index using data from February 1990 to December 2001. A stepwise regression procedure is employed using an F-statistic for entry and exit of 1.0. The resulting coefficients and levels of significance are shown in Table 6–13. Nonsignificant factors excluded from the model have blank entries in the table.

The two hedge fund categories shown in Table 6–2 to have strong serial correlation—convertible arbitrage and fixed-income arbitrage—obtain significant coefficients for the previous level of the hedge fund index. The only factor to affect all hedge fund categories is the cost of crude oil. This factor was also identified by Amenc, El Bied, and Martellini (2003) to have a significant effect on all hedge fund categories considered. The default spread affects each category except for market-neutral. The default spread has a very significant effect on the fixed-income arbitrage index. The impact of the default spread on bond returns is similarly noted in Chapter 4 on factors influencing bond returns.

The small-minus-big and high-minus-low coefficients in Table 6–13 all have negative signs where they are shown to apply. This is opposite to the direction of impact of these factors shown in Tables 6–6 and 6–7. But it must be remembered that all the research used to determine the impact shown in these two tables is based on concurrent models and not on forecasting models.

The standard deviation factors that are surrogates for options prices are not universally consistent across the five hedge fund categories. If hedge funds behave as options on the underlying investments, this process is not evident.

Judging by the R^2 of each category regression, the convertible arbitrage and fixed-income arbitrage categories are the most explainable. In contrast, the global macro and market-neutral categories are the least explainable. This is somewhat related to the

T A B L E 6-13

Coefficients of Factor Models for Indices of Hedge Fund Categories

Factor	Convertible Arbitrage	Fixed-Income Arbitrage	Event-Driven	Global Macro	Market-Neutral
Previous hedge fund index return (1)	0.3866 (5.3315)***	0.1551 (1.9023)*	0.1105 (1.3890)	0.1027 (1.2077)	-0.1395 (-1.6411)
S&P 500 price index return (1–3)		0.1654 (3.6528)***			0.0533 (1.4400)
Cost of crude oil (1–3)	0.0785 (3.4489)***	0.0964 (4.0227)***	0.1557 (3.4159)***	0.0945 (1.7466)*	0.0761 (3.7981)***
90-day Treasury bill change (1–2)		1.5994 (2.3229)*			
S&P 500 monthly standard deviation (1–24)	0.3582 (3.3871)***	-0.1643 (-1.3219)			
SMB stock return (1–12)	-0.3501 (-3.4475)***		-0.7170 (-3.7938)***		
HML stock return (1–7)	-0.1065 (-2.3203)**		-0.2670 (-2.6699)**		
NYSE volume in trillions of shares (1)	0.0921 (2.2876)***	-0.2461 (-4.0476)***			
90-day Treasury bill rate (1–2)	0.2248 (2.2290)**				

Default spread Baa–10-year govt. (1–3)	−0.5785 (−1.7341)*	1.8392 (4.3819)***	0.9238 (1.8588)*	1.6312 (2.4433)**	−0.1467 (−2.2362)*
NYSE turnover ratio (1)		0.7375 (2.7854)**		−1.1055 (−3.6215)***	
S&P 500 daily standard deviation (1)	−0.6919 (−2.7230)**			1.1276 (1.5776)	
10-year bond daily standard deviation (1)	0.8280 (3.1511)***		1.0044 (2.0210)*		0.3433 (1.1301)
90-day T-bill daily standard deviation (1)	0.1373 (1.0279)	0.5292 (2.8381)**			−0.3503 (−2.3015)*
S&P 500 dividend yield (1)	2.2705 (4.6184)***		2.7283 (3.7294)***		
S&P finance stocks dividend yield (1)	−1.6864 (−5.6693)***		−2.2924 (−4.1473)***	−0.8560 (−2.4305)**	
FRB currency index (1)	−0.0300 (−1.4017)		−0.0462 (−1.1457)	−0.1021 (−1.9346)*	
Alpha	−1.5203	−6.0567	−0.5571	12.5714	0.3135
R^2	0.4743	0.3633	0.2079	0.1331	0.1122
Residual standard error	0.7020	1.1008	1.6412	2.4132	0.8956

This table provides the expected value of each coefficient. Corresponding t-statistics are provided in parentheses. Significance is indicated by *** at the 0.001 level, ** at the 0.01 level, and * at the 0.05 level for one-tailed t-statistic tests.

degree of serial correlation for each of these categories. The categories with the strongest serial correlation are the most explainable. It is also worth noting that the global macro index has the largest residual error. This class of hedge funds which changes from one investment to another on a regular basis proves to be the most challenging to predict.

For predictive models based on monthly data, these models of hedge fund performance seem to have very large R^2 compared with the monthly models for stocks and bonds. The apparent strength of the degree of fit of these hedge fund models is partly dependent on the short 12 years of data available. Had 25 years of data been available, these R^2 probably would not have been as strong.

REFERENCES

Agarwal, Vikas, and Narayan Y. Naik. "Performance Evaluation of Hedge Funds with Option-Based and Buy-and-Hold Strategies." Working paper, London Business School (2000a).

Agarwal, Vikas, and Narayan Y. Naik. "Generalized Style Analysis of Hedge Funds." *Journal of Asset Management* 1, no. 1 (July 2000b): 93–109.

Agarwal, Vikas, and Narayan Y. Naik. "Risks and Portfolio Decisions Involving Hedge Funds." Working paper, London Business School (2002).

Amenc, Noël, Sina El Bied, and Lionel Martellini. "Evidence of Predictability in Hedge Fund Returns and Multi-Style Multi-Class Style Allocation Decisions." *Financial Analysts Journal* (2003 forthcoming).

Bürki, Valentin, and Rodolphe Larqué. "Hedge Funds Returns and Their Drivers." Master's Thesis, Ecole des HEC, University of Lausanne (2001).

Capocci, Daniel. "An Analysis of Hedge Fund Performance, 1984–2000." Working paper, University of Liege (November 2001).

Edwards, Franklin R., and Mustafa Onur Caglayan. "Hedge Fund Performance and Manager Skill." *Journal of Futures Markets* 21, no. 11 (2001): 1003–1028.

Fama, Eugene F., and Kenneth F. French. "The Cross-Section of Expected Stock Returns." *Journal of Finance* 47, no. 2 (1992): 427–465.

Fama, Eugene F., and Kenneth F. French. "Common Risk Factors in the Returns on Stocks and Bonds." *Journal of Financial Economics* 33 (1993): 3–56.

Fung, William, and David A. Hsieh. "Empirical Characteristics of Dynamic Trading Strategies: The Case of Hedge Funds." *Review of Financial Studies* 10 (1997): 275–302.

Fung, William, and David A. Hsieh. "The Risk in Hedge Fund Strategies: Theory and Evidence from Trend Followers." *Review of Financial Studies* 14, no. 2 (Summer 2001): 313–341.

Fung, William, and David A. Hsieh. "Asset-Based Style Factors for Hedge Funds." *Financial Analyst Journal* 58, no. 5 (September/October 2002): 16–27.

Gregoriou, Greg N., Fabrice Rouah, and Komlan Sedzro. "On the Market Timing of Hedge Fund Managers." *Journal of Wealth Management* (Summer 2002): 1–13.

Kat, Harry M., and Joelle Miffre. "Performance Evaluation and Conditioning Information: The Case of Hedge Funds." Discussion paper in Finance 2002-10, International Securities Market Associations, University of Reading (April 2002).

Schneeweis, Thomas, Hossein Kazemi, and George Martin. "Understanding Hedge Fund Performance." Research report sponsored by Lehman Brothers Capital Introductions Group (November 2001).

Schneeweis, Thomas, and Richard Spurgin. "Multi-Factor Models of Hedge Fund, Managed Futures, and Mutual Fund Return and Risk Characteristics." *Journal of Alternative Investments* (Fall 1998): 1–24.

Sharpe, William. "Asset Allocation: Management Style and Performance Measurement." *Journal of Portfolio Management* 8 (1992): 7–19.

CHAPTER 7

Predictability of Market Returns

> I remember the rage I used to feel when a prediction went awry. I could have shouted at the subjects of my experiments, "Behave, damn you, behave as you ought!" Eventually I realized that the subjects were always right. It was I who was wrong. I had made a bad prediction.
>
> *Burrhus Frederic Skinner*
> *Walden Two (1948)*

Having a regression model that closely fits the performance of market returns over a specific date range by employing a set of explanatory factors is not very useful if the degree of fit does not persist into following time intervals. The distinction between an in-sample fit and an out-of-sample prediction is an important one. It all hinges on model stationarity. If all the factors that influenced a market were identified and if the model coefficients were constant across all time intervals, then we would be able to generate accurate and profitable performance forecasts. Yet we may not be completely confident that we have identified all the important factors influencing the market. If an important independent factor is missing in a linear model, fitting the market returns to a set of incomplete factors incorporates the average effect of the missing factor in the constant term of the model. If the average value for this factor is different for another time interval, then the average forecasted performance for the follow-on time interval would be biased. The average forecasted performance would be off by the difference in the averages of the missing independent factor between the two time intervals multiplied by the true but undetermined linear coefficient for that factor.

Not knowing to include an important factor is certainly a troublesome problem. But even more vexing problems are possible. Consider the case in which we suspect a factor is theoretically important but the factor is nearly constant over the interval we employ to fit the model. The coefficient for this factor will most likely be estimated at something close to zero. Had the factor taken on a wide range of values, we would have been able to form a reasonable estimate for its coefficient. Should this factor change value in a following interval, it is sure to cause forecasting errors.

If there are a large number of causative factors that have had constant values in the past and can take on new constant values or become random variables in the future, we will have a forecasting error whenever one of these factors becomes active. Our hope is that we have identified the most important factors and have estimated the impact of changes in their values as coefficients in a model. If we have missed an important factor or have not been able to estimate its impact in the past, we must continue to strive to discover its impact in the future.

MEASURES OF PREDICTABILITY

Many studies developing models of investment market returns and the factors influencing those returns refer to the model as a prediction equation. This obviously refers to the intention of the researcher to have the developed equation be used in a forecasting capacity. But the degree of fit between the market return and the factors should not really be referred to as a measure of predictability. The strength of the relationship based on the time interval used to estimate the values of the unknown model coefficients is properly referred to as the degree of fit of the model to the available data. This in-sample goodness of fit should technically not be termed a measure of predictability.

The use of the term *predictability* should be reserved for an out-of-sample evaluation of the model employing a data set not used to determine any of the model coefficients. For example, if the model coefficients were estimated through a fitting process using monthly data from January 1960 to December 1989, then the data from January 1990 to December 2000 could be used to determine one estimate of the model's level of predictability.

We should recognize this distinction between model fit and model predictability. We can convert a model-fit process to a model-predictability process simply by developing the model parameters based on one time period and then evaluating out of sample using another time period. The measure of fit from the fitting process gives us some idea of possible predictability, but it is far safer to reserve the measure of predictability for an independent data set. In the discussion that follows, if we refer to a predictability estimate based on the fit data set, we shall be careful to refer to it as the in-sample predictability.

There are a number of mathematical measures of predictability. Some of the most popular measures are provided in the discussion that follows. Several of these predictability measures require the use of common statistical factors. These common statistical factors are defined before proceeding. First, following Pesaran and Timmermann (1995), assume that the periodic rate of return is predicted as a linear function of a number of macroeconomic factors.

$$\rho_{\tau+1} = \beta_i X_{\tau i} + \varepsilon_{\tau+1,i} \qquad (7\text{-}1)$$

where:

ρ_τ = rate of return for the investment for time period τ
β_i = unknown regression coefficients for $\kappa + 1$ factors including a constant term for model permutation i
$X_{\tau i}$ = values of factors used to predict the investment performance for time period τ for model permutation i
$\varepsilon_{\tau+1,i}$ = an error term representing the portion of ρ_τ that is not explained by the factors

When utilizing (7–1) as a prediction model, the predictability equations that follow are measures of in-sample predictability as long as the time period τ used for the determination of the regression coefficients β is the same time period used to evaluate the predictability measures.

Various model prediction criteria are based on likelihood estimates that assign different weights to the concepts of fit and parsimony of the prediction models. The fit of the model is measured by the log-likelihood function LL_{ti}, and the parsimony of the model is measured by the number of freely estimated coefficients. Eventually we will use these concepts in a composite weighted function to attempt to maximize the model fit and simultaneously minimize the use of degrees of freedom. The value of the log-likelihood function is determined by

$$\sigma^2{}_{ti} = \sum_{\tau=0}^{t-1} \frac{(\rho_{\tau+1} - X'_{\tau i}\beta_{ti})^2}{t} \tag{7-2}$$

$$LL_{ti} = \frac{-t[1 + \log(2\pi\sigma^2{}_{ti})]}{2} \tag{7-3}$$

where:

LL_{ti} = log-likelihood function representing the "fit" of the model
t = number of time periods of data available
κ = number of factors used to predict the investment performance
i = number of permutations of the factors that can be in or out of the model = 2^κ

Based on the κ factors available for inclusion in (7–1), there are a number of model permutations depending on the inclusion or exclusion of particular factors. For each of the following performance criteria, the permutation of included factors that generates the largest algebraic value of the performance criterion defines the best predictive model.

Akaike Information Criterion

Using the model defined in (7–1) and the statistics defined in (7–2) and (7–3), it can be shown that the Akaike information criterion $AIC_{t,i}$ is a function of these statistics and the number of model factors employed. For a performance history that has time periods from time 0 to time t, the Akaike information criterion at time t for a model i that has κ_i factors in the model is just

$$\text{AIC}_{ti} = \text{LL}_{ti} - (\kappa_i + 1) \tag{7-4}$$

where κ_i = number of participating factors used in model i to predict the investment performance and LL_{ti} is defined in (7–3). For more details on the Akaike information criterion, see Akaike (1973).

Schwarz's Bayesian Information Criterion

Similarly, using the same model and statistics defined in (7–1) to (7–3), it can be shown that Schwarz's Bayesian information criterion $\text{BIC}_{t,i}$ is also a function of these statistics, the number of model factors employed, and the number of time periods available. For a performance history that has time periods from time 0 to time t, Schwarz's information criterion at time t for a model i that has κ_i factors is just

$$\text{BIC}_{ti} = \frac{\text{LL}_{ti} - (\kappa_i + 1) \log(t)}{2} \tag{7-5}$$

For more details on Schwarz's Bayesian information criterion, see Schwarz (1978).

Theil's R^2 Criterion of Predictability

The R^2 criterion defined by Theil (1958) is normally calculated as a fraction of the variance of the investment returns explained by the linear model shown in (7–1). That is,

$$\tilde{\sigma}^2{}_{ti} = \sum_{\tau=0}^{t-1} \frac{(\rho_{\tau+1} - X'_{\tau i}\beta_{\tau i})^2}{t - \kappa_i - 1} \tag{7-6}$$

$$\bar{\rho}_\tau = \sum_{\tau=1}^{t} \frac{\rho_\tau}{t} \tag{7-7}$$

$$S^2{}_{\rho t} = \sum_{\tau=1}^{t} \frac{(\rho_\tau - \bar{\rho}_\tau)^2}{t - 1} \tag{7-8}$$

$$R^2 = 1 - \frac{\sigma^2{}_{ti}}{S^2{}_{\rho t}} \tag{7-9}$$

While (7–9) is the most common expression for R^2, it can be shown that an alternative expression for R^2 is the following equation in terms of fit and parsimony:

$$\text{THEIL}_{ti} = \text{LL}_{ti} - \frac{\log[t/(t - \kappa_i - 1)]}{2} \tag{7-10}$$

Note that the only differences among the Akaike, Schwarz, and Theil criteria are related to the second term of each of the equations (7–4), (7–5), and (7–10). These second terms are just functions of the number of time intervals τ available and the number of factors κ employed.

Cumby and Modest Predictability of Market Return Direction

A measurement of predictability in terms of forecasting the correct direction of the market is treated by Cumby and Modest (1987) as a linear model evaluated on a regression basis. This method is not based on the fit and parsimony of the prediction model. The model is based on a trading methodology that indicates whether the investor should be 100 percent invested in the market or 100 percent invested in a risk-free instrument.

$$R_{Mt} - R_{Ct} = b_0 + b_1 X(T)_t + e_t \qquad (7\text{--}11)$$

where:

$F(T)_t =$ forecast of the T-period excess return of the market made in advance for time t

If $F(T)_t > 0$, then be fully invested in the market and receive the market return for time t

If $F(T)_t \le 0$, then be out of the market and receive the risk-free rate for time t

$X(T)_t = 1$ when the forecast for the market return exceeds the risk-free return, $F(T)_t > 0$

$X(T)_t = 0$ when the forecast for the market return does not exceed the risk-free return, $F(T)_t \le 0$

$R_{Mt} =$ random variable representing the actual return on the market M for time t

$R_{Ct} =$ certain return on the risk-free investment C for time t, known in advance

$b_0 =$ regression coefficient, interpreted as the expected difference in returns between the buy-and-hold strategy and the trading strategy—a negative value would be expected

$b_1 =$ regression coefficient, interpreted as the expected incremental return whenever the market return is forecasted to be above the risk-free return

$e_t =$ unexplained model error at time t

If the prediction method can successfully determine those time periods during which $F(T)_t$ is greater than the unconditional average of $F(T)_t$, then the value of b_1 will be statistically different from zero.

DIFFICULTIES LEADING TO POOR PREDICTABILITY

Developing a model for predicting the returns of any given market is half science and half intuition. Model development is complicated by the fact that, during any selected time interval, some controlling factors may not make themselves known by taking on a significant range of values. The discovery of the most basic fundamental factors is the goal of the modeling effort. New factors will certainly present themselves in the future, and old factors may appear to become unimportant. As long as this is caused by previously active factors becoming dormant due to the factor becoming invariant, there is no problem. The same is true for a previously dormant factor becoming active. If all the important factors have been identified and incorporated into a nearly correct model structure, the model should perform well under a range of market conditions. Alternatively, there are many ways to specify an inadequate model that performs poorly out of sample. This section attempts to enumerate the various causes of developing a model with weak predictability.

Missing Factors

If the basic structure of the model is wrong, then all analysis based on that structure is likely to be flawed. Leaving out an important factor can cause the most serious problems. If a fundamentally important factor is missing because it was invariant in the past, it is sure to cause poor predictability in the future should it become variable. The failure to include a significant variable in the model is a profound modeling flaw.

Unnecessary or Spurious Factors

Similarly, putting a variable in the model that should not be there is the obverse of the same coin. Given a sufficient amount of available data to fit, it is not very likely to allow a completely spurious variable in the model. It is more likely that the wrong measure of the right fundamental concept might be included in a model. For example, consider the case in which the correct variable required is a measure of general price inflation. If a measure of commodity price inflation is employed, this factor may do a credible job in some circumstances during the model-fitting process. But if it is the wrong concept, the out-of-sample goodness of fit is likely to suffer.

Incorrect Data Lags

Employing explanatory factors with the wrong data lag can provide seemingly good fits whenever these factors exhibit strong serial correlation. If the month-to-month changes in factors are very small, the selection of the time lag is not very critical. But as soon as the monthly changes in the factor accelerate or exhibit more volatility, then the determination of the correct lag becomes more important. It is worthwhile to devote some effort to the empirical determination of the lag that presents the best model fit.

Incorrect Accumulation Intervals

Some factors must be accumulated for a length of time other than the basic frequency of the data. The inflation rate averaged over the last 60 months will be different from the average inflation over the last 36 months or 12 months. While there may be some theoretical reason to try a particular accumulation interval, most model building will involve a good deal of empirical scanning for the most effective interval for each factor.

Faulty Mathematical Form

Another basic type of model misspecification is the basic mathematical form of the model itself. Many models are specified in a linear form because no better logical form is suspected or because determining the coefficients of linear models is easier than nonlinear models. If the true nature of the model is nonlinear, then an independent linear formulation may only give a rough directional indication to the effect of the factors. If cross-product terms are missing, then important interactions between factors may not be available. An example of a nonlinear model is the dividend discount model.

$$V_0 = \sum_{t=1}^{t=\infty} b_t \pi_t \prod_{k=1}^{k=t} c_k v_k \qquad (7\text{--}12)$$

where:

π_t = dividend yield for year t

v_k = discount factor in year $t = 1/(1 + i_t)$

i_t = interest rate for year t

b_t, c_k = unknown coefficients

An example of a purely linear model might be specified as

$$R(T)_{it} = a_0 + a_1 f_1 + a_2 f_2 + a_3 f_3 + a_4 f_4 \qquad (7\text{--}13)$$

If these two models were used to fit the same performance history, then the degree of model fit and the impact of the various factors could be substantially different between the two model structures.

A wide range of structures is available for formulating prediction models. The structures include linear regression, vector autoregression, Kalman filters, and neural networks plus many others. One of these structures may prove to be more successful than the others under particular market regimes, even when using the same macroeconomic factors. Priestley (1996) finds that Kalman filters generate superior factors over first differences and vector autoregression for use in conjunction with the arbitrage pricing theory. Ming Qi (1999) demonstrates that the use of a flexible nonlinear model such as a neural network marginally outperforms the use of a linear regression model for both in-sample fits and out-of-sample forecasts.

Actual Values versus Expectations

Most predictive performance models involve measures of actual reported values of macroeconomic factors. A number of investigators have suggested the use of changes in expectations of macroeconomic factors instead of the actual measure of the factors themselves. Luckily, for some factors, surveys are available that attempt to measure expectations. Expectations of inflation, interest rates, and foreign exchange rates are available from a number of sources.

Lags in the Availability of Reported Numbers

The use of actual measures can have its own set of problems such as the lag between the end of a time interval and the subsequent availability of the reported number. Lags of 1 to 2 months are common. For predictive purposes, the length of such reporting delays must be considered in model formulations. The model formulation lag for a given variable must not be less than the reporting lag.

Revisions to Reported Time Series

Reported values of macroeconomic factors are subject to revision by the reporting authority. Unfortunately, what tends to be permanently recorded in long-term time series is the ultimate result after all revisions. The initial and intermediate estimates of the factor value are not recorded in the permanent time series. If it is the reported value of the factor that causes the investment performance to change, then the initial impact of a revised factor is lost after the revision is made. If it is the true underlying value of the factor that causes changes in the investment performance, then the initial values may not be important at all. Of course, there is always the chance that there is a permanent error in the reported value of a factor that is never found and corrected. This possibility will simply contribute to model error.

Insufficient Variation in Independent Variables

A factor that can have a significant impact on the performance of an investment may never be measured empirically if the value of the factor is relatively constant over the interval used to fit the model. Frequently this is the result of simply using too short a time interval. Other times it is the result of having a factor go dormant for a long time. The factor may be controlled by changes in legislative or regulatory considerations that are activated infrequently. The values of macroeconomic factors are not the subject of planning or experimental design. We must take the values of the factors as we find them for any specific historical interval. We cannot contrive to have all factors take on a wide range of values as one might design into an agricultural experiment.

Impact of the Underlying Data Frequency

There is a very significant effect on predictability due to changing the frequency of the data. Building models on monthly, quarterly, or annual data produces considerable differences in results. Certain unmeasured factors can have a significant impact for shorter horizons. For example, technical trading, market forces, or news events can have a short-term impact. However, for longer horizons, the impact of these factors is washed out. Building models based on annual data may be more accurate by avoiding the model error introduced by these unstructured short-term factors. Conversely, using annual data will severely restrict the number of data points available for model-building purposes. Using daily data would produce a larger number of data points although there are few macroeconomic variables available with daily frequency. Using monthly data seems to be the best compromise to achieve a reasonably large number of data points for macroeconomic factors.

Impact of the Prediction Horizon

Fama and French (1989) evaluate the use of term spread and dividend yield to predict value-weighted stock returns over a range of prediction horizons. Using data from 1927 to 1987, as the horizon is increased from 1 month to 48 months, they show that the R^2 increases from 1 to 25 percent. They conclude from this dramatic increase in R^2 that longer horizon intervals are more predictable. Alternatively, Bekaert and Hodrick (1992) claim that such increases in R^2 are the result of negative serial correlation in the long-term returns.

The Fama and French regression results obtained for their horizons longer than 12 months make use of overlapping annual return observations. Kirby (1997) demonstrates that serial correlation resulting from the use of overlapping returns data can produce seeming increases in predictability for longer forecasting horizons when there is little or no actual predictability. Using Monte Carlo simulations, Kirby shows that when the true population R^2 is small, the value of a derived sample R^2 or t-statistics for long overlapping horizons can be misleadingly large. To avoid making misleading conclusions about long-term predictability, it would be better to use the resulting standard deviations of predicted returns rather than using the apparent R^2 or t-statistics.

Structural Changes in the Prediction Model

Pesaran and Timmerman (2002) suggest that structural changes in prediction models need to be considered due to the impact of major changes in market sentiment, the appearance of irrational speculative bubbles, or regime switches in monetary or debt management policies. They determine that the time interval from 1954 to 1997 exhibited three breakpoints requiring changes in the coefficients of a model consisting of the dividend yield, the short-run interest rate, and the default premium.

The failure of a single set of model coefficients to accurately fit their entire 44-year interval could be attributed to one of two causes. The market could be adaptive and learn from past relationships. Market participants might then arbitrage away any apparent opportunities and thereby change the values of previously effective coefficients. This would result in the need for structural model changes proposed by Pesaran and Timmerman.

On the other hand, there could be important factors having an influence on the market performance that are missing from the model formulation. If the values of one of these factors were relatively constant for a long interval, then it would not be required to help explain that interval. But as soon as the factor became variable, then its presence in the model would be required. Thus, the apparent need for structural model changes could result from nothing more than an incomplete model specification.

Allowing the possibility of sudden structural changes in the model at unknown points in the future would severely handicap the usefulness of any predictive process. In order to preserve the opportunity for a successful prediction process, searching for additional factors or alternative model formulations would seem to offer a more useful path to finding the "model for all seasons."

REPORTS OF GOOD PREDICTABILIY

Many of the reports of good *predictability* available in the literature are actually indications of the in-sample goodness of fit rather than out-of-sample forecasts. In this section, results involving both in-sample fits of a forecasting equation and out-of-sample forecasts are presented. The research based on in-sample goodness of fit alone is included for those cases in which the investigators have used significant statistical measures to estimate the degree of in-sample predictability.

Bekaert and Hodrick (1992) conduct in-sample predictability studies on vector autoregressive forecasts involving two-country stock market returns, an exchange rate between the two countries, a forward currency premium, and the two-country dividend yields. For measures of predictability, they use the Schwarz (1978) Bayesian information criterion and the Cumby and Huizinga (1992) l-test for serial correlation in the error process. They also employ a more traditional χ^2 test for determining if all coefficients in the model are zero. For a 1-month forecasting horizon, they find that there is evidence of predictability, but the level of the predictability is small judging from the adjusted R^2 values. Using horizons as long as 60 months provides only marginal increases in the adjusted R^2 values for forecasting equity returns. On the other hand, there is a consistently large increase in the adjusted R^2 values when forecasting currency markets. This research was based on a very short time interval of 108 months from 1981 to 1989.

Bossaerts and Hillion (1999) confirm an indication of significant in-sample predictability for stocks in 9 out of 14 countries evaluated. The factors used to predict the market are the January effect, the dividend yield, a short-term interest rate, and a bond yield. They allow each factor to be considered for inclusion in the model using an assortment of predictability measures. A simple constant-return model is also evaluated. They evaluate various predictability measures including Theil's R^2, the Akaike information criterion, and Schwarz's Bayesian information criterion. Bossaerts and Hillion also include four additional criteria for which they provide detailed descriptions. These additional factors are the Fisher information criterion, the posterior criterion, the predictive least squares criterion, and the predictive least squares criterion with Markov dimension criterion. If the model with a simple constant return demonstrates the highest predictability measures, then there is no predictability for that country. They show that for the measures of predictability evaluated, across a wide range of countries, there is ample evidence of in-sample predictability. The amount of data available varied by country from 62 months to 411 months in the in-sample time interval.

Ferson and Korajczyk (1995) conduct an extensive test on the predictability of an index based on all firms listed on the New York Stock Exchange and the American Stock Exchange for two time intervals: 1927–1988 and 1961–1988. Using time horizons from 1 month to 24 months, they investigate a model based on arbitrage pricing theory to predict stock market returns. They question whether the factor coefficients are constant or need to be time-varying. Recognizing that overlapping time intervals can cause significant statistical problems by inducing autocorrelation into the error terms, they only employ nonoverlapping time intervals. For the 1961–1988 subperiod, their tests strongly reject the null hypothesis of no predictability. For the longer interval, their tests produce weaker results. For the longer-horizon returns, they find that a constant beta model is useful for making predictions. For shorter-horizon returns during the 1927–1988 interval, they reject the constant beta approach. On the other hand, allowing the betas to vary provides hardly any improvement. While Ferson and Korajczyk set out to examine the question of constant versus variable betas, they manage to show that the APT model explains up to 80 percent of the predictability over most time horizons from 1 to 24 months using 5 macroeconomic factors.

Pesaran and Timmermann (1995) estimate predictability using 39 years of monthly data for the U.S. stock market. They employ a wide range of prediction factors including the dividend yield, the earnings-price ratio, the 1-month T-bill rate, the 12-month T-bond rate, a 1-year rate of inflation, a 1-year change in industrial output, and a 1-year growth in a narrow money stock. The predictability measures include R^2, the Akaike information criterion, Schwarz's Bayesian information criterion, and a sign criterion developed by the authors. All predictability measures considered are shown to indicate successful forecasts except for Schwarz's Bayesian information criterion. Overall, Pesaran and Timmermann conclude that the best forecasting models must allow for economic regime switches that would permit new factors to be introduced into the model as they become evident. Examples of such new factors include inflation after the first oil shock in the 1970s and the commencement of the Federal Reserve policy of targeting interest rates. They also find that the degree of predictability is dependent on the volatility of the market. Highly volatile markets appear to be associated with stronger measures of predictability. This is consistent with the idea that markets with strongly changing conditions allow better estimates of factor coefficients.

Qi (1999) utilizes neural networks to demonstrate that this kind of nonlinear model provides better predictability than linear models. Using the same set of macroeconomic factors and the same date range employed by Pesaran and Timmermann (1995), Qi shows that neural networks outperform a linear prediction model for all five measures of model accuracy that are considered. Moreover, this is done for both an in-sample time interval and an out-of-sample interval. The five measures of prediction accuracy all involve direct comparison of the actual value of the return against the predicted return.

If the actual return for time interval i is ρ_i and if the predicted return for the time interval i is $\hat{\rho}_i$, the following measures of forecasting accuracy are evaluated by Qi:

$$\text{The root mean square error} = \left[\frac{1}{T} \sum_{i=1}^{T} (\rho_i - \hat{\rho}_i)^2 \right]^{1/2} \tag{7-14}$$

$$\text{The mean absolute error} = \frac{1}{T} \sum_{i=1}^{T} |\rho_i - \hat{\rho}_i| \tag{7-15}$$

$$\text{The mean absolute percentage error} = \frac{1}{T} \sum_{i=1}^{T} \left| \frac{(\rho_i - \hat{\rho}_i)}{\rho_i} \right| \tag{7-16}$$

The Pearson correlation coefficient =

$$\frac{\sum_{i=1}^{T} (\rho_i - \hat{\rho}_i)(\hat{\rho}_i - \bar{\hat{\rho}}_i)}{\left[\sum_{i=1}^{T} (\rho_i - \hat{\rho}_i)^2 \right]^{1/2} \left[\sum_{i=1}^{T} (\hat{\rho}_i - \bar{\hat{\rho}}_i)^2 \right]^{1/2}} \tag{7-17}$$

$$\begin{array}{l} \text{Proportion of times that the} \\ \text{sign is correctly forecast} \end{array} = \frac{1}{T} \sum_{i=1}^{T} z_i \tag{7-18}$$

$$\text{where} \quad z_i = \begin{cases} 1 & \text{if } (\rho_{i+1})(\hat{\rho}_{i+1}) > 0 \\ 0 & \text{otherwise} \end{cases}$$

Lo and MacKinlay (1997) devise procedures for estimating the maximally predictable portfolio, or MPP. Using various macroeconomic factors, models are devised for stock and bond asset classes that contain time-varying risk premiums that maximize the predictability of the portfolio. They specify an investment return model as a linear function of dividend yield, the default spread, the term spread, past stock market returns, and an interest rate trend. From these linear return functions, estimates of the maximally predictable portfolio asset allocations are calculated. These allocations are found to change substantially as the return horizon is increased from monthly to semiannual to annual horizons. On an out-of-sample basis, they compare the performance of the MPP with three other measures of predictability. Using these comparisons, they confirm the presence of predictability in the MPP method. They conclude that stock market prices do not follow a random walk and that the MPP model has significant predictive power.

REPORTS OF POOR PREDICTABILITY

Bossaerts and Hillion (1999) established significant in-sample predictability, as described previously. Yet the same procedure, when applied to 60 months of out-of-sample data, showed no predictive power. Over a wide range of model selection criteria, no criterion demonstrates a significant out-of-sample prediction capability. They suggest that the failure to establish out-of-sample predictability indicates that the underlying models must be nonstationary, possibly caused by learning in the marketplace. It may be true that the values of the model coefficients are changing with time. As pointed out previously, it may also be true that the apparent nonstationarity may be due to a model misspecification caused by one or more missing factors.

Fuller and Kling (1994) apply the Cumby-Modest methodology to the 51-year period from 1938 to 1988 in order to test for predictability for several types of bonds and for U.S. common stocks. By using forecasting horizon values of $T = 1, 3, 12, 24, 36,$ and 48 months, forecasting equations are developed using the default premium $DPREM_t$ and the term premium $TPREM_t$. The forecasting equation employed has the form

$$r(T)_t = a(T)_t + B(T)_t[\text{DPREM}_t] + C(T)_t[\text{TPREM}_t] + e(T)_t \quad (7\text{–}19)$$

where:

> T = length of the return horizon
> t = current month
> $r(T)_t$ = annualized compounded return for the market from the end of month t to the end of $t + T$
> $a(T)_t$ = forecasting equation intercept
> $B(T)_t$ = coefficient for DPREM$_t$ in the forecasting equation
> $C(T)_t$ = coefficient for TPREM$_t$ in the forecasting equation
> DPREM$_t$ = default premium between bonds chosen regardless of rating and Aaa bonds at month t
> TPREM$_t$ = term premium between Aaa bonds and 1-month Treasury bills at month t
> $e(T)_t$ = unexplained error in T-month return at month t

The results of Fuller and Kling's study show that forecasting Aaa bonds and A bonds results in significant forecasting ability. Forecasting junk bonds and common stocks results in no significant forecasting ability using equation (7–19) as a forecasting model. The failure to identify significant forecasting power for common stocks is most likely due to an incomplete model specification. Limiting the model to include only the default premium and the term premium is somewhat restrictive. Had factors such as dividend yield, inflation, and changes in Treasury bill rates been included, the model may have demonstrated significant predictability.

Handa and Tiwari (2000) pose a number of interesting predictability questions. Do stable relationships exist between predictive factors and the out-of-sample performance of the stock market? Is the factor combination of lagged stock returns, dividend yield, and book-to-market ratios sufficient to demonstrate stock market predictability? How is the issue of predictability affected by involving two, three, or more investments in the portfolio allocation process? In order to generate robust answers to these and other questions, only out-of-sample evaluations are employed. Two kinds of investors are defined. The first is the *i.i.d. investor* (independent and identically distributed performance). In this case, only the averages of a historic interval are used for the expected returns for each investment. There is no allowance for conditioning factors. The second type of investor is the *mutual fund strategy investor*, who believes that certain market factors can be used to prepare better estimates of future market returns through a linear factor model. In the case of a single risky asset plus a risk-free investment, Handa and Tiwari find that the mutual fund strategy outperforms the i.i.d. strategy for 1972–1984 and underperforms the i.i.d. strategy for 1985–1998. They then conclude that the linear factor relationships must be unstable. When multiple risky assets are considered, the mutual fund strategy is found consistently better for the entire 1972–1998 interval. By adopting a boot-strapping method that randomly draws quarterly performance data from history, with replacement, they conclude that the reported superiority of the mutual fund strategy is an apparent artifact of the specific interval of history evaluated.

Neeley and Weller (2000) investigate the stability of the vector autoregressive (VAR) approach of Bekaert and Hodrick (1992) previously described. A VAR model is established for the long-horizon predictability of stocks and currencies for the United States, Japan, the United Kingdom, and Germany. For each two-country pair, Neeley and Weller generate vector autoregressions employing the excess stock market return for each country, the exchange rate between the countries, the dividend yield in each country, and the 1-month interest rate differential between the countries. While it is demonstrated that there is a certain amount of in-sample predictability, the purpose of this study is to determine if the VAR model has any out-of-sample predictive power. The coefficients of the VAR model are determined over the time interval 1981–1989. Out-of-sample predictability tests are conducted for 1990–1996. A substantial bias in the out-of-sample forecasts produced is taken as a sign of poor predictability. Finally, it is shown that a simple benchmark forecast equal to the average returns in the in-sample time interval has better predictability measures than the VAR forecasts.

PREDICTABILITY VERSUS PROFITABILITY

Qi (1999) makes the point that predictability does not necessarily guarantee profitability. Profitability is also controlled by the trading system that is implemented, by dynamic asset allocations to multiple investments in a portfolio, by transaction costs, and by any changes in leveraging. If two investments each have their direction correctly forecast for a sequence of months, the decision mechanism used to allocate capital to the two investments can play a large role in the level of the long-term profitability. For example, in a portfolio with a stock and a bond asset, even if the return for stocks is forecast to be up 10 percent next month, the allocation given to stocks might not be 100 percent. If the forecast for bonds were 0, 10, or 20 percent, stocks might be allocated 100, 50, or 0 percent, respectively, of the portfolio. The allocation to stocks must depend on the level of the bond forecast and the uncertainty associated with each forecast. The prediction process and the asset allocation process will both bear on the profitability.

Furthermore, if asset allocations procedure requires frequent as well as very large changes in the allocations, then transaction costs may consume much of the gains attainable by following a sequence of optimal one-period allocations. The same is also true if the investment model allows borrowing to leverage up the portfolio. Changes in the leverage ratio would also incur additional transaction costs.

Qi adopts a simple switching strategy that gives 100 percent of a stock/bond portfolio to the investment that has the highest expected return for each time interval. Even under high transaction costs, Qi shows that over the 33-year interval from 1960 to 1992, a linear prediction model outperforms a buy-and-hold stock market portfolio. The nonlinear neural network model developed by Qi is shown to produce substantially higher returns than the market portfolio under the same high transaction costs. While these results were generally true over the full 33-year interval, there were 10-year time intervals during which the buy-and-hold market portfolio outperformed the linear prediction model. Pesaran and Timmermann (1995) suggest that during periods with low investment volatility, such as the 1960s, there is little profitability in dynamic asset allocation.

WHAT CAN BE DONE TO INCREASE PREDICTABILITY?

Armed with some knowledge of the conditions that might influence the quality of investment return predictions, we can now describe several principles to follow when constructing prediction models.

Include Every Theoretically and Empirically Important Factor

No matter how satisfying an in-sample fit seems, a prediction model is doomed to provide poor out-of-sample forecasts if a significant factor is missing. Starting from the point of view of a theoretically sound model should provide a useful set of prediction factors. Yet this may not provide all the factors to fit a long range of market returns. There are times when new factors present themselves because the market is reacting to a new concept or to a long-dormant variable. There is nothing wrong with an empirical procedure to test the validity of a proposed factor.

Use a Long Data Set to Establish Model Coefficients

To have some assurance that the set of factors used to predict the market will work under future market conditions, it is best to have many historical combinations of the factors. Since we cannot set up an experiment to force a stratified sample of factor values, the best we can hope for is to use a long range of history that has experienced many market cycles. A long history can undergo what might be considered regime switches or market structure changes. The temptation to split the data into independently fitted time intervals should be resisted. This will reduce the level of out-of-sample predictability. We are seeking universal models. If the causes for any apparent structural shifts can be identified and measured, then these factors should be tested for inclusion in the model.

Employ the Most Accurate Model Structure Possible

The theoretical model for combining the significant factors that influence investment returns may be highly complex and nonlinear. Determining unknown coefficients for such models may be time-consuming and mathematically challenging. But it has been shown that nonlinear models have the potential for providing more accurate out-of-sample forecasts. On the other hand, linear models allow the inclusion of more factors in practical solution methodologies. Frequently, linear models can guarantee the determination of optimal solutions, whereas nonlinear models may only find local optima. A practical compromise might be to use linear models for investigative work to discover the identity of the most significant factors. Then a nonlinear model could be utilized incorporating these same factors for generating working forecasts.

Use Long Prediction Horizons to Discover Important Factors

When searching for the factors that have the largest influence on market returns, it may be best to use long prediction horizons for the discovery process. Trying to predict 1-month rates of return is more difficult than trying to predict annual returns even from the same values of macroeconomic factors. This could be caused by the serial correlation that many researchers have noted in the predictive factors. It could also be caused by a number of nonrecurring news-related factors such as rumors of war, strikes, and short-term political instability, as well as the impact of certain types of technical trading systems. These kinds of short-term factors cause volatility in 1-month returns but tend to be washed out of annualized performance data.

Continuously Monitor Forecasting Errors

Monitoring the stream of differences between forecasted returns and actual returns would help indicate when a model is out of kilter. Having a model produce large errors when the average error is near zero suggests that there may be a problem with the model structure. Large errors can also result from using the wrong variation of one of the factors, an incorrect lag, or an unsuitable accumulation interval. Having the model produce strings of serially correlated errors (many positive errors or many negative errors in a row) suggests that there is a significant factor missing from the model. If the errors are related to some new factor, then that factor is a good candidate for inclusion in the model. While counterexamples might be generated for these rules of thumb, they represent a good starting point for follow-on research.

Incorporate a Learning Capability into the Forecasting Process

Xia (2001) shows that when returns are somewhat predictable but model parameters are not known with certainty, there is a reward for learning better estimates of the model coefficients. Without learning, the changes in the predictive factors produce monotonic changes in the allocations. In the presence of learning, the optimal allocations become less sensitive to changes in the predictive factors leading to higher expected returns. For example, when the expected return of stocks increases, more capital is used to hedge away the uncertainty of the value of the model coefficients. The impact of the causative factors ceases to be monotonic. If investors follow an optimal learning process, this might make it appear that the coefficients of a factor model are changing with time.

REFERENCES

Akaike, H. "Information Theory and an Extension of the Maximum Likelihood Principle." In *Second International Symposium on Information Theory*, edited by B. N. Petrov and C. Csaki. (Budapest, Hungary): Akademiai Kiado, 1973, 267–281.

Bekaert, Geert, and Robert J. Hodrick. "Characterizing Predictable Components in Excess Returns on Equity and Foreign Exchange Markets." *Journal of Finance* 47, no. 2 (June 1992): 467–509.

Bossaerts, Peter, and Pierre Hillion. "Implementing Statistical Criteria to Select Return Forecasting Models: What Do We Learn?" *Review of Financial Studies* 12, no. 2 (Summer 1999): 405–428.

Cumby, Robert E., and John Huizinga. "Testing the Autocorrelation Structure of Disturbances in Ordinary Least Squares and Instrumental Variables Regressions." *Econometrica* 60 (1992): 185–219.

Cumby, Robert E., and David M. Modest. "Test for Market-Timing Ability: A Framework for Forecast Evaluation." *Journal of Financial Economics* 19 (1987): 169–189.

Fama, Eugene F., and Kenneth R. French. "Business Conditions and Expected Returns on Stocks and Bonds." *Journal of Financial Economics* 25 (1989): 23–50.

Ferson, Wayne E., and Robert A. Korajczyk. "Do Arbitrage Pricing Models Explain the Predictability of Stock Returns?" *Journal of Business* 68, no. 3 (July 1995): 309–349.

Fuller, Russell J., and John L. Kling. "Can Regression-Based Models Predict Stock and Bond Returns?" *Journal of Portfolio Management* (Spring 1994): 56–63.

Handa, Puneet, and Ashish Tiwari. "Does Stock Return Predictability Imply Improved Asset Allocation and Performance?" Working paper, Henry B. Tippie College of Business, University of Iowa (November 2000).

Kirby, Chris. "Measuring the Predictable Variation in Stock and Bond Returns." *Review of Financial Studies* 10, no. 3 (Fall 1997): 579–630.

Lo, Andrew W., and A. Craig MacKinlay. "Maximizing Predictability in the Stock and Bond Markets." *Macroeconomic Dynamics* 1 (1997): 102–134.

Neeley, Christopher J., and Paul Weller. "Predictability in International Asset Returns: A Reexamination." *Journal of Financial and Quantitative Analysis* 35 (December 2000): 601–620.

Pesaran, M. Hachem, and Allan Timmermann. "Predictability of Stock Returns: Robustness and Economic Significance." *Journal of Finance* 50 (1995): 1201–1228.

Pesaran, M. Hachem, and Allan Timmermann. "Market Timing and Return Prediction under Model Instability." *Journal of Empirical Finance* 9 (2002): 495–510.

Priestley, Richard. "The Arbitrage Pricing Theory, Macroeconomic and Financial Factors, and Expectations Generating Processes." *Journal of Banking and Finance* 20 (June 1996): 869–890.

Qi, Ming. "Nonlinear Predictability of Stock Returns Using Financial and Economic Variables." *Journal of Business & Economic Statistics* 17 (October 1999): 419–429.

Schwarz, Gideon. "Estimating the Dimension of a Model." *Annals of Statistics* 6 (1978): 461–464.

Theil, H. *Economic Forecasts and Policy.* Amsterdam: North Holland, 1958.

Xia, Yihong. "Learning about Predictability: The Effects of Parameter Uncertainty on Dynamic Asset Allocation." *Journal of Finance* 56 (2001): 205–246.

CHAPTER 8

Market Timing Methods and Results

It is circumstance and proper timing that give an
action its character and make it either good or bad.

Plato
From Plutarch, Lives (444–400 B.C.)

Time-varying asset allocation is motivated by return enhancement
or by risk avoidance or by some combination of the two concepts.
Otherwise a static portfolio with the most acceptable reward and
risk expectations would be implemented and never revised. In the
urgent world of investing there is always some pressure to consider
modifying the portfolio allocations as the investment climate
changes. Whether motivated by a sudden lowering of interest rates
by the Fed, by an oil production announcement by OPEC, or by a
surge in reported industrial capacity utilization, there are frequent
temptations to consider portfolio alteration.

Any investor considering the adoption of a model to change
allocations frequently should have an interest in the maximum
potential for better portfolio performance. There are many
questions to be resolved. For example, how does the frequency of
portfolio revisions affect the outcome? How does the number of
investments considered in the portfolio alter performance? What is
the influence of transaction costs? How does the prediction
accuracy affect the potential return? How does the size of allocation
changes influence the results? What types of timing models hold
some promise for increasing return over buy and hold? How

successful have models or actual money managers been at altering portfolios and against what benchmark? This chapter addresses some of these issues in order to evaluate the potential reward for market timing.

MARKET TIMING VERSUS DYNAMIC ASSET ALLOCATION

Before we attempt to answer any of the open questions, let us address the difference between *market timing* and *dynamic asset allocation*. Unfortunately, some consider the words *market timing* to carry a bad connotation, as if it were only conducted by unsuccessful or disreputable investment managers. But the concept of market timing is just a tool. How it is applied or misapplied is another matter. We are interested in whether there is likely profitability in a system that alters asset allocations on a regular basis.

Following the lead of Phillips and Lee (1989) and Kester (1990), let us define *market timing* as the method of switching between a 100 percent allocation to a risky asset such as stocks and a 100 percent allocation to another investment such as cash. The procedure normally involves only two investments, a risky and a riskless investment. It also involves an exclusive allocation to one or the other. No partial allocations are undertaken. Generally, the policy for deciding when to switch is determined by being in the investment with the highest expected return in each time interval. This is considered the path to the highest terminal wealth. In addition to the terminal wealth objective, a secondary objective is often established by considering the market timing performance relative to some benchmark. Having a high return and beating a stock market benchmark at the same time is better than just having a high return.

The risk of the path to get to the highest terminal wealth is often not an issue. The risks normally considered by market timers are the risk of being out of the risky asset when there is a large gain to be made or the risk of being in the risky asset when a large loss might occur. Market timers' regret has to do with being in the wrong state and the resulting return that might be lost by not being in the other state. In order to estimate the expected return for each time period, the total return to the investor must be considered after all investment expenses. Therefore, transaction costs associated with switching from one investment to another should be included in thorough market timing evaluations.

Dynamic asset allocation, on the other hand, allows any number of investments and allows any combination of partial allocations to each investment. The risk of the portfolio should be considered in addition to the average return or terminal wealth. The risk associated with the path to arrive at the terminal wealth is important. The range of possibilities for trading off risk versus return is just as important for dynamic asset allocation as it is for the static Markowitz formulation of modern portfolio theory. A frequent objective utilized for dynamic asset allocation is to generate a better return at the same level of risk as that of a static buy-and-hold portfolio. Just as in market timing, the total return to the investor must be considered. Therefore, realistic transaction costs must be accounted for in a dynamic asset allocation strategy.

MAXIMUM POSSIBLE GAIN FROM MARKET TIMING

For any particular market timing model employed, it is worthwhile to consider the likelihood of being able to make significant returns given the degree of market fluctuations. If good returns cannot be made, or if they can only be made when models must have an unrealistically high forecasting accuracy, then profitable market timing may be too difficult to realize.

Sharpe (1975) proposes estimating an upper limit for the potential value of market timing by evaluating a clairvoyant investor who invests each year in either stocks or cash equivalents, depending on which has the higher return for the year. In any year involving a switch, a 2 percent transaction cost is imposed. Between 1934 and 1972 this results in a 15.25 percent annual return for perfect timing compared with 12.76 percent for buy and hold in the stock market, a gain of 2.49 percent. Of course, no procedure will perfectly predict which of the two will be the higher each year. So Sharpe calculates that a prediction accuracy of 83 percent must be achieved to overcome transaction costs in order to attain the same return as the stock market for this 1934–1972 interval. But the stock market risk, as measured by standard deviation, is not the same as the risk associated with the market timing approach. So it is further determined that a market timing prediction accuracy of 74 percent is required for a mixture of stock and cash equivalents to achieve the same standard deviation as the market timing results. The conclusion is that unless a market timing procedure can result in at least a 74 percent accuracy of selecting the better-performing investment on an annual basis, then market timing should not be undertaken. This is a serious warning indeed.

As if this were not enough of a warning, Jeffrey (1984) conducts a similar evaluation using data from 1926 to 1982, with special emphasis on comparing the results of a best case, 100 percent forecasting accuracy, versus a worst case, 0 percent forecasting accuracy. Because of the effects of compounding, he finds that, using annual data, the incremental impact of the worst case is 2.23 times as bad as the incremental impact on terminal wealth when compared with buy and hold in the stock market. Jeffrey finds that about a 72 percent annual forecasting accuracy employing 1 percent transaction costs would be required to achieve a parity between the worst-case and the best-case incremental impact.

Jeffrey cautions that there is a serious risk involved with market timing by being out of the market when it is important to be in the market. If the 10 best-performing stock market years are missed out of 57 years, then the resulting return devolves to just the T-bill return. Chandy and Reichenstein (1993), using monthly data from 1926 to 1990, also conclude that if an investor is not in the market during the best 7.1 percent of all months, then the remaining 92.9 percent of the months provide a 0.0 percent return. The risk of being out of the market at the wrong time can have serious consequences. Chua and Woodward (1986) investigate the relative importance of being correct during bull markets versus bear markets. They conclude that it is far more important to correctly forecast bull markets. Using data from 1926 to 1983 at 1 percent stock transaction costs, they find that predicting bull markets correctly 50 percent of the time does not beat a buy-and-hold strategy even if 100 percent of bear markets are correctly forecast.

As others considered Sharpe's suggestion of requiring a 74 percent forecasting accuracy, several additional conclusions were reached. Sy (1990) demonstrates that adding the 5 additional years of 1929 to 1933 to the data set used by Sharpe results in a drop of the required prediction accuracy to 65 percent. Sy concludes that the particular historical data range selected can have a significant impact on the results. As an example, he demonstrates that if only the years of 1970 to 1988 are employed, the breakeven accuracy relative to the equity market drops to 58 percent.

Several investigators point out that the annual revision frequency used by Sharpe requires very high levels of forecasting accuracy when compared with what quarterly or monthly revision frequencies require. Droms (1989) uses data from 1946 to 1986 to show that, in the presence of 1 percent transaction costs, annual timing requires a breakeven accuracy of 75 percent. Similarly, quarterly timing requires a breakeven accuracy of 65 percent, and monthly timing requires a breakeven accuracy of only 58 percent. Shortening the revision frequency provides more opportunities within the year to get on the right side of the market. This leads to higher returns and lowers the required accuracy.

In a very thorough evaluation of the impact of commission costs, revision frequency, and forecasting accuracy, Lam and Li (2002) employ recent data from January 1986 to December 2000. Market timing is evaluated using the S&P 500 with dividends included and a short-term T-bill rate. During this interval, a buy-and-hold strategy using the S&P 500 obtains an average annual return of 13.85 percent. Using a transaction cost of 0.4 percent, Lam and Li obtain the prediction accuracy required to match the S&P 500 buy-and-hold return at different revision frequencies, as shown in Table 8–1. At this transaction cost of 0.4 percent, the monthly revision frequency obtains the lowest required prediction accuracy. At transaction costs of 0.6 percent, the monthly revision frequency also has the lowest required prediction accuracy. At transaction costs of 0.2 percent, the lowest prediction accuracy 0.63 percent occurs using a weekly revision frequency. In this case, the prediction accuracy for the monthly revision frequency is 0.65 percent, only modestly higher. These results indicate that using monthly revision frequencies generally leads to the lowest required

T A B L E 8-1

Prediction Accuracy Required for
Varying Revision Frequencies, 1986 to
2000

Revision Frequency	Prediction Accuracy
Daily	0.80
Weekly	0.69
Monthly	0.68
Quarterly	0.73
Annually	0.90

prediction accuracy over a range of realistic institutional transaction costs.

All the evaluations considered to this point involve market timing between large-cap stocks and cash equivalents. Of course, it is possible to market-time any other pair of investments. Kester (1990) evaluates market timing using large-firm stocks versus cash equivalents and again using small-firm stocks versus cash equivalents. Over a range of transaction costs from 0.25 to 2.00 percent, the rate of return from timing small-firm stocks and cash equivalents dominates the potential timing return using large-firm stocks and cash equivalents. This is demonstrated to be true for monthly, quarterly, and annual portfolio revision frequencies using data from 1934 to 1988. Kester concludes that small-firm stocks are a better investment vehicle to use for market timing than large-firm stocks.

All of the preceding analysis produces one of two results:

- An estimate of the maximum returns achievable using perfect market timing
- An estimate of the required market timing forecasting accuracy in order to match a buy-and-hold benchmark

We can use these results to evaluate the effectiveness of various market timing models. The closer that the model performance comes to the perfect timing performance, the more efficient the model must be.

As a guide to the maximum performance achievable by a market timing methodology, Table 8–2 summarizes the perfect annual market timing return using large-cap stocks and cash equivalents. This is obtained from results of a number of investigators using various revision frequencies and transaction costs. These numbers are based on nominal returns after the deduction of transaction costs. Several investigators report results for a range of transaction costs. Where this was true, a transaction cost is selected nearest to 0.5 percent per switch. Where investigators report real returns above a benchmark, the return of the benchmark is added back to bring the returns to a nominal level.

Of course, the perfect timing returns reported in Table 8–2 reflect different date ranges. This certainly influences the reported numbers. The *typical value* shown in the last row in the table represents a set of values based on the results of the various investigations. It could be used as a standard for perfect timing when evaluating specific market timing models using transaction costs near 0.5 percent per switch.

All the perfect timing research presented so far involves correctly selecting the better performing of two investments at each point in time. If three or more investments are available, then the result of selecting the best of these investments at each time period significantly increases the benefit of timing. For example, assume

T A B L E 8–2

Nominal Perfect Timing Returns

Investigator	Historical Date Range	Transaction Cost, %	Annual Revision	Quarterly Revision	Monthly Revision
Chua and Woodward	1926–1983	1.0%	16.00%		
Droms	1926–1986	None	16.45%	25.21%	35.99%
Jeffrey	1926–1982	1.0%	15.20%	22.40%	
Kester[a]	1934–1988	0.5%	14.37%	20.08%	25.88%
Lam and Li	1986–2000	0.6%	14.98%	20.03%	25.52%
Sharpe	1929–1972	2.0%	14.86%		
Typical value		0.5%	14–16%	20–24%	25–35%

[a]A value of 8.10% was added to the Kester results to bring them from a relative to a nominal level.

T A B L E 8-3

Results of Perfect Market Timing

Investments Employed	Annual Return from Buy-and-Hold	Annual Return from Perfect Monthly Timing
U.S. stocks–S&P 500	12.04%	
Bonds–long-term government	9.30%	
Non-U.S. stocks–MSCI EAFE	10.97%	
T-bills–90-day	6.50%	
Stocks and T-bills		34.51%
Stocks, bonds, T-bills		42.84%
Stocks, bonds, non-U.S. stocks, T-bills		58.65%

that four investments are available: the S&P 500 total return with dividends reinvested, long-term U.S. government bonds, non-U.S. stocks represented by the MSCI EAFE index with dividends included, and 90-day U.S. T-bills. For the time interval from January 1970 to December 2001, Table 8–3 shows the performance of each of the individual investments as well as the perfect timing results for two, three, and four investments. These results are calculated using no transaction costs. The benefit of market timing increases as each additional investment is added for consideration.

MARKET TIMING MODEL PERFORMANCE

A number of hypothetical market timing models are evaluated. These models are hypothetical because they are not evaluated in real time but are determined after the fact by applying a set of trading rules against market prices. Only true market timing models are evaluated in the sense that they must switch between a 100 percent allocation to one of two investments. Each model is briefly described. Then a number of descriptive and result factors are displayed in a table in order to provide easy comparison across models.

Market timing models can be evaluated in an *ex ante* or in an *ex post* framework. Since we will provide comparisons between these two resulting frameworks when they are available, these two terms are defined first. In an ex ante framework, the market timer estimates in advance whether the stock market return or the cash equivalent return is expected to be the higher of the two. The market timer then waits to observe whether the forecast is correct. Success is achieved if the forecast turns out to be true. This framework starts with the forecast and then proceeds to evaluate the resulting performance conditioned on which forecast was made. Four ex ante probabilities result for success or failure given that either of the two investments was forecast to be above the other. The ex ante approach is considered an appropriate method for a market timer to evaluate and revise the methodology employed.

In an ex post framework, the resulting performance of the market timing model is evaluated first. Then the forecasts that were made are evaluated for each resulting performance level. Success is achieved if the result was preceded by a correct forecast. This framework starts with the performance result and then proceeds to evaluate the forecast that was made conditioned on the result obtained. Four ex post probabilities are obtained for success or failure given either of the two possible investment results. The ex post approach is generally considered the better method for an investor to evaluate a market timer.

Clarke, FitzGerald, Berent, and Statman (1989) design a simulation procedure to demonstrate that a factor influencing the stock market rate of return can provide sufficient information to outperform a stock market buy-and-hold investment. They assume that the stock market return is a linear function of GNP with a positive coefficient, as shown in equation (8–1):

$$S_{t+1} = \bar{S} + \beta \text{GNP}_t + e_{t+1} \qquad (8\text{–}1)$$

where:

S_{t+1} = rate of return on the stock market at time period $t + 1$
$\bar{S}$ = average rate of return per time period over all time periods considered
GNP_t = percent change in the GNP during time period t

β = sensitivity coefficient representing the change in S per unit change in GNP

e_{t+1} = error term at time period $t + 1$, with an expected value of zero

By defining that the market return, the GNP, and the error term are all normally distributed and allowing the correlation between the GNP and the market return to take various values, they have precise control over the data used for the simulation. The mean stock market return is set to 15.5 percent per year plus 6.15 percent for each 1 percent change in the GNP. The standard deviation of the stock return is set to 20.5 percent. The cash instrument is defined to be T-bills with a constant return of 7 percent per year. The simulation starts by randomly drawing a GNP value and then looking at the influence this has on the conditional expected stock market return using (8-1). Randomly drawing the conditional annual or monthly stock market returns, a decision is made to invest in the stock market in the next time interval if the market return for the current time interval is above the constant cash return. It is then simple to observe results such as the percentage of successful forecasts and the average timing model return for a given value of the correlation between GNP and the market return. The results of this simulation approach are shown in Table 8–4. For this table, all ex ante and ex post results are calculated at a 0.3 correlation between GNP and stock market returns. Higher correlation levels lead to larger market timing advantages.

The results of the simulation indicate that if the correlation between the GNP and the market return is zero, the timing model should always allocate 100 percent to the stock market. As the correlation with the GNP increases, the expected return for stocks increases as the timing model attempts to avoid stock market losses. In this case, the percentage of time periods that the timing methodology invests in stocks deceases. The net effect on the market timing portfolio is to generate higher portfolio returns as the GNP increases.

The generation of the GNP numbers for this simulation is based on an independent random draw for each time period with a mean GNP change of zero. It is well known that there is strong serial correlation in macroeconomic time series such as GNP

T A B L E 8-4

Clarke, FitzGerald, Berent, and Statman Market Timing Results

Investments considered	Stocks = S&P 500, Cash = T-bills
Transaction costs used	0.1% and 1.0%
Revision frequency	Annual and monthly
Predicted variable	S&P 500 return
Factors used	GNP alone
Model structure	$R_{stocks} = A + B^*GNP$, $R_{cash} = 7\%$ per year
Timing rules	Buy stocks when forecasted $R_{stocks} > R_{cash}$
Use of leverage	None
Date range used	No date range. Simulation based on a distribution
Percent of time that actual $R_{stocks} > R_{cash}$	66%
Percent of time that actual $R_{cash} > R_{stocks}$	34%
Ex ante result for stocks, annual switch	Stocks forecast is correct 68% of the time
Ex ante result for cash, annual switch	Cash forecast is correct 56% of the time
Ex post result for stocks, annual switch	Stocks result had correct forecast 94% of the time
Ex post result for cash, annual swtich	Cash forecast had correct forecast 14% of the time
Buy-and-hold benchmark	100% in S&P 500
Advantage over benchmark, annual switch	0.2% per year at 0% transaction cost
Advantage over benchmark, monthly switch	5.9% per year at 0% transaction cost

values. And it is strongly so on a monthly basis. Had this serial correlation effect been added to the simulation, an even stronger market timing advantage would have been found. The conservative approach employed makes the point well enough that a factor model influencing returns can provide a strong market timing advantage when monthly switching is allowed.

Larsen and Wozniak (1994–1995) employ a discrete regression model (DRM) approach that estimates the probability that one asset class return is greater than another during time period t. This probability called Y_t has a value of 1 when the stock return exceeds cash and 0 otherwise. Y_t represents the probability that the return on stocks R_{stocks} is greater than the return on cash R_{cash}. A regression model using multiple factors is defined to estimate the value of Y_t.

$$Y_t = b_0 + b_1 X_{1t} + b_2 X_{2t} + b_3 X_{3t} + \cdots + b_n X_{nt} + e_t$$

$$= BX_t + e_t \tag{8-2}$$

where:

Y_t = probability that the stock return is greater than the cash return during time period t

b_0 = constant term

X_{nt} = value of a macroeconomic factor n influencing Y during time period t, where the X_{nt} are evaluated at multiple lag intervals

b_n = sensitivity coefficient representing the change in Y per unit change in X_n

e_t = error term at time period t

In order to keep the estimated probabilities in the range of 0 to 1, a logit regression model approach is adopted. In a logit regression,

$$\text{Prob}(Y_t = 1) = \text{Prob}(R_{stocks} > R_{cash}) = \frac{\exp(BX_t)}{1 + \exp(BX_t)} \tag{8-3}$$

The logit function is an S-shaped curve with the useful properties that when BX_t is $-\infty$, then $\text{Prob}(Y_t = 1)$ equals 0, and when BX_t is $+\infty$, then $\text{Prob}(Y_t = 1)$ equals 1. For more information on logit regressions, see Greene (1999).

After the coefficients are found for equation (8–2), this equation can be used to determine the probability that $R_{stocks} > R_{cash}$. The DRM market timing approach applied by Larsen and Wozniak commits 100 percent to stocks whenever $\text{Prob}(R_{stocks} > R_{cash}) > 0.5$ and 100 percent to cash otherwise.

The factors considered for the explanatory variables are shown in Table 8–5. All these factors are investigated for lags

T A B L E 8-5

Larsen and Wozniak Logit Model Factor

The term spread between long-term government bonds and 3-month T-bills
The default spread between long-term Baa corporate bonds and long-term
  government bonds
The default spread between long-term Baa corporate bonds and 3-month T-bills
The real earnings yield on the S&P 500 less 3-month T-bills
The 24-month variance on the S&P 500 returns
The 24-month growth in the S&P 500
The annual percent change in industrial production
Inflation, measured as the annual percent change in the consumer price index
Dividend yield of the S&P 500 index

between 1 and 12 months using data from 1977 to 1992. A number of estimation intervals of 48, 72, 96, and 120 months are used to forecast performance for the following 1, 3, and 6 months.

Once a forecast is made, the process is shifted forward 6 months and another forecast is made. The Akaike information criterion is used to determine which combination of the factors, factor lags, and estimation interval produces the best market timing model. The results of the Larsen and Wozniak DRM market timing model using logit regressions are shown in Table 8–6. This market timing evaluation allows the coefficients of equation (8–2) to be revised every 6 months. Not only can the coefficients change, but also the variables and lags are allowed to change. This permits a great deal of flexibility that allows the model to adapt to changing market conditions. Because the coefficients are changing every 6 months, Larsen and Wozniak provide no indication of the values and significance of the coefficients.

In a subsequent version of this research, Larsen and Wozniak (1995) comment that using the DRM approach naturally reduces the number of transactions since transactions only occur when the probability of ($R_{\text{stocks}} > R_{\text{cash}}$) crosses the value of 0.50. They also report that even if transaction costs were considered at a level of 0.50 percent per year, consistent with the cost of mutual fund timing, then the procedure would still be profitable.

Nam and Branch (1994) also evaluate a market timing model based on a logit function to control the switching from the stock

TABLE 8-6

Larsen and Wozniak Market Timing Results

Investments considered	Stocks = S&P 500, Cash = T-bills
Transaction costs used	0%
Revision frequency	1, 3, and 6 months
Predicted variable	Probability that $R_{stocks} > R_{cash}$
Factors used	Up to 8 factors shown in Table 8–5
Model structure	$Y_t = b_0 + b_1X_{1t} + b_2X_{2t} + b_3X_{3t} + \cdots + b_nX_{nt} + e_t$
Timing rules	Buy stocks when Prob $(R_{stocks} > R_{cash}) > 0.5$
Use of leverage	None
Date range used	1977–1992 and 1987–1991
Percent of time that actual $R_{stocks} > R_{cash}$	60% (based on 1987–1991)
Percent of time that actual $R_{cash} > R_{stocks}$	40% (based on 1987–1991)
Ex ante result for stocks, monthly switch	80.6% (based on 1987–1991)
Ex ante result for cash, monthly switch	37.5% (based on 1987–1991)
Ex post result for stocks, monthly switch	65.9% (based on 1987–1991)
Ex post result for cash, monthly switch	56.3% (based on 1987–1991)
Buy-and-hold benchmark	100% in S&P 500
Advantage over benchmark, monthly switch	3.1% per year based on 1977–1992, no transactions costs

market, represented by the S&P 500 index, to cash, represented by 30-day T-bills. Given the logit basis for determining the probability of being in the stock market, there is some similarity between the Nam and Branch approach and the Larsen and Wozniak (1994–1995) approach. But the similarity does not persist into the methods of using the estimated probability to control the switching between stocks and cash. Furthermore, Nam and Branch explicitly evaluate the effects of two different levels of transaction costs.

Data are employed from February 1962 to December 1976. The factors used in the logit regression to estimate the probability of being in the stock market are shown in Table 8–7. Note that there is very little overlap with the factors used in the Larsen and Wozniak model. The significance of the regression results is also shown in

T A B L E 8-7

Nam and Branch Logit Model Factors

Factor	t-Statistic	Significance
Change in the Treasury bill rate	− 2.155	5% level
T-bill rate in previous months	− 2.828	1% level
Dividend yield (dividend/price)	1.546	Over 10% level
Earnings growth rate	− 1.210	Over 10% level

this table. In previous research Nam (1990) evaluates other factors that showed little promise in reducing the logit model error. These factors are Baa-rated long-term corporate bond yield, monthly growth in industrial production, and the index of leading economic indicators.

Using a 0.46 probability cutoff point to switch from stocks to cash, the in-sample accuracy of the logit regression is 64.8 percent. In order to test this level of accuracy, a holdout sample from 1977 to 1987 is used to evaluate the predictive capability of the model. Using 180-month rolling intervals, logit regressions are generated to use as forecasting equations for the next month. The average accuracy of predicting the correct switching direction on an out-of-sample basis is 60.1 percent.

The 0.46 cutoff point is determined to be the optimal switching point in order to obtain maximum switching accuracy. Nam and Branch question the use of automatic switching whenever the logit probability crosses the 0.46 level. Because switching involves transaction costs, Nam and Branch propose a "neutral-market" probability zone between 0.20 and 0.65 in which no changes in asset allocation are allowed. If the switching model is 100 percent committed to stocks, the probability must drop below 0.20 before switching to cash. If the switching model is 100 percent committed to cash, the probability must go above 0.65 before switching to stocks. At transaction costs of 1 and 2 percent, for the in-sample interval from 1962 to 1976, this switching scheme outperforms switching at the 0.46 probability cutoff point. At transaction costs of 0, 1, and 2 percent for the out-of-sample evaluations, this switching scheme also outperforms switching at the 0.46 level. Avoiding unnecessary switches appears to be a useful control. The results of the Nam and Branch market timing model using logit regressions are shown in Table 8–8.

T A B L E   8-8

Nam and Branch Market Timing Results

Investments considered	Stocks = S&P 500, Cash = T-bills
Transaction costs used	0%, 1%, and 2%
Revision frequency	Monthly
Predicted variable	Probability that $R_{stocks} > R_{cash}$
Factors used	The four factors shown in Table 8–7
Model structure	$Y_t = b_0 + b_1X_{1t} + b_2X_{2t} + b_2X_{2t} + \cdots$ $+ b_nX_{nt} + e_t$
Timing rules	Buy stocks when Prob > 0.65; buy cash when Prob < 0.20
Use of leverage	None
Date range used	In-sample 1962–1976. Out-of-sample 1977–1987
Percent of time that actual $R_{stocks} > R_{cash}$	54.2% (based on 1962–1976)
Percent of time that actual $R_{cash} > R_{stocks}$	45.8% (based on 1962–1976)
Ex ante result for all monthly forecasts	64.8% (based on 1962–1976)
Buy-and-hold benchmark	100% in S&P 500
Advantage over benchmark, monthly switch	4.4% at 0% transaction costs, 3.3% at 1%, 2.2% at 2%

Pesaran and Timmermann (1994) propose a market timing methodology based on a regression model of the excess return of the stock market. When the expected excess stock market return above 30-day T-bills exceeds zero, their timing model invests 100 percent in stocks, otherwise 100 percent in government bonds. The model for estimating the stock market return, represented by the S&P 500, utilizes the regression factors shown in Table 8–9.

The effect of using annual, quarterly, and monthly data frequencies is evaluated by developing a regression model for the S&P 500 at each one of these frequencies. The regression models employ nonoverlapping data from January 1954 to January 1991. The coefficient, t-statistic, and significance level for each factor, and adjusted R^2 of the regression are displayed in Table 8–10. Since

T A B L E 8-9

Pesaran and Timmermann Regression Model Factors

Dividend yield
Inflation based on the producer price index
Term premium = 6-month commercial paper rate less 3-month T-bill rate
The 3-month or 1-month T-bill rate itself
The change in industrial production

T A B L E 8-10

Pesaran and Timmerman Regression Results

Factor	Annual Coefficient (*t*-Statistic) [Significance]	Quarterly Coefficient (*t*-Statistic) [Significance]	Monthly Coefficient (*t*-Statistic) [Significance]
Dividend yield	9.17	14.40	14.19
(dividend/price)	(4.5)	(4.2)	4.2
	[0.1%]	[0.1%]	[0.1%]
Inflation	−1.72	−0.73	−0.279
(producer price index)	(−3.9)	(−3.5)	−4.4
	[0.1%]	[0.1%]	[0.1%]
T-bill rate	−0.06	−0.0075	−0.0072
(3 month or 1 month)	(−2.6)	(−2.0)	−2.9
	[5%]	[5%]	[1%]
Term premium	0.11	Not	Not
(6 month−3 month)	(2.8)	significant	significant
	[1%]		
Change in industrial	Not	−0.32	−0.155
production	significant	(−2.3)	−3.7
		[5%]	[0.1%]
Number of time periods	37	148	444
Adjusted R^2	0.590	0.194	0.082

only sequential date ranges are employed, no correction is required for overlapping time intervals. For each factor, the results seem quite consistent across the three data frequencies. Note that the dividend yield and the inflation rate have very significant coefficients at each of the data frequencies.

The regression model for predicting stock returns is the first step in the market timing procedure. The second step is the definition of a trading rule. Pesaran and Timmerman employ a simple rule of committing 100 percent to the stock market if the excess stock return forecast is greater than zero and committing 100 percent to government bonds otherwise. Performance of this timing model is determined for each one of the annual, quarterly, and monthly data frequencies. The effect of stock market transaction costs is also evaluated. Transaction costs are set to 0.0, 0.5, and 1.0 percent. The evaluation at a 0.0 percent transaction cost is provided for comparison to other research. The 0.5 percent transaction cost for stocks is suggested as typical for institutional investors. The 1.0 percent transaction cost is suggested as typical for small private investors.

The results vary widely depending on the transaction cost and on the market timing revision frequency. Table 8–11 shows the annual arithmetic rate of return for the market timing process using the S&P 500 and 12-month T-bills for the annual, quarterly, and monthly revision frequencies and for various transaction costs. The data employed are from January 1960 to December 1990. The average annual return for the S&P 500 based on monthly transactions is 10.90 percent for this same time interval. All market timing combinations beat the buy-and-hold return for the S&P 500 except for the monthly revision frequency at a 1.0 percent transaction cost. It appears that using an annual revision frequency is a profitable procedure under any level of cost. In this evaluation, using 0.0 percent transaction costs, quarterly or monthly revision

T A B L E 8-11

Pesaran and Timmerman Market Timing Returns

Stock Transaction Cost	Bond Transaction Cost	Annual Revision	Quarterly Revision	Monthly Revision
0.0%	0.0%	12.70%	13.04%	13.08%
0.5%	0.1%	12.43%	12.43%	11.14%
1.0%	0.1%	12.21%	11.91%	9.74%

frequencies produce results only slightly better than an annual revision frequency.

A summary of the Pesaran and Timmerman market timing model is shown in Table 8–12.

T A B L E 8-12

Pesaran and Timmerman Market Timing Results

Investments considered	Stocks = S&P 500, Cash = 12-month T-bills
Transaction costs used	0.0% 0.5%, and 1.0%
Revision frequency	Annual, quarterly, and monthly
Predicted variable	Stock market return less the 3-month T-bill rate
Factors used	The five factors shown in Table 8–9
Model structure	$Y_t = b_0 + b_1 X_{1t} + b_2 X_{2t} + b_3 X_{3t} + \cdots + b_n X_{nt} + e_t$
Timing rules	Buy stocks when $Y_t > 0.0$; otherwise go to cash
Use of leverage	None
Date range used	1960–1990
Buy-and-hold benchmark	100% in S&P 500
Advantage over benchmark, annual switch	1.92% at 0% transaction costs, 1.71% at 0.5%, 1.54% at 1.0%
Advantage over benchmark, monthly switch	2.18% at 0% transaction costs, 0.29% at 0.5%, − 1.11% at 1.0%

Summary of Market Timing Models. Three of the preceding market timing models evaluate the impact of monthly switching. It might be useful to summarize their performance relative to a buy-and-hold benchmark at various levels of transaction costs. Table 8–13 provides the returns obtained from these three market timing models in excess of the buy-and-hold stock market performance.

Two observations based on this summary are worth noting. First, transaction costs can substantially lower the returns obtainable from market timing, a result not totally unexpected. Pesaran and Timmerman show that the benefits of market timing models can be completely eroded by transaction fees as little as 1 percent. Second, the excess returns achievable by market timing models are quite small compared with the level of the stock market

T A B L E 8-13

Monthly Market Timing Model Annualized Excess Returns

Investigators	Date Range	Advantage at 0% Transaction Cost	Advantage at Medium Transaction Cost	Advantage at High Transaction Cost
Larsen and Wozniak	1977–1992	3.1%		
Nam and Branch	1977–1987	4.4%	3.3 at 1%	2.2 at 2%
Pesaran and Timmerman	1960–1990	2.18%	0.29 at 0.5%	− 1.05 at 1%

buy-and-hold portfolio. When the stock market average annual return is near 13 percent, market timing models only add roughly 2 to 4 percent even at zero transaction costs. On an unleveraged basis, the impact of these types of market timing concepts is very modest. An investor wishing to double the buy-and-hold performance should not expect such a dramatic performance increase by using market timing.

The reasons for such modest gains for 100 percent switching models include the following:

The factor models might be missing one or more important factors.

The best market timing models correctly predict stocks as the higher return only 60 to 80 percent of the time.

Switching from 100 percent stocks to 100 percent cash might be a less-than-optimal decision rule.

Only two investments are considered for the portfolio.

Leverage is not considered.

MARKET TIMING MONEY MANAGER PERFORMANCE

The performance of the market timing models presented in the last section is based on hypothetical models, not the actual results of money managers dealing with the day-to-day realities of money management. If we want to know how successful market timing methodologies can be, then the direct approach of observing the performance of market timers should be the most informative.

Three sources of market timing indications have been evaluated in the literature of money management. The first involves mutual funds that allow allocation changes between equities and fixed income. There is a large body of research evaluating the market timing abilities of mutual funds, including Kon (1983), Chang and Lewellen (1984), Henriksson (1984), Chua and Woodward (1986), and Goetzmann, Ingersoll, and Ivkovic (2000).

Generally, this research finds that there is very little market timing skill demonstrated by mutual funds. Evaluations are conducted by Ferson and Schadt (1996) and Becker, Ferson, Myers, and Schill (1999) of possible conditional market timing skill on the part of mutual funds when the influence of public information such as macroeconomic or market factors is considered. This research also fails to establish any significant market timing skill by mutual funds. It is not very surprising that mutual funds cannot be shown to demonstrate strong market timing skill. Most mutual funds simply do not attempt to do market timing. They are more interested in security selection techniques to obtain the best returns. Even funds whose prospectus allows them to participate in changing asset allocations as a strategy are shown by Goetzman, Ingersoll, and Ivkovic (2000) to exhibit no significant market timing skill. Since our definition of market timing involves switching from 100 percent stocks to 100 percent cash or bonds, it would be unlikely to find any mutual funds at all that invest in this way. Funds that participate in dynamic asset allocation would tend to make gradual shifts in allocation and would not be likely to switch instantaneously from 100 percent stocks to 100 percent cash. So mutual funds do not appear to provide fertile ground for the evaluation of market timing.

The second sector in which the measurement of market timing is undertaken involves the performance of recommendations contained in investment newsletters. Evaluating the recommendations of newsletters for their market timing skill presents significant analytical problems. The recommendations in these newsletters are generally not executed by the publisher on behalf of clients. So there is no *actual* performance history. The delay between the time that the publisher forms an opinion, puts it in the newsletter, and then delivers it to the client can be considerable. Are evaluations of market timing to be made on market information from the day of decision, publication, or delivery? The very fact that many newsletters are published on a monthly frequency means that the performance evaluation could be monthly at best, even when the publisher intends the market timing changes to be midmonth, as sometimes provided through telephone updates. In addition to this time-of-execution problem, the performance of newsletter recommendations should be adjusted for commissions and slippage. Beyond these measurement problems, studies by Graham and Harvey (1996) and Jaffe and Mahoney (1999) conclude that newsletters containing asset allocation recommendations exhibit little market timing skill. This means newsletters' recommendations are also not very useful for evaluating market timing methodologies, just as we found for mutual funds.

The third area considered for market timing evaluations comprises money managers who offer market timing products. These managers make actual investments on behalf of the investor suffering all the costs of slippage, commissions, and the manager's fees. Money managers of this sort consist of market timers who make 100 percent allocations and asset allocators who may consider two or more investments and may make partial allocations. Looking for market timing skill among money managers seems to offer the best opportunity for measuring actual skill. Unfortunately, performance tracking information on market timers is not as plentiful as it is for mutual funds. Although it appears that there may be several hundred market timers currently offering their services, three published studies of market timers—those by Wagner, Shellans, and Paul (1992), Philips, Rogers, and Capaldi (1996), and Chance and Hemler (2001)—evaluate only 25, 11, and 30 market timers, respectively. This small number is due to the limited number of manager track records available for the time intervals studied, 1985–1990, 1977–1994, and 1986–1994.

Wagner, Shellans, and Paul (1992) employ data on the timing signals of money managers who invest in no-load mutual funds. In order to eliminate the differences among managers due to the specific mutual funds employed, the timing signals are applied to the S&P 500 index with dividends reinvested. When out of the stock market, the market timing procedure invests in a proxy for a money-market fund (25 basis points above a 91-day T-bill rate). Monthly returns for 25 timers having continuous track records from October 1, 1985, to September 30, 1990, are calculated using management fees from 0.5 to 2.11 percent per year.

The average total return of the S&P 500 during this interval is 14.85 percent per year. The average return for the 25 timers at 0.5 percent fees is slightly higher at 14.94 percent. The range of timer returns is 8.71 to 22.31 percent. The average risk associated with the timers, measured as standard deviation, is 3.35 percent per year compared with the S&P 500 at 5.42 percent. This means that the market timers deliver modestly higher returns at a substantially lower risk. This reduction in risk is attributed to success at going to cash during a major portion of bear market intervals. The average timer outperforms the S&P 500 91 percent of the time when the S&P 500 monthly return is down. Because the market timers are out of the market in some months when the market is up, the market timers obtain only 62 percent of the returns achieved by the S&P 500 in up-market months. On the other hand, the market timers only suffer 34 percent of the losses obtained by the S&P 500 during down-market months. During this same interval, long-term government bonds achieve about the same level of standard deviation as the average market timer. But the government bonds only return 11.18 percent per year. Thus, the market timers returned an excess return of 3.76 percent above bonds with similar risk.

This research by Wagner, Shellans, and Paul is critically reviewed by Brocato and Chandy (1994). They point out that this research may be subject to survivor bias and may include commissions lower than what actual timers charge.

It is true that the performance of market timers reported by Wagner, Shellans, and Paul is not dramatically higher than buy and hold for the S&P 500. Yet it is enough to suggest that selecting the better timers offers an opportunity of obtaining superior performance in terms of a risk-reward trade-off. If the length of the evaluation interval could only be extended, this would also give more confidence in the assessment of market timing skill.

Philips, Rogers, and Capaldi (1996) evaluate 11 money managers they identify as tactical asset allocators. Technically, these managers are not market timers because they invest in stocks, bonds, and cash with changing fractional asset allocations. But they are included in this evaluation of timing managers because there are so few studies of actual two-investment market timers.

This performance evaluation is broken into two intervals: inception to 1987 and 1988 to 1994. Of the eleven managers, only nine have a performance history for the first time interval. Each manager has a declared benchmark of 50 to 65 percent in equities and the balance in bonds or cash. The performance for each manager is evaluated as the excess return against individual benchmarks. For the first time interval up through 1987, all nine of the managers exceed their benchmark by 1.10 to 7.34 percent per year, with an average excess return of 3.93 percent. Five of the nine managers exceed their benchmarks by confidence levels at 10 percent or better. The second time interval is another matter. Of the eleven managers having data from 1988 to 1994, five beat their benchmarks and only one does so by a significant amount. For the second interval, the average manager actually underperforms its benchmark by 6 basis points per year. The market timing ability during this second interval is considerably lower than in the first interval. The authors theorize that the difference in performance is due to a much smaller opportunity to market-time in the second interval. Perfect market timing in the first interval would lead to an annual excess return of 23.5 percent over a 60-40 stocks-to-bonds benchmark. In the second interval, perfect market timing provides only 14.8 percent excess return over the same benchmark. The authors also indicate that the correlation between stocks and bonds changed significantly between the two intervals from 0.20 to 0.60. Because of this correlation change, trading methodologies based on consistent relationships between stocks and bonds could have gone awry.

This study confirms market timing skill in the first interval and denies it in the second interval. This inconsistency between time intervals clouds the significance of the findings. The fact that only 11 managers are evaluated also adds some uncertainty to the results.

Chance and Hemler (2001) examine the market timing ability of 30 managers from 1986 to 1994. Fifteen of these managers are true market timers, and the other fifteen are tactical asset allocators who assign fractional allocations to stocks and cash. Just as in the

Wagner, Shellans, and Paul study, these managers actually invest in no-load mutual funds. But their timing signals are abstracted and then used to market-time stock market indices to remove the impact of investing in different equity instruments. Three separate evaluations are made using the signals against the NASDAQ index, the combined NYSE/AMEX/NASDAQ index, and the S&P 500 index as stock market proxies. Not all the manager track records start in January 1986. In fact, half the performance histories do not begin until after January 1990. The timing signals are evaluated daily, and profit or loss is determined for the performance of the three stock market indices between signal entry and exit dates. When not in the stock market, holdings are placed in 1-month T-bills.

The initial results without any transaction fees or management fees are based on a Cumby-Modest unconditional regression test of the timing ability of the manager. See Chapter 7 for a description of this test. For market performance using the NASDAQ index, 17 of the 30 managers show significant market timing ability at the 5 percent confidence level, and 21 show market timing ability at the 10 percent confidence level.

The effects of transaction costs are evaluated by using costs of 0.25 and 0.50 percent per switch. Depending on the level of transaction fees, the number of managers with returns exceeding 1-month T-bills ranges from 26 to 15 managers. This research indicates that about half of market timing managers demonstrate significant skill in their investment performance.

REVIEW

The potential return available from market-timing two or more investments can be quite large. As shown in Table 8–2, perfect monthly market timing of stocks and T-bills can achieve 25–35 percent returns under 0.5 percent transaction costs. Assuming that the stock market return is in the range of 10–16 percent, this implies that perfect timing leads to an excess return over stocks of about 17 percent.

This perfect timing potential is not easy to achieve. At less than perfect timing results, for monthly investment revisions and including reasonable transaction costs, somewhere between 65 and 70 percent forecasting accuracy is required to beat a buy-and-hold stock market benchmark. Therefore, a market timing manager must be able to demonstrate considerable skill to avoid being on the wrong side of the market and to overcome transaction costs.

Market timing models evaluated after the fact by a number of researchers indicate just how difficult it is to conduct profitable market timing. Carefully considered models are able to achieve excess returns of only 2 to 3 percent above the buy-and-hold stock market return. This means that less than 20 percent of the potentially perfect excess return of 17 percent is achievable, even by hypothetical trading models applied after the fact.

Actual market timing managers, investing in real time, demonstrate mixed ability to successfully outperform stock market benchmarks. On average, market timers can outperform the stock market by 0 to 3 percent excess return depending on the time interval evaluated. Roughly 50 to 70 percent of timers show significant skill at being able to obtain positive excess returns. This leaves the other 30 to 50 percent who are not able to demonstrate market timing skill.

These results show that the potential for market timing conducted by some professional managers can lead to expectations of as high as 3 percent excess returns. These return expectations are realistic for timing considering only stocks and cash, committing 100 percent to one investment or the other, including modest transaction costs and not employing the use of leverage. Using more than two investments, allowing fractional asset allocation, and employing the use of leverage may generate more than the 3 percent maximum excess return demonstrated by successful market timing managers.

REFERENCES

Becker, Connie, Wayne Ferson, David H. Myers, and Michael J. Schill. "Conditional Market Timing with Benchmark Investors." *Journal of Financial Economics* 52 (1999): 119–148.

Brocato, Joe, and P. R. Chandy. "Does Market Timing Really Work in the Real World?" *Journal of Portfolio Management* (Winter 1994): 39–44.

Chance, Don M., and Michael L. Hemler. "The Performance of Professional Market Timers: Daily Evidence from Executed Strategies." *Journal of Financial Economics* 62 (November 2001): 377–411.

Chandy, P. R., and William Reichenstein. "Market Surges and Market Timing." *Journal of Investing* (Summer 1993): 41–45.

Chang, Eric C., and Wilbur G. Lewellen. "Market Timing and Mutual Fund Performance." *Journal of Business* 57, no. 1 (1984): 57–72.

Chua, Jess H., and Richard S. Woodward. "Gains from Stock Market Timing." *Monograph Series in Finance and Economics.* Salomon Brothers Center for the Study of Financial Institutions, Graduate School of Business Administration, New York University, New York, 1986.

Clarke, Roger G., Michael T. FitzGerald, Philip Berent, and Meir Statman. "Market Timing with Imperfect Information." *Financial Analysts Journal* (November–December 1989): 27–36.

Droms, William G. "Market Timing as an Investment Policy." *Financial Analysts Journal* (January–February 1989): 73–78.

Ferson, Wayne E., and Rudi W. Schadt. "Measuring Fund Strategy and Performance in Changing Economic Conditions." *Journal of Finance* 51, no. 2 (June 1996): 425–461.

Goetzmann, William N., Jonathan Ingersoll, Jr., and Zoran Ivkovic. "Monthly Measurement of Daily Timers." *Journal of Financial and Quantitative Analysis* 35 (2000): 257–290.

Graham, John R., and Campbell R. Harvey. "Market Timing Ability and the Volatility Implied in Investment Newsletters' Asset Allocation Recommendations." *Journal of Financial Economics* 42 (1996): 397–421.

Greene, William H. *Econometric Analysis*, 4th ed. Upper Saddle River, N.J.: Prentice Hall, 1999.

Henriksson, Roy D. "Market Timing and Mutual Fund Performance: An Empirical Investigation." *Journal of Business* 57, no. 1 (1984): 73–96.

Jaffe, Jeffrey F., and James M. Mahoney. "The Performance of Investment Newsletters." *Journal of Financial Economics* 53 (1999): 289–307.

Jeffrey, Robert H. "The Folly of Stock Market Timing." *Harvard Business Review* (July/August 1984): 689–706.

Kester, George W. "Market Timing with Small versus Large-Firm Stocks: Potential Gains and Required Predictive Ability." *Financial Analysts Journal* (September–October 1990): 63–69.

Kon, S. J. "The Market-Timing Performance of Mutual Fund Managers." *Journal of Business* 56, no. 3 (1983): 323–347.

Lam, Kin, and Wei Li. "Is the 'Perfect' Timing Strategy Really Perfect?" Working paper, Department of Finance and Decision Sciences, School of Business, Hong Kong Baptist University (2002).

Larsen, Glen A., Jr., and Gregory D. Wozniak. "Market Timing for Active Asset Allocation: A Discrete Regression Model Approach." *Journal of Applied Business Research* 11, no. 1 (1994–1995): 125–134.

Larsen, Glen A., Jr., and Gregory D. Wozniak. "Market Timing Can Work in the Real World." *Journal of Portfolio Management* (Spring 1995): 74–81.

Nam, Joong-soo. "Enhancing the Timing of the Asset Allocation Process." Dissertation, University of Massachusetts, 1990.

Nam, Joong-soo, and Ben Branch. "Tactical Asset Allocation: Can It Work?" *Journal of Financial Research* (Winter 1994): 465–479.

Pesaran, M. Hashem, and Allan Timmermann. "Forecasting Stock Returns: An Examination of Stock Market Trading in the Presence of Transaction Costs." *Journal of Forecasting* 13 (1994): 335–367.

Philips, Thomas K., Greg. T. Rogers, and Robert E. Capaldi. "Tactical Asset Allocation: 1977–1994." *Journal of Portfolio Management* (Fall 1996): 57–64.

Phillips, Don, and Joan Lee. "Differentiating Tactical Asset Allocation from Market Timing." *Financial Analysts Journal* 45, no. 2 (1989): 14–16.

Sharpe, William F. "Likely Gains from Market Timing." *Financial Analysts Journal* (March–April 1975): 60–69.

Sy, Wilson. "Market Timing: Is It a Folly?" *Journal of Portfolio Management* (Summer 1990): 11–16.

Wagner, Jerry, Steve Shellans, and Richard Paul. "Market Timing Works Where It Matters Most ... In the Real World." *Journal of Portfolio Management* (Summer 1992): 86–90.

CHAPTER 9

Multiperiod Portfolio Theory

For a moment of night we have a glimpse of ourselves
and of our world islanded in its stream of stars—
pilgrims of mortality, voyaging between horizons
across the eternal seas of space and time.

Henry Beston
The Outermost House (1928)

The Markowitz mean-variance portfolio model assumes a single time period for the determination of optimal asset allocation. For an investor with a long-term investment horizon, the question arises whether the optimal multiperiod portfolio has any relationship to optimal holdings in a single-period setting. Should the portfolio holdings change as time passes? The solution to this problem depends on the future expectations of performance for each of the investments in the portfolio. If the expected performance distribution of an investment is constant for each future time period, then research has shown that the allocations obtained from the single-period mean-variance problem should be maintained for every future period. If the return distributions are changing with time, then in order to maximize terminal wealth, it would be prudent to change the allocations with time as well.

If the moments of future return distributions are assumed to be accurately known, then solutions to the optimal set of changing asset allocations can be determined. If the future return distributions are subject to uncertainty or subject to learning on the part of participants, then the value of a multiperiod approach begins to erode. But it is still worthwhile to review the research undertaken in this area in order to understand the impact of future expectations on the formation of current optimized portfolio holdings.

MULTIPERIOD MODELS WITH PREDICTABLE RETURNS

The point of departure for multiperiod portfolio optimization is to assume that returns at each period of the horizon are not constant but vary conditionally with a set of exogenous factors in accordance with some model. Let us apply the name *multiperiod portfolio theory*, or MPPT, to this body of knowledge concerning conditional multiperiod portfolio optimization.

The specific model of interest for what follows is to assume that the returns, or the asset allocations themselves, are a linear function of a set of macroeconomic factors. Since 1980, an avalanche of research has shown that many types of investments have returns that can be related to previous values of macroeconomic factors. For a review of this research, see Chapters 3 to 6 on stocks, bonds, interest rates, and hedge funds (respectively).

Another concept common to these models is the budget constraint between one time period and the next. This equation calculates the change in wealth between the two time periods as a function of the allocations to the investments and the state variables. This change in wealth considers both the periodic rate of return on the underlying investments and the periodic capital consumption of a portion of the portfolio.

Assume that:

W_t = investor's wealth at time t
C_t = capital consumption occurring during time t
r_{jt} = return of investment j at time t
x_{jt} = portfolio allocation given to investment j during time t

Considering both portfolio growth and capital consumption, the value of the investor's portfolio at the end of time $t + 1$ is

$$W_{t+1} = (W_t - C_t) \sum_{j=1}^{n} (x_{jt} r_{jt}) \qquad (9\text{--}1)$$

When investment returns are not independent and identically distributed (i.i.d.) over the investment horizon, the asset allocations at each point in time can be calculated as a function of macroeconomic factors in order to maximize the resulting terminal wealth. Investors who are able to anticipate the level of future returns may alter their current allocations to be better positioned to take advantage of the returns to come. The difference in asset allocations between a dynamic and myopic portfolio policy is referred to as *hedging demand.* This process is termed the hedging demand because it may lead to ignoring the single-period (myopic) optimal allocations in order to hedge against future changes in investment opportunities.

The methodologies for solving MPPT problems cover a wide range of techniques. Most of these techniques employ discrete-time formulations although there are several continuous-time approaches. Solution tools include dynamic programming, stochastic processes, and Monte Carlo simulation. We shall proceed by surveying several of the MPPT approaches in very broad terms. Covering these methodologies in detail is not required for what follows. We simply want to place the DynaPorte model into context. DynaPorte involves multiple past periods and only a single future period. Therefore, the use of multiple future periods by the MPPT models is not directly relevant.

RISK MEASURES

It is a well-known result from Samuelson (1969) and Merton (1969, 1971, 1973) that if return distributions are constant over a multiperiod investment horizon, then optimal asset allocations may be constant over the horizon. This is certainly true for an investor who rebalances portfolios optimally and cares about mean variance or constant relative risk aversion (CRRA). A CRRA investor cares only about terminal wealth W according to the power utility function $v(W)$ which employs γ, the coefficient of relative risk aversion,

where: $$v(W) = \frac{W^{1-\gamma}}{1 - \gamma} \qquad \text{if } \gamma > 1 \qquad (9\text{--}2)$$

or: $$v(W) = \ln W \qquad \text{if } \gamma = 1$$

The CRRA investor does not care about the path taken to arrive at the terminal wealth. This means the investor is not concerned about the volatility of the returns to arrive at the terminal value. Much research on multiperiod portfolio optimization uses the power utility function of terminal wealth as the objective function.

MERTON (1969, 1971, 1973)

In a continuous-time setting, Merton develops a stochastic dynamic programming formulation for capital growth and capital consumption. A complex stochastic partial differential equation is derived that describes the optimal control process for changing the asset allocations and the capital consumption rate over time. The objective is to maximize a utility function of consumption plus terminal wealth of the investor. Following Merton (1973), the variables for this model include:

U = utility function for consumption
B = utility of terminal wealth or "bequest" function
T = distribution of age of death of investor
$C(t)$ = consumption flow of assets at time t
$W(t)$ = wealth at time t
r = return on riskless asset
w_i = fraction of wealth invested in asset i at each point in time
s = time variable during lifetime
$\mathcal{J}(W, X, t)$ = "derived" utility of wealth function
P_i = instantaneous price of asset i
α_i = instantaneous rate of return on asset i
σ_{ij} = instantaneous covariances between asset i and asset j
X = vector of m state variables including P_i, α_i, and σ_{ij}
f_k = Itô process time function for state vector element k
F = vector of Itô process time function $[f_1, f_2, \ldots f_m]$
g_k = diagonal elements of Itô process for state vector element k
G = diagonal matrix of Wiener process functions $[g_1, g_2, \ldots g_m]$
dQ = vector of Wiener process elements $[dq_1, dq_2, \ldots dq_m]$

dz_k = a stochastic process with independent
   increments for element k
η_{kh} = instantaneous correlation between dq_k and dz_h
v_{kh} = instantaneous correlation between dq_k and dq_h
U_C = notation for $\delta U/\delta C$
$\mathcal{J}_t$ = notation for $\delta \mathcal{J}/\delta t$
$\mathcal{J}_w$ = notation for $\delta \mathcal{J}/\delta W$
$\mathcal{J}_j$ = notation for $\delta \mathcal{J}/\delta j$
$\mathcal{J}_{WW}$ = notation for $\delta^2 \mathcal{J}/\delta^2 W$
$\mathcal{J}_{ij}$ = notation for $\delta^2 \mathcal{J}/\delta i\, \delta j$
$\mathcal{J}_{jW}$ = notation for $\delta^2 \mathcal{J}/\delta j\, \delta W$

The investor controls the decision variables w_i and C for each point in time in order to maximize the "derived" utility of wealth function that has components for consumption of assets and the terminal value of residual assets.

$$\mathcal{J}(W, X, t) = \max E_0\left(\int_{s=0}^{T} U[C(s), s]\, ds + B[W(T), T]\right) \quad (9\text{--}3)$$

where E_0 is the conditional expectation operator.

The elements of the state vector X are written as a vector Itô process defined as

$$dX = F(X)dt + G(X)dQ \quad (9\text{--}4)$$

The optimality condition for the utility of wealth function is given by the partial differential equation (9–5):

$$0 = \max_{(c,w)} \left\{ U(C, t) + \mathcal{J}_t + \mathcal{J}_W\left[\left(\sum_{i=1}^{n} w_i(\alpha_i - r) + r\right)W - C\right]\right.$$

$$+ \sum_{k=1}^{m} \mathcal{J}_k f_k + \tfrac{1}{2}\mathcal{J}_{WW} \sum_{i=1}^{n}\sum_{j=1}^{n} w_i\, w_j\, \sigma_{ij}\, W^2$$

$$\left. + \sum_{k=1}^{m}\sum_{i=1}^{n} \mathcal{J}_{kW}\, w_i\, W g_k\, \sigma_i\, \eta_{ki} + \tfrac{1}{2}\sum_{k=1}^{m}\sum_{h=1}^{m} \mathcal{J}_{kh}\, g_k\, g_h\, v_{kh}\right\} \quad (9\text{--}5)$$

This equation contains terms for the time-varying decision variables w_i and C. These variables can be eliminated by substituting the following $n + 2$ equations into (9–5) and solving for $\mathcal{J}$.

The boundary condition must be met:

$$\mathcal{J}(W, T, X) = B(W, T) \tag{9–6}$$

The first-order consumption condition must be met:

$$0 = U(C, t) - \mathcal{J}(W, t, X) \tag{9–7}$$

And the $(i = 1, 2, \ldots, n)$ additional first-order conditions must be met:

$$0 = \mathcal{J}_W(\alpha_i - r) + \mathcal{J}_{WW} \sum_{j=1}^{n} w_j W \, \sigma_{ij} + \sum_{k=1}^{m} \mathcal{J}_{kW} \, g_k \, \sigma_i \, \eta_{ki} \tag{9–8}$$

The rationale is that once having solved (9–5) for $\mathcal{J}$, then $\mathcal{J}$ can be inserted into (9–7) and (9–8) to determine the values of w_i and C. But actually solving the revised version of (9–5) in closed form is difficult under most circumstances. Because of its complexity, this differential equation has proved difficult to apply to realistic models involving the relationship between macroeconomic state variables and asset returns.

Yet despite the mathematical difficulties, Merton manages to coax considerable results from the formulation. He shows that if the investment opportunity set is constant over time (expected returns and the covariance matrix are constant), then the asset allocations are constant over time and equal to the one-period solutions for a mean-variance investor. In this case, there is no intertemporal hedging demand.

Merton's formulation proves to be a watershed for additional work in the area of multiperiod asset allocation. The challenge has been to find formulations that allow two concepts: The investment returns are tractable functions of a number of controlling state variables, and the functions have significant historical fit to investment performance data.

BRENNAN, SCHWARTZ, AND LAGNADO (1997)

Employing a set of continuous differential equations, Brennan, Schwartz, and Lagnado (1997) are able to define a stochastic optimal control problem for stocks, long-term bonds, and cash. Three state variables are assumed to control the process: the interest rate level, the stock dividend yield, and the bond yield. The values of these factors are assumed to be known over all time intervals with certainty. The means and standard deviations of the investment returns are defined to be functions of three conditional factors. A joint stochastic process is defined in which the continuously rebalanced time changes in the investment returns and the dividend yield are functions of the exogenous factors as well as the returns of the other investments.

The coefficients for the joint stochastic process are estimated using nonlinear seemingly unrelated regressions. Then the optimal control formulation is solved using a discrete approximation grid for the continuous process. Results are obtained under a CRRA model of terminal wealth over a 20-year horizon. A comparison is made between results allowing short selling and results inhibiting short selling. In an out-of-sample evaluation, results for the no-short-selling case obtain returns roughly equivalent to the stock market average return but at a much lower standard deviation. The out-of-sample evaluation of the short-selling case shows that the procedure can deliver returns half again as big as the stock market but with a proportionate increase in the standard deviation. An interesting result of this model is that the average monthly turnover is 89.6 percent for the short-selling case and only 22.5 percent for the constrained case.

The authors point out that solution times increase linearly with the number of investments and geometrically with the number of state variables. Problems employing more than three state variables prove to be impractical to solve. Transaction costs are not considered in their formulation because this would add a new state variable for each time interval, generating a problem of unworkable size.

Comparing the results of a 20-year horizon and a one-period horizon, it is found that the longer horizon case generally commits more capital to stocks and long-term bonds than for the myopic horizon case. This is found to be caused by mean reversion in stock and bond returns over the long horizon.

BRANDT (1999)

In order to avoid errors due to model misspecification, Brandt (1999) formulates a nonparametric Euler equation approach to the determination of investment decision rules. In a traditional approach, Euler equations are normally used to prove that, for a CRRA investor, the asset allocation decisions are the same irrespective of the length of the investment horizon. Brandt formulates a conditional-method-of-moments approach in which the portfolio asset allocation to stocks and Treasury bills is a nonparametric conditional function of the values of the selected state variables. For each period of history that the state variables are observed being in a "similar" state, a sample observation is generated. These sample observations are used to trace out the shape of the function relating the state variables to the resulting asset allocations. This procedure avoids the requirement of specifying a functional form relating the state variables to the optimal asset allocations. Brandt indicates that the Euler equations could be modified to account for transaction costs, but they are not included in this analysis.

To validate the methodology, a solution is first obtained for the case where there are no state variables, the unconditional case. The results for stock and Treasury bill allocations indicate, as they should, that the asset allocations are not statistically different across all investment horizons for a given level of risk aversion.

A conditional case is then evaluated using the following state variables: the NYSE dividend yield, the default premium between Baa and Aaa corporate bonds, and the term premium between long-term government bonds and 90-day Treasury bills. The future values of the state variables required to determine the allocations over the forward time horizon are assumed to be known with certainty. Any uncertainty in estimating these state variables is not considered.

When the model is evaluated for a one-period horizon, the one-at-a-time effect of each of the state variables produces stock allocations 25 to 50 percent higher than the unconditional case. When the horizon is extended to two or more time periods, the allocation to stocks as well as the effect of hedging demand increases substantially, especially when dividend yield is used as the state variable. Of course, achieving these results is predicated on knowing the forward values of the state variables with certainty. Only one of the four state variables is used for each evaluation of the objective function. Just as in Brennan, Schwartz, and Lagnado (1997), the number of state variables causes geometric growth in the size of the problem formulation.

BARBERIS (2000)

The relationship between future values of the state variables and future values of returns is subject to uncertainty. There are actually two problems: the uncertainty of the future values of the state variables themselves and the uncertainty of the relationship between the state variables and the future rates of return. The first problem is *state variable risk*, and the last problem is a combination of *model risk* and *estimation risk*. Barberis (2000) manages to evaluate part of the problem by calculating the impact of estimation risk on asset allocation over a range of horizons for an investor with preferences over terminal wealth that are CRRA. In this analysis, no accommodation is made for transaction costs.

For this evaluation, two investments are employed, the NYSE stock index and Treasury bills. Only two state variables are employed, the stock dividend yield and the Treasury bill rate. No short selling or buying on margin is allowed. Using a dynamic programming formulation for the asset allocations as a function of the state variables, Barberis considers two model formulations. The first has no estimation risk of the model coefficients affecting future returns, and the second is a Bayesian approach admitting uncertainty of the coefficients. Simulation methods are then used to evaluate the distribution of return uncertainties.

Barberis finds that investors should increase stock allocations at longer horizons. For example, based on data from 1986 to 1995, an investor with a risk aversion of $\gamma = 5$ who rebalances annually should allocate 35 percent to stocks at a 1-year horizon and 75 percent to stocks at a 10-year horizon if dividend yields are near

2.86 percent. This increase in allocation to stocks is due to the hedging demand effect as described in Merton (1973).

When the possibility of learning better estimates of the model coefficients is accounted for, the allocation to stocks reverses course and decreases with the length of the horizon. For example, an investor with a risk aversion of $\gamma = 5$ who rebalances annually, and who takes no account of estimation risk, allocates about 80 percent to stocks irrespective of the length of the horizon. If both coefficient uncertainty and the possibility of learning are considered, the allocation to stocks is reduced to about 40 percent at a 10-year horizon.

While these results are useful, the impact of state variable risk may be much more important. Barberis does not address the question of state variable risk.

LYNCH AND BALDUZZI (2000)

By applying a dynamic programming approach expanded to consider both fixed and proportional transaction costs, Lynch and Balduzzi (2000) add an important new feature to the MPPT landscape. Two investments are considered: the NYSE stock index and 1-month Treasury bills. Only one state variable is employed, the 12-month dividend yield. Asset allocations are determined over a 240-month horizon, with no short sales allowed. The investor is assumed to have constant relative risk aversion, with $\gamma = 4$ employing terminal wealth as an objective.

Transaction costs for stocks are set at 0.25 percent for both purchases and sales, indicating a round-trip cost of 0.50 percent. No transaction cost is assigned to Treasury bills. The fixed costs are taken as 0.10 percent in any month incurring a change in allocation from the previous month.

The conclusions reached by others are confirmed in the presence of transaction costs, but the dynamics are different. At each time period, the model considers how much might be gained by changing the asset allocations as well as the cost of making the change. A no-trade region is determined for the stock asset allocation in which the costs of changing allocations are more than the benefit to the rate of return. This no-trade region prohibits small changes in allocations.

Simulating 100,000 times over a performance history from 1927 to 1996, Lynch and Balduzzi are able to generate averages for the following variables: rebalancing frequency, transaction costs per month, width of the no-trade region, and the average allocation to the stock index.

In the presence of transaction costs, the average stock allocation for an investor early in life, assuming returns are not predictable, is 57.4 percent. Assuming returns are predictable leads to an average allocation of 71.1 percent. This difference is similar to the results obtained with no transaction costs. The surprise is just how similar it is. Without transaction costs, the investor allocates 56.2 percent to stocks under the unpredictable assumption and 69.4 percent assuming predictability. The asset allocations seem to arrive at similar numbers despite an average transaction cost of 0.571 percent per month. Another unexpected result is the large size of the average width of the no-trade region, 25.8 percent assuming predictability of returns. This means that suggested changes in allocation typically must be ± 12.9 percent in order to allow a transaction to take place.

No direct calculation is made of state variable uncertainty. Future values of the state variable are assumed to be known with certainty. They are generated using an autoregressive process assuming 0.962 as a persistence value. Lynch and Balduzzi demonstrate the result of changing this persistence to 0.32 and 0.00. In the face of lower persistence, the state variable returns to its long-term average more quickly. As a result, the no-trade region is shown to increase dramatically from approximately 25 to 45 percent for very large or very small values of the state variable. In the middle of this U-shaped function, the no-trade region is about the same as for the high-persistence case. Only allocation changes caused by extreme values of the state variable are affected.

AÏT-SAHALIA AND BRANDT (2001)

As noted in Brennan, Schwartz, and Lagnado (1997) and Brandt (1999), incorporating more than a few state variables in the dynamic programming formulation leads to unworkable problem size. In order to alleviate this problem, Aït-Sahalia and Brandt (2001) devise a method to employ only one effective state variable that is an index of multiple fundamental state variables. This composite index is determined by using a generalized method of moments (GMM) formulation to determine the weights of the underlying state variables in the index. The innovation provided by Aït-Sahalia and Brandt is the determination of the asset allocations without an intermediate estimate of the expected investment returns. The allocations are estimated nonparametrically directly from the composite index. The index is parametric but the asset allocation decision is not. In the evaluation of this model, short sales are prohibited and transaction costs are not considered.

The investments selected are the S&P 500 stock index, a U.S. government bond index of maturities greater than 10 years, and a maturity-matched Treasury bill. The state variables considered are the default spread, the log of the dividend-to-price ratio, the term spread, and the trend in the investment return. Data from 1954 through 1997 are used to evaluate the terminal wealth of the investor using a range of horizons from 1 to 10 years.

Unfortunately, this date range includes a portion of the 1990s during which the relationship between stock returns and dividend yields seems to lose significance. As a result, the composite index of state variables loads very poorly on dividend yields. This in turn causes the resulting solution to the conditional objective function to display virtually no hedging demand. For any selected risk level, the allocation to stocks is virtually constant across investment horizons. In fact, the little hedging demand that is observed works in the opposite direction to conventional thinking. The allocation to stocks decreases modestly at longer horizons. This is attributed by the authors to the low load on the dividend yield in the composite state variable.

Another interesting result from this study is the virtual absence of significant allocation to bonds at any level of risk or any value of the composite state variable. Aït-Sahalia and Brandt attribute this to a negative relationship between bond returns and the term spread component of the weighted state variable. This results in a hedging demand that works against holding bonds in the long term.

CAMPBELL, CHAN, AND VICEIRA (2003)

A procedure that can handle a large number of investments and state variables is defined in Campbell, Chan, and Viceira (2003). Their approach assumes that asset allocations are linear functions of the state variables and that capital consumption is a quadratic function of the state variables. No borrowing or short selling restrictions are included in the formulation. Transaction costs are also not considered. The investments include a value-weighted index on the combination of the NYSE, NASDAQ, and AMEX as a proxy for stock returns, a 5-year Treasury bond return, and a 90-day Treasury bill rate. The exogenous state variables employed include the Treasury bill yield, stock dividend yield, and the term spread between a 5-year zero-coupon bond and the Treasury bill rate.

Future values of the state variables required for each point in time are assumed to follow a first-order vector autoregressive (VAR) process. For this purpose, the state variables are considered to be the original exogenous state variables plus the returns on each of the investments. The VAR estimates obtained are based on quarterly data from 1952 to 1999. These estimates show that the quarterly stock and bond VAR equations obtain R^2 just under 0.10, which is typical for this type of forecasting model. The R^2 for the exogenous state variables are comfortably strong, between 0.53 and 0.93. But each exogenous state variable only relates significantly to its own previous value. This means that a state variable such as dividend yield only relates strongly to past values of itself. Other variables do not help much.

Using numerical procedures to solve a set of nonlinear equations resulting from assumptions about asset allocation and capital consumption dynamics, the asset allocations are determined at each point in time. Because the allocations are not subject to short-selling constraints, the stock and bond allocations achieve values over 400 percent at various times between 1954 to 1999.

One of the advantages of the Campbell, Chan, and Viceira methodology is that the asset allocation to each investment can be split at any time into components due to the myopic allocation and due to the hedging demand allocation. This is useful for evaluating how much hedging demand has to do with terminal wealth.

BRANDT, GOYAL, AND SANTA-CLARA (2001)

An approach to circumvent the problem of treating many state variables is the simulation approach by Brandt, Goyal, and Santa-Clara (2001). In this procedure, the relationship between asset returns and the state variables can take on any form, including forms that result in the path being wealth-dependent, something defined away in the CRRA assumption used by many others. Virtually any feature of realistic portfolio evaluation can be accommodated. This includes transaction costs, taxes, and intermediate capital consumption. Additional constraints can easily be added to the system, such as constraints on borrowing and short selling. The joint dynamics of the asset returns and the state variables can also be evaluated in a Bayesian framework if desired, with the result that state variable uncertainty and return model uncertainty can be specifically incorporated.

The investor's utility function need not be CRRA. Any function such as maximizing Sharpe ratios, minimizing maximum drawdowns, or minimizing deviations below a target return can be accommodated. The only requirement is that the objective function must be four times differentiable.

There are several steps to the simulation process. First, the investor's expected utility function is defined as a Taylor series expansion. This type of function lends itself to closed-form solution techniques. Fourth-order expansions are found useful in order to accommodate the effects of skewness and kurtosis of investment returns on the investor's utility function. Then a large number of random simulated investment paths are generated following the assumed rules involving the state variables and the asset returns. For each simulated path, the optimal portfolio weights at each time period are recursively determined using dynamic programming to maximize the Taylor series utility function. In order to accomplish this, a regression analysis is conducted at each time period on the moments of the utility function to determine their dependence on the values of the state variables.

This is a computation-intensive approach. Nevertheless, it has two big advantages. First, virtually any functional form relating the state variables to the investment returns is possible, allowing the ability to incorporate many investment management details such as transaction costs. Second, a large number of investments, state variables, and time intervals can easily be handled within modest solution times. Brandt, Goyal, and Santa-Clara report solving a problem using 10,000 simulations of 10 risky securities and 40 state variables over 20 time periods in less than 30 minutes on a standard PC.

For a simple problem, the authors go through an evaluation to demonstrate that the simulation methodology produces answers very similar to an exact solution based on quadrature integration. Part of this evaluation indicates that a fourth-order expansion of the utility function gives noticeably better results than a second-order expansion.

In an evaluation of a multiperiod problem for stocks plus cash, the stock returns are considered as a function of dividend yield. Assuming a CRRA investor for comparison purposes, the results are very similar to those obtained in Barberis (2000) and Campbell and Viceira (1999). Thus, this more flexible simulation approach appears to be able to handle a variety of objective functions and investment return functions. It also obtains results similar to those of other implementations of MPPT when the model structure assumptions are the same.

KLEMKOSKY AND BHARATI (1995)

Most of the models evaluated so far have involved the Merton formulation for maximizing terminal wealth using the solution to a dynamic programming problem. Klemkosky and Bharti (1995) take a more pragmatic approach by using the Markowitz mean-variance model on a rolling basis. Using 60 months of data ending December 1963, a linear model is formed to predict the rate of return for January 1964 for each investment using 11 potential state variables. The best parsimonious model is selected from all possible model combinations, resulting in only a subset of the state variables being employed. The most parsimonious model is determined according to Mallow's criterion for the selection of predictive models. Each possible combination of the state variables is evaluated according to equation (9–9), and the model with the lowest criterion value is selected.

$$C_p = \frac{(T - K_i)\sigma_i^2}{\sigma^2} + 2K_i - T \qquad (9\text{–}9)$$

where:

C_p = Mallow's predictive criterion
T = number of observations
K_i = number of explanatory variables in model i
σ^2 = mean squared error using all variables
σ_i^2 = mean squared error using K_i variables

Expected returns are then predicted for the next month using the conditional linear factor model. Standard deviations and covariances are calculated for the last 60 months on an unconditional basis. Using these values as inputs to the Markowitz model, the optimal portfolio with the highest Sharpe ratio is determined. The resulting 1-month return for the next month is recorded as the portfolio predicted return. Then the time window is moved forward 1 month and the entire process is repeated until the forecasted month is December 1990.

This experiment is repeated twice, with and without transaction costs of 0.48 percent per round-turn. The benchmarks for one experiment are the S&P 500 stock index and the Salomon Brothers High Grade Corporate Bond Index. Table 9–1 shows a

T A B L E 9-1

Klemkosky and Bharati Dynamic Portfolio Performance versus Benchmarks

Investment	Annualized Return	Annualized Standard Deviation
Stock index benchmark	10.64	15.27
Bond index benchmark	7.27	9.89
Dynamic portfolio without transaction costs	16.06	9.25
Dynamic portfolio with transaction costs	13.27	9.12

comparison of the rolling dynamic portfolio results against the benchmark performance averaged over the entire interval from January 1964 to December 1990.

The dynamic portfolio, with or without transaction costs, outperforms both benchmarks on a return and a standard deviation basis. This out-of-sample experiment indicates that a rolling Markowitz model employing a conditional forecast of expected returns is capable of providing superior returns over a static buy-and-hold portfolio.

THE EFFECT OF UNCERTAINTY IN THE PREDICTIVE RELATIONSHIPS

When future returns are functionally conditional on selected state variables, three types of uncertainty are involved with the use of a predictive model. Consider the linear model form commonly used to represent the relationship between the investment return at time t, R_t, and the values of K conditional exogenous state variables s_{kt} preferably with a time lag of $n < 0$.

$$R_t = \alpha + \sum_{k=1}^{K} \beta_k s_{k,t-n} + e_t \qquad (9\text{--}10)$$

Uncertainties about the form of equation (9–10) and the values of the variables in the equation lead to three types of risk. Accounting for these uncertainties can change the relationship between the length of the horizon and the resulting asset allocations. That is, the very nature of the hedging demand can be altered. In fact, depending on the degree of uncertainty, the hedging demand can become zero or can reverse direction. The impact of each one of these uncertainties is worth considering in more detail.

Model Risk

Uncertainty over the functional form of equation (9–10) is termed *model risk*. This includes two concepts: the mathematical structure of the equation and the list of state variables s_k that are employed. While model risk is recognized, no research has been identified for this concept.

Estimation Risk

The uncertainty of the unknown coefficients of the model, α and β_k, is termed *estimation risk*. A specific random sample of historic values of the investment returns R_t and the factor values s_k leads to an estimate of the values of the coefficients. Another random sample will lead to a different estimate of the coefficients. We are interested in discovering the true population estimates of the values of the coefficients. We would also like to know how much impact there is on the hedging demand due to this estimation risk.

Barberis (2000) includes estimation risk in his analysis by looking at the distribution of possible asset allocations that results from considering the distribution of the possible values of the coefficients. The expected value of allocations based on the distribution of coefficients is different from the allocations resulting from using the expected values of the coefficients.

Xia (2001) goes a step further and considers the possibility of learning more about the values of the coefficients over time. He shows that hedging demand can come from three sources: the direct impact of the coefficients not being equal to zero, future changes in the state variables, and uncertainty in the true values of the coefficients. Each of these components can independently warp the hedging demand. Consequently, changes in the state variables may no longer have monotonic effects on the hedging demand. At one level of a state variable, the hedging demand can go up with increasing horizons, and at another level of this state variable, the hedging demand can go down with increasing horizons. The optimal portfolio strategy in accordance with Xia (2001) is contained in equation (9–11).

$$x^* = \frac{\bar{\mu} + b(s - \bar{s}) - r}{\gamma \sigma_P^2} \qquad \text{(myopic portion of asset allocation)}$$

$$+ \frac{\phi_b v(s - \bar{s})}{\gamma \sigma_P^2 \phi} \qquad \text{(learning portion of asset allocation)}$$

$$+ \frac{\phi_s \sigma_P \sigma_s \rho_{sP}}{\gamma \sigma_P^2 \phi} \qquad \text{(hedging demand due to state variables)}$$

$$+ \frac{\phi_b \sigma_P \sigma_b \rho_{\beta P}}{\gamma \sigma_P^2 \phi} \qquad \text{(hedging demand due to coefficient}$$

$$\text{uncertainty)} \qquad (9\text{–}11)$$

where:

x^* = asset allocation to each investment at time t
$\bar{\mu}$ = mean return for each investment
β = coefficient of state variable in return function
b = mean value of β
s = value of state variable at time t
$\bar{s}$ = mean value of state variable
r = risk-free interest rate
γ = coefficient of relative risk aversion
σ_P = standard deviation of investment price
ϕ = optimality function of investment and capital consumption
ϕ_b = partial derivative of optimality function with respect to b
ϕ_s = partial derivative of optimality function with respect to s
v = variance of β
σ_s = standard deviation of state variable
σ_b = standard deviation of β
ρ_{sP} = correlation between state variable and investment price
$\rho_{\beta P}$ = correlation between β and investment price

State Variable Risk

Most research on MPPT assumes that the values of the state variables are known with certainty. This third risk comes from using equation (9–10) for distant future estimates of investment return beyond the natural lag n in the predictive equation. When this occurs, the values of the factors s_{kt} must also be estimated. In this case, uncertainty in the future factor values gives rise to uncertainty in the predicted returns. Many of the MPPT approaches assume that future values of the state variables can be generated though a vector autoregressive approach. Lynch and Balduzzi (2000), Campbell, Chan, and Viceira (2003), and Barberis (2000) employ this VAR approach.

At first glance, it appears that there is a strong relationship between the present and future values of the state variables using these VAR equations. For example, Campbell, Chan, and Viceira (2003) find that the R^2 of the dividend yield forecasting 1 quarter ahead is 0.932. Independent results, using data from the early 1950s to the end of 2001, forecasting 1 month ahead produces an adjusted

R^2 of 0.986, a seemingly powerful forecasting result. When attempting to use monthly data to forecast out 36 months, this R^2 reduces to 0.557 and gets much worse at longer horizons. The most significant variables found useful for fitting the 1-month stocks are shown in Table 3–19 in Chapter 3. The lagged effect of these state variables predicting future values of themselves is shown in the first five rows of Table 9–2 at various forecasting horizons. The adjusted R^2 to predict the stock return various months into the future using a model including all the state variables from Table 3–19 is shown in the last row of Table 9–2. The number of accumulation months for each factor in the "State Variable" column is shown in parentheses. For example, "Stock return (48)" indicates that a 48-month compounded stock return is used to predict the various forecast horizons. For this mean-reversion variable there is a large overlap in the data. This is guaranteed to induce strong serial correlation. On the other hand, the dividend yield only employs 1 month of data, and yet it still has a strong natural persistence.

Despite the fact that several of the state variables employed have strong persistence, the ability of these factors to forecast the stock return more than 6 months into the future is nonexistent. This stems from the low adjusted R^2 for the prediction model for a 1-month lag. While these factors are significant for predicting stock returns at the 1-month lag, they still leave the lion's share of the variance of stock returns unexplained. These state variables simply

T A B L E 9–2

Forecasting Power of State Variables and Price Model (Adjusted R^2) at Various Forecast Horizons

State Variable	1 Month	3 Months	6 Months	12 Months	24 Months	36 Months
Dividend yield (1)	0.986	0.944	0.976	0.752	0.630	0.557
Industrial capacity (2)	0.994	0.952	0.835	0.585	0.290	0.081
NYSE turnover (52)	0.999	0.999	0.996	0.986	0.947	0.893
Capacity utilization (12)	0.991	0.922	0.731	0.319	0.028	−0.002
Stock return (48)	0.946	0.847	0.730	0.542	0.322	0.203
Stock price model	0.094	0.053	0.034	0.009	−0.010	−0.003

do not prove very satisfactory for forecasting long-horizon returns or for setting long-horizon asset allocations for investment portfolios. The errors associated with distant forecasts are just too large to accurately determine asset allocations for many months into the future.

The values of the state variables s are not very predictable more than 6 months forward. The best prediction of their value would then devolve to their historical mean value $\bar{s}$. Referring to equation (9–11), the second term of the myopic portion is limited to those few months in which $(s - \bar{s})$ is not equal to zero. The effect of the learning portion of (9–11) will also disappear after 6 months. Similarly, the last row of Table 9–2 indicates that the value of ρ_{sP} is zero after 6 months. Therefore, the hedging demand due to state variables will become nonexistent after 6 months. The last term in (9–11), the hedging demand due to coefficient uncertainty, is simply a constant. It will just raise or lower the investment allocation relative to the myopic allocation but does not cause time variation. Even when the state variables are predictable, the last term in (9–11) remains a constant that does not vary with time. Therefore, every time-varying term in (9–11) disappears after 6 months, leaving only the myopic term due to the investment mean and variance.

We can draw the conclusion that the use of MPPT for horizons longer than a few months is not very effective because we cannot forecast the values of the required state variables. The hedging demand portions of (9–11) simply cannot be determined very far out. Thus, it seems reasonable for investors to lock in portfolio allocations using a myopic model for a single time period. Then investors can adapt to fresh updates of the state variables at the beginning of the next time period. The worst that happens is the loss of a few months of small hedging demand benefit. This is confirmed by Barberis (2000) and Xia (2001), who show that the impact of including the effect of the hedging demand in the face of parameter uncertainty for a range of assumptions is less than 2 percent on the allocation to stocks for time horizons under 6 months.

The small asset allocation effect coupled with the difficulties in solving the required numerical procedures and the practical limitations on the number of assets and state variables does not make MPPT very attractive. The difficulties of incorporating transaction costs, borrowing, and short selling into the formulation are a concern. Finally, the fact that most of MPPT uses constant relative risk aversion as the risk aversion function, which implies no consideration of the path of the wealth growth, is also troublesome.

REFERENCES

Aït-Sahalia, Yacine, and Michael W. Brandt. "Variable Selection for Portfolio Choice." *Journal of Finance* 56, no. 4 (August 2001): 1297–1351.
Barberis, Nicholas. "Investing for the Long Run When Returns Are Predictable." *Journal of Finance* 55, no. 1 (February 2000): 225–264.
Brandt, Michael W. "Estimating Portfolio and Consumption Choice: A Conditional Euler Equations Approach." *Journal of Finance* 54, no. 5 (October 1999): 1609–1645.
Brandt, Michael W., Amit Goyal, and Pedro Santa-Clara. "A Simulation Approach to Dynamic Portfolio Choice with an Application to Industry Momentum." Working paper, Wharton School, University of Pennsylvania (2001).
Brennan, Michael J., Eduardo S. Schwartz, and Ronald Lagnado. "Strategic Asset Allocation." *Journal of Economic Dynamics and Control* 21 (1997): 1377–1403.
Campbell, John Y., Yeung Lewis Chan, and Luis M. Viceira. "A Multivariate Model of Strategic Asset Allocation." *Journal of Financial Economics* 67, Issue 1 (January 2003), 41–80.
Campbell, John Y., and Luis M. Viceira. "Consumption and Portfolio Decisions When Expected Returns Are Time Varying." *Quarterly Journal of Economics* 114 (1999): 433–495.
Klemkosky, Robert C., and Rakesh Bharati. "Time-Varying Expected Returns and Asset Allocation." *Journal of Portfolio Management* (Summer 1995): 80–87.
Lynch, Anthony W., and Pierluigi Balduzzi. "Predictability and Transaction Costs: The Impact on Rebalancing Rules and Behavior." *Journal of Finance* 50, no. 5 (October 2000): 2285–2309.
Merton, Robert C. "Lifetime Portfolio Selection under Uncertainty: The Continuous Time Case." *Review of Economics and Statistics* 51, no. 3 (August 1969): 247–257.
Merton, Robert C. "Optimum Consumption and Portfolio Rules in a Continuous-Time Model." *Journal of Economic Theory* 3 (1971): 373–413.
Merton, Robert C. "An Intertemporal Asset Pricing Model." *Econometrica* 41 (1973): 867–887.
Samuelson, Paul A. "Lifetime Portfolio Selection by Dynamic Stochastic Programming." *Review of Economics and Statistics* 51 (1969): 238–246.
Xia, Yihong. "Learning about Predictability: The Effects of Parameter Uncertainty on Dynamic Asset Allocation." *Journal of Finance* 56 (2001): 205–246.

DynaPorte™ Model Description*

> Give all thou canst; high Heaven rejects the lore
> Of nicely calculated less or more
>
> *William Wordsworth*
> *Inside of King's College Chapel, Cambridge*

This chapter describes the formulation of a dynamic portfolio optimization system called DynaPorte. The need for the development of this system is rooted in the observation that a static portfolio optimization methodology does not provide a sense of confident investing even when rigorously applied. The Markowitz mean-variance model provides an elegant solution to the problem of trading off risk versus return. But generating the required inputs of returns, standard deviations, and a correlation matrix for the expected performance for all the investments places a heavy burden on the user. It is not obvious how to generate these inputs. It is obvious that no two users of the Markowitz model having access to the same historical performance data would generate the same set of expectations for a given list of investments. Therefore, they would not obtain the same set of asset allocations.

Beyond the problem of generating a single set of expectations in order to utilize the mean-variance model lies the question of how

---

*The formulation described in this chapter, plus additional formulations using other objective functions, are protected against commercial infringement under U.S. patent application number 10/120,121. All rights are strictly reserved. Employing this formulation for commercial purposes is specifically reserved.

often these expectations should be updated. What seems to be needed to get around these problems is a system that can automatically formulate these expectations based on macroeconomic factors that influence investment performance. But developing factor models that explain investment returns alone is not going far enough. A more useful approach would be a system that directly obtains time-varying asset allocations by taking into account the influence of macroeconomic factors. The approach of DynaPorte is to make the asset allocations be linear functions of the influential factors in a linear programming framework.

MODEL OBJECTIVES

In Chapter 9, we mention a number of approaches to multiperiod investment models. In many of these cases the mathematical statement of the problem is challenging, the solution methodologies are difficult, and numerous simplifying assumptions must be made. The number of investments that can be treated is frequently very small, and the number of controlling factors is limited. In addition to these problems, the impact of skewed performance distributions can cause difficulties with many solution methodologies. With all these difficulties in mind, the following model objectives are proposed.

Handle a Reasonably Large Number of Investments

The investments in the portfolio should be considered to be investment classes rather than individual securities. The DynaPorte methodology is not suited to determining allocations to hundreds of stocks. The methodology is better suited to determining allocations to tens of asset classes. This is true because macroeconomic factors have a stronger relationship with asset classes than they do with individual securities. The difference in performance between two individual securities in the same asset class is related to differences in company specifics, not to macroeconomic factors. Using the DynaPorte formulation, up to 20 or 30 asset classes might be the largest allocation problem that can be solved in a practical amount of time, although larger problems are feasible.

Make the Allocations a Function of Macroeconomic Factors

Instead of making the portfolio returns, standard deviations, and correlation coefficients be functions of influential factors, the idea is to make the asset allocations be direct linear functions of these factors. This approach of making the asset allocations a linear function of the influential factors has been incorporated in other asset allocation formulations, including Brandt (1999) and Campbell, Chan, and Viceira (2003). These other formulations deal with more complex problems and are not linear programming structures, but they support the concept of using linear functions of exogenous factors to represent time-varying asset allocations.

Using this procedure avoids the two-stage process of determining the performance expectations from the influential factors and then using these expectations to generate the asset allocations. It also avoids the problem of building a consistent set of expectations based on the factors. A correlation matrix in which each covariance term is independently developed based on a factor model while remaining consistent with each other covariance term could prove difficult. For implementations of the mean-variance model with linear return functions of influential factors, see Perold (1984) and Robertsson (2000). In the formulation that follows, making the allocation to each investment be a function of a set of macroeconomic factors does not present any consistency problem.

Retain the Periodic Nature of the Performance History

The Markowitz model and other models employ first and second moments of the original performance history. Solution guarantees partly depend on shapes of distributions or risk tolerance characteristics. It would be useful to avoid these problems and to be able to deal with any possible performance distribution. It would also be useful to obtain a solution by dealing with actual monthly or quarterly performance numbers rather than with moments of distributions. This allows us to utilize a wide range of objective functions calculated from the performance of time series.

Allow the Evaluation of a Large Amount of Performance History

In order to discover underlying relationships between investment performance and influential macroeconomic factors, a number of expansion-recession business cycles need to be evaluated. This assumes that each business cycle provides an opportunity for each factor to move through a wide range of values. Following Haimowitz (1998), the range of business-cycle durations since 1945 has been on the order of 2 to 10 years. With this in mind, 20 to 50 years of monthly investment returns and factor values should provide a sufficient number of business cycles to measure the effect of influential factors. Thus, the ideal model might need to explicitly consider up to 600 months of history. The optimal length of history employed will depend on the consistency of the relationships between macroeconomic factors and investment performance over the interval.

Allow a Reasonably Large Number of Influential Factors

The number of macroeconomic factors that can be used is dependent on three concepts. The first is the true number of factors that might actually influence the performance of an investment. The second is the number of independent factors that we can discriminate in attempting to fit the model. And the third is the amount of solution time required to deal with an increasing number of factors. As a practical limit, let us assume that a model capable of handling 10 to 30 factors would provide ample flexibility, although 50 might be better.

Allow for Upper and Lower Allocation Bounds

Since we are seeking a model structure that has the asset allocations as the solution variables, it would be prudent to allow for a user-specified upper and lower bound on the allocations for each investment. This practical pair of allocation bound constraints lets the user superimpose restrictions on the range of allocations that can be generated.

Allow Borrowing for Portfolio Leveraging within Selected Bounds

Borrowing to leverage up portfolio assets can be a useful tool to gear up portfolio performance. It is possible to incorporate a method that allows for the borrowing of capital in order to leverage up the portfolio. Of course, any capital borrowed would need to be paid for, at either a fixed or variable rate. Borrowing to leverage is not mandatory, but it can be allowed at the user's discretion. In the same way that the allocations are allowed to have upper and lower bounds, the leveraging can be constrained within an upper and lower bound as well. We define a leverage ratio of 1 to indicate that there is no leveraging and a value greater than 1 to indicate the leverage ratio. Setting both the upper and lower leveraging bounds to a value of 1 would effectively switch off the leveraging capability.

Allow the Leverage Ratio to Be a Function of Macroeconomic Factors

In order to achieve better portfolio performance, there may be times during which leveraging should be increased or decreased in response to macroeconomic factors. In the same way that we allow the allocations to be functions of the influential factors, we can allow the leverage ratio to be a separate function of the same set of factors.

Include the Cost of Transactions

Changing the asset allocations from period to period may require paying transaction costs. These costs can be incurred from commissions, fees, or slippage in periods when the allocation is increasing as well as in periods when the allocation is decreasing. A separate cost is allowed for purchases and for sales, with the possibility that the costs are different for each investment in the portfolio. The transaction costs are specified as a percentage of the value of the investment purchase or sale. The periodic return for each investment is adjusted for the cost of the allocation change for that investment between the last time period and the current time period.

Allow for Nonnormality in the Return Distributions

As we saw in Chapter 1, skewness and kurtosis values departing from the normal distribution can make the use of variance unsuitable as a portfolio objective. Another objective function should be chosen to allow for skewed distributions in the underlying investment returns. While this is true for many traditional investment types, it is especially important for derivatives products such as options.

Minimize Mean Absolute Deviation While Targeting an Average Return

The most practical goal of the portfolio optimization model is a linear objective function. The objective function chosen is the minimum mean absolute deviation below a threshold return. This choice is practical because it allows us to work on strictly linear portfolio problems incorporating more investments, more factors, and longer performance histories. Quadratic objective functions would limit the problem to a much smaller size in order to obtain solutions in a reasonable time. While the choice of this particular objective function stems from a desire to keep the entire portfolio model linear, there are circumstances for which this linear goal is actually preferable to the traditional sum-of-squares objective. On the other hand, there are circumstances for which the sum of squares can be shown to be better. But there is probably no circumstance for which the sum-of-squares objective is dramatically dominant over the mean absolute deviation. For more details concerning linear versus quadratic objective functions, see Chapter 12. Given the simplifying assumption that the asset allocations are constrained to be linear functions of the influential factors, using a linear objective function is not a very large modeling fault. This minimum mean absolute deviation objective is coupled with a target rate of return to obtain one point along an efficient frontier.

Allow for Other Objective Functions

A host of other objective functions are feasible including maximizing the average portfolio return, absolutely or at a constrained value of the mean absolute deviation. For the purposes of this book, we shall just acknowledge that such approaches are possible and continue to focus on the mean absolute deviation as a desirable and workable objective.

DYNAPORTE MODEL FORMULATION

The DynaPorte model is a linear programming formulation of a portfolio optimization problem. The approach is to define the asset allocation to each investment in terms of a time-variant linear function of a set of macroeconomic variables. Constraints are established to keep the allocations within selected bounds, such as 0 to 1, at each point of history. The sum of the allocations at each point of history can be maintained at 1 or a selected leverage level. The leverage level can also be a linear function of the macroeconomic factors subject to upper and lower bounds. In the following formulation, a target average return over all history is established as a constraint. The set of linear allocation coefficients and linear leverage coefficients that satisfies all these constraints and minimizes the sum of losing months below a threshold return is found using linear programming techniques. In order to aid in the formulation of the problem, the model variables are defined in Table 10–1.

T A B L E   10-1

Definition of Variables for DynaPorte Model

Variable	Description
j	index representing each investment
N	maximum number of investments
t	index representing each time period, normally in months
M	maximum number of time periods
Y_{jt}	rate of return of investment j in time period t
k	index representing each influential macroeconomic factor
K	maximum number of influential macroeconomic factors
F_{kt}	value of influential macroeconomic factor k in time period t
AA_{jt}	asset allocation to investment j in time period t
A_j	constant portion of the allocation function for investment j
B_{kj}	coefficient for factor k in the allocation function for investment j
R_t	portfolio rate of return in time period t
T_t	portfolio rate of return value that is the threshold for downside deviations at time period t
V_t	portfolio return minus threshold in time period t when this difference is positive, else 0
Z_t	portfolio return minus threshold in time period t when this difference is negative, else 0
$amin_j$	minimum allocation allowed to investment j as a proportion of all allocated assets
$amax_j$	maximum allocation allowed to investment j as a proportion of all allocated assets
R_{avg}	portfolio average return per period
I_t	interest rate per time period t that must be paid to borrow money for leveraging
LEV_t	leverage ratio employed during time period t
C	constant term in the leverage function
D_k	coefficient for factor k in the leverage function
LEV_{min}	minimum leverage allowed (lower bound)
LEV_{max}	maximum leverage allowed (upper bound)
DEL_{jt}	change in asset allocation to investment j between time period $t-1$ and time period t
DP_{jt}	change in asset allocation to investment j between $t-1$ and t when change is positive
DN_{jt}	change in asset allocation to investment j between $t-1$ and t when change is negative
CP_j	cost for 1 unit change in investment j when change is positivie
CN_j	cost for 1 unit change in investment j when change is negative

The Mean Absolute Deviation Objective Function

To maintain the problem as a pure linear program, the mean absolute deviation (MAD) objective function is defined to be the average of the returns below a selected threshold for all time periods. This objective function is a linear function in terms of the periodic rates of return of the portfolio. It is referred to as an L_1 risk measure since it involves first-order differences from a central value. It avoids the standard deviation, an L_2 risk measure, used in the Markowitz mean-variance model, which requires quadratic programming methods. Defining the objective function as the sum or average of losses below a threshold is based on concepts developed by Konno and Yamazaki (1991) with extensions by Feinstein and Thapa (1993). For a successful utilization of a MAD objective function in a portfolio model, see Zenios and Kang (1993). For more details about the efficacy of L_1 as a risk measure, see Chapter 12 on mean absolute deviation.

The ability to formulate the objective function in this manner is based on a well-known linear programming device. The rate of return of the portfolio R_t less the threshold value T_t during one time period is broken into two components: a positive component above the threshold V_t and a negative component below the threshold Z_t. Mathematically,

$$R_t - T_t = +V_t - Z_t \qquad (10\text{--}1)$$

Since solution variables in linear programming normally only take positive values, only one of V_t or Z_t is in the solution. Either the positive component V_t has a nonzero value and the negative component Z_t has a zero value, or vice versa. Splitting the return about the threshold into positive and negative components provides the ability to concentrate on the downside variable Z_t. Setting the objective function to the average loss below the selected threshold produces a linear function. Remember that the value of Z_t is zero in time periods in which $(R_t - T_t) > 0$. The mean absolute deviation objective function can be expressed as

$$\frac{1}{M}\sum_{t=1}^{M} Z_t \qquad (10\text{--}2)$$

Asset Allocation Constraint

The time-varying asset allocation AA_{jt} for each investment j for each time period t is defined as a linear function of the time-changing values of the K influential macroeconomic factors F_{kt}. This equation represents the heart of the DynaPorte methodology. It states that the allocation to each investment changes linearly as the factors change. It also implies that the impact of each of the multiple factors is independent and additive.

$$AA_{jt} = A_j + \sum_{k=1}^{K} B_{kj}F_{kt} \qquad (10\text{--}3)$$

This function applies to all time periods. While the values of the asset allocations change in response to the influential factors, the allocation coefficients remain constant over all time.

Asset Allocation Change

In order to calculate the transaction costs associated with a change in the allocation between time period $t - 1$ and time period t, there must be a calculation of this difference. For every time period t except for time period $t = 1$, there is a change in allocation DEL_{jt} for investment j.

$$DEL_{jt} = AA_{jt} - AA_{j,t-1} \qquad (10\text{--}4)$$

The value of DEL_{jt} for $t = 1$ is defined to be zero.

It is convenient to calculate separate costs for positive changes in the allocation and for negative changes in the allocation. The value of DEL_{jt} is broken into two components: DP_{jt} for those time periods when DEL_{jt} is positive and DN_{jt} for those time periods when DEL_{jt} is negative. If DP_{jt} has a value greater than zero, then DN_{jt} equals zero. If DN_{jt} has a value greater than zero, then DP_{jt}

equals zero. Only one of the two will have a nonzero value depending on whether DEL_{jt} is positive or negative. This feature is accomplished with the following equation:

$$DEL_{jt} = DP_{jt} - DN_{jt} \qquad (10\text{-}5)$$

The variables DP_{jt} and DN_{jt} do not need to be considered if the associated transaction costs are zero. When these costs are zero, equations (10–4) and (10–5) are not added to the model formulation. Specifying nonzero transaction costs can add substantially to the model solution time.

Leverage Ratio Constraint

Leveraging involves borrowing to increase the amount of capital to invest in the available investments. The amount borrowed must be paid for at the interest rate I_t, which could be time-varying. The leverage ratio LEV_t for each time period t is determined by the linear leverage function. This leverage function is affected by the time-changing values of the K influential factors, F_{kt}.

$$LEV_t = C + \sum_{k=1}^{K} D_k F_{kt} \qquad (10\text{-}6)$$

An unleveraged portfolio at time t has a value of $LEV_t = 1$. An unleveraged portfolio employs no borrowing. A leveraged portfolio at time t has a value of $LEV_t > 1$. A leveraged portfolio in period t implies that borrowing takes place during that period. The portion of the portfolio that is borrowed is just $(LEV_t - 1)$. The total capital available to be allocated to the N investments is LEV_t.

Portfolio Return Constraint for Each Time Period

The portfolio return R_t for each time period t is equal to the sum of the product of the allocation AA_{jt} to each investment j multiplied by the rate of return Y_{jt} for the investment and then adjusted for the cost of borrowing for leverage and also adjusted for the periodic transaction costs.

Any amount borrowed ($LEV_t - 1$) becomes a portfolio liability and reduces the portfolio performance at the cost of I_t percent per period.

The return for time period t is adjusted for transaction costs. Each new unit of investment j purchased costs CP_j. Each new unit of investment j sold costs CN_j. There is no transaction cost taken for the initial purchase of the investments at the beginning of time period 1. This is a fixed cost that has nothing to do with portfolio optimization. If it were calculated and charged to the first time period, there would be a large impact on the return in the first period. If the value of CP_j were the same across all j investments, then it would make no difference what the initial asset allocations are. The total cost of the initial portfolio purchase would be a constant that could be spread across the entire period that the portfolio is held. Similarly, there is no transaction cost associated with the possible sale of the entire portfolio at the end of the portfolio horizon, $t = M$. If a liquidating transaction were calculated and charged solely to time period M, there would be a large negative impact on the performance of this last period. Another reason not to take this liquidation cost is that the portfolio may continue to be invested after the time period M. The size of such a final cost to liquidate the portfolio does have something to do with portfolio optimization because its value depends on the size the portfolio grows to. Despite this observation, for the other reasons given it will not be included in this formulation.

The range of realistic costs for CP_j and CN_j are reported by Clarke, FitzGerald, Berent, and Statman (1989) as 0.1 percent each way if futures are used as the investment instrument and 1.0 percent each way when using physicals. Kester (1990) indicates that for large professional stock funds 0.25 percent is possible for large funds and as much as 2.0 percent is incurred by small investors. From current commonly available commission rates, for stock transactions involving $25,000 or more, the one-way cost is near 0.5 percent. Pesaran and Timmerman (1994) report that the transaction cost for bonds is close to zero. They also find that the transaction cost for stocks is approximately 0.5 percent for institutional investors and 1.0 percent for small private investors.

The total return per period over all investments including the cost of borrowing plus purchase and sales transaction costs is

$$R_t = \left(\sum_{j=1}^{N} AA_{jt}Y_{jt}\right) - (LEV_t - 1)I_t - \sum_{j=1}^{N} DP_{jt}CP_j$$

$$- \sum_{j=1}^{N} DN_{jt}CN_j \tag{10-7}$$

Performance Deviation Constraint

The splitting of the performance above and below the threshold level into a positive and negative component as shown in (10–1) must be defined as a formal constraint. The values of V_t and Z_t are treated as unknowns in the linear programming formulation. This equation is repeated here to emphasize that it is a true constraint of the model formulation. For each time period t:

$$R_t - T_t = +V_t - Z_t \tag{10-8}$$

Allocation Summation Constraint

For each time period t, the sum of allocations across each of the j investments must equal that period's leverage ratio, LEV_t. In an unleveraged situation, the sum of the allocations would simply be 1.

$$\sum_{j=1}^{N} AA_{jt} = LEV_t \tag{10-9}$$

Although it is not a part of the formulation of the model, combining equations (10–3) and (10–9) produces the following two useful results.

$$\sum_{j=1}^{N} A_j = C \tag{10-10}$$

and for each factor k

$$\sum_{j=1}^{N} B_{kj} = D_k \qquad (10\text{--}11)$$

Equation (10–11) indicates that a change in the allocation to investment j due to the change in factor k must be offset by changes in the allocations to one or more other investments. The sum of all changes in allocation due to a change in factor k must be zero across all investments if there is no change in leverage.

Average Portfolio Return Constraint over All Time Periods

The average portfolio return over all time periods R_{avg} is the simple average of the portfolio returns for each time period R_t. Since there are M time periods, the average portfolio return is

$$R_{avg} = \frac{1}{M}\sum_{t=1}^{M} R_t \qquad (10\text{--}12)$$

When minimizing the objective function (10–2), the value of R_{avg} is a specified value within the range of feasible average portfolio returns.

Asset Allocation Upper Bounds

The asset allocation upper bound for each investment j must be less than or equal to the same maximum proportion of the leverage ratio for each time period t. The upper bounds are not strictly constants. They are constants $amax_j$ multiplied by the leverage ratio LEV_t in effect for the time period t.

$$AA_{jt} \le amax_j LEV_t \qquad (10\text{--}13)$$

Asset Allocation Lower Bounds

The asset allocation lower bound for each investment j must be greater than or equal to the same minimum proportion of the leverage ratio for each time period t. The lower bounds are not strictly constants. They are constants $amin_j$ multiplied by the leverage ratio LEV_t in effect for the time period t.

$$AA_{jt} \geq amin_j LEV_t \qquad (10\text{–}14)$$

Leverage Ratio Upper Bounds

The leverage ratio at each time period t must be less than or equal to a specified leverage upper bound, LEV_{max}.

$$LEV_t \leq LEV_{max} \qquad (10\text{–}15)$$

Leverage Ratio Lower Bounds

The leverage ratio at each time period t must be greater than or equal to a specified leverage lower bound, LEV_{min}. The value of LEV_{min} should never be specified less than 1.

$$LEV_t \geq LEV_{min} \qquad (10\text{–}16)$$

The problem is to find the values of the unknown A_j, B_{kj}, C, D_k, DP_{jt}, DN_{jt}, V_t, and Z_t such that all constraints and bounds (10–3) to (10–9) and (10–12) to (10–16) are satisfied and the objective function (10–2) is minimized.

Solving the linear programming problem represented by these equations results in the determination of one point along an efficient frontier. Other points along the efficient frontier can be determined by selecting other feasible values for the average portfolio return. The maximum possible portfolio return can be determined by solving a separate linear program in which equation (10–2) is ignored and equation (10–12) is maximized. Similarly, the minimum portfolio return can be determined by solving a linear program in which equation (10–2) is ignored and equation (10–12) is minimized.

DYNAPORTE ADVANTAGES

Compared with other dynamic portfolio optimization models, DynaPorte is capable of handling very large problems in terms of the number of investments, the number of factors, and the number of explicit time periods. This occurs because the model is formulated as a linear program. The computational speed and power of linear programming are brought to bear on a problem that may contain thousands of variables and constraints.

Since there are N investments, M time periods, and K macroeconomic factors, the number of unknown variables in the formulation (assuming upper and lower bounds, leverage, and transaction costs are all in effect), A_j, B_{kj}, C, D_k, DP_{jt}, DN_{jt}, V_t, Z_t, AA_{jt}, DEL_{jt}, and R_t is

$$6MN + 4M + (N+1)(K+1) \qquad (10\text{--}17)$$

The number of constraints in the formulation, in equations (10–3) to (10–9), and in (10–12) to (10–16) is

$$5MN + 6M + 1 \qquad (10\text{--}18)$$

For a problem with $N = 6$ investments, $K = 10$ factors, and $M = 500$ time periods, this would result in 20,077 unknowns and 18,001 constraint equations. By linear programming standards this is a relatively easy problem to solve. If the objective function were nonlinear, this problem size would present more of a challenge.

Another advantage of the DynaPorte formulation is that there is no requirement or prohibition on the shape of the investment performance distributions or the macroeconomic factor value distributions. Since the formulation deals directly with the periodic investment returns Y_{jt} and the macroeconomic factor values F_{kt}, there are no restrictions on the distributions from which the Y_{jt} and F_{kt} are drawn. There is also no need to utilize second or higher moments of these distributions.

At first, it might seem unusual that there is no direct analog for the correlation matrix in the DynaPorte formulation. The linkage between the performance of one investment and the performance of another investment is controlled through the nature of the allocation equations that are functions of the macroeconomic factors. If the change in one factor causes a number of investments to increase in allocation, then there must be an offsetting decrease in allocation to one or more other investments, in accordance with equation (10–11). This linkage takes the place of the correlation matrix used in the Markowitz mean-variance formulation.

DYNAPORTE SHORTCOMINGS

No model is a perfect representation of the system it describes. These are always assumptions and simplifications in a model structure. Several of the shortcomings of the DynaPorte formulation are worth noting. The first possible shortcoming is that the true impact of the macroeconomic factors may be nonlinear. There are two ways around this difficulty. Either formulate the problem as a nonlinear model and then use nonlinear optimization techniques or structure the problem so that the asset allocation functions of the macroeconomic factors are piecewise linear. Neither one of these approaches will be undertaken in this book.

Another possible shortcoming is based on the comparison of estimation error between the mean absolute deviation (MAD) model and the Markowitz mean-variance (MV) model. Simaan (1997) defines estimation error as the difference between a known average return of a portfolio and a random sample of n monthly returns. Simaan shows that for normally distributed returns the MV model has a lower estimation error than the MAD model for small values of n and for investors with high risk tolerance. Simaan demonstrates that there is a clear advantage to the MV model when $n = 30$ as measured by an opportunity cost of 2.43 percent per year. When $n = 120$ this opportunity cost diminishes to 0.34 percent per year. Fortunately, for the number of time periods recommended for the DynaPorte formulation, from $n = 240$ to $n = 600$, the effect of this type of estimation error should be minimal.

The next shortcoming has to do with the allocation functions themselves. For each historical time period used to fit the model, the allocation to each investment will lie between the chosen upper and lower bounds. Furthermore, in the time interval over which the model is developed, the sum of allocations for each time period is constrained to sum to the value LEV_t. Assuming that there is a feasible solution for the target return R_{avg} then these constraints are guaranteed to be satisfied for every time period used to develop the coefficients. When the allocation equations are used as a forecasting tool, these constraints can fail. Future values of the macroeconomic factors can lead to asset allocations that do not satisfy these constraints. When this occurs, certain renormalization processes can be applied to alter the projected allocations to satisfy the constraints.

An additional shortcoming is the failure to deal with minimum transaction sizes. For a selected investment, the change in allocation between one time period and the next might be a very small change. Placing an order to implement this change in the portfolio could conflict with a minimum order-size restriction. Or it might incur a punitive transaction cost per unit. Including a constraint to deal with minimum transaction sizes can lead to a requirement for an integer programming approach. Such an approach would add dramatically to the solution time for the problem sizes considered here. For a model allowing the inclusion of minimum transaction sizes, see Perold (1984).

A final shortcoming of the DynaPorte formulation has to do with the implementation of the transaction costs. The costs are assumed to be a constant percentage of the change in allocated assets at each time period irrespective of the size of the allocation change. These costs per unit may not always be constant. There could be a series of volume discounts for large transactions. There could also be a fixed cost associated with a minimum transaction size.

REVIEW

Despite the potential shortcomings mentioned above, the capabilities of the DynaPorte formulation should provide a very workable approach to a complex dynamic portfolio problem. Practically, portfolios up to 50 investments can be considered for reasonable solution times. And as many as 50 macroeconomic variables might be included to influence the changing asset allocations. As many as 600 months of history could be used to determine the unknown model variables. Leveraging is allowed, and the cost of leveraging is included in the periodic returns. Linear transaction costs are incorporated for both new purchase and new sales transactions each month. The inclusion of nonzero transaction costs can add substantially to the required solution times due to the number of new variables and constraints added to the model. The discovery and evaluation of the influential factors on the time-varying asset allocations would seem to make DynaPorte a practical portfolio development and maintenance methodology.

DynaPorte is an approach for determining asset allocation functions that will fit historical data. It can be used as a forecasting tool by using the generated equations on an out-of-sample basis. It differs both in form and in intention from the multiperiod portfolio theory discussed in Chapter 9. DynaPorte contains a methodology for determining the asset allocation functions in a way that minimizes the impact of performance below a selected target return.

REFERENCES

Brandt, Michael W. "Estimating Portfolio and Consumption Choice: A Conditional Euler Equations Approach." *Journal of Finance* 54, no. 5 (October 1999): 1609–1645.

Campbell, Yeung, Lewis Chan, and Luis M. Viceira. "A Multivariate Model of Strategic Asset Allocation." *Journal of Financial Economics* 100 (January 2003).

Clarke, Roger G., Michael T. FitzGerald, Philip Berent, and Meir Statman. "Market Timing with Imperfect Information." *Financial Analysts Journal* (November–December 1989): 27–36.

Feinstein, Charles D., and Mukund N. Thapa. "Notes: A Reformulation of a Mean-Absolute Deviation Portfolio Optimization Model." *Management Science* 39, no. 12 (December 1993): 1552–1553.

Haimowitz, Joseph H. "The Longevity of Expansions." *Federal Reserve Bank of Kansas City Economic Review* (Fourth Quarter 1998): 13–34.

Kester, George W. "Market Timing with Small versus Large-Firm Stocks: Potential Gains and Required Predictive Ability." *Financial Analysts Journal* (September–October 1990): 63–69.

Konno, Hiroshi, and Hiroaki Yamazaki. "Mean-Absolute Deviation Portfolio Optimization Model and Its Applications to Tokyo Stock Market." *Management Science* 37, no. 5 (May 1991): 519–531.

Perold, Andre F. "Large-Scale Portfolio Optimization." *Management Science* 30, no. 10 (October 1984): 1143–1160.

Pesaran, M. Hashem, and Allan Timmermann. "Forecasting Stock Returns: An Examination of Stock Market Trading in the Presence of Transaction Costs." *Journal of Forecasting* 13 (1994): 335–367.

Robertsson, Göran. "Conditioning Information in Tactical Asset Allocation." Working paper, Department of Finance, Stockholm School of Economics, Stockholm (September 2000).

Simaan, Yusif. "Estimation Risk in Portfolio Selection: The Mean Variance Model versus the Mean Absolute Deviation Model." *Management Science* 43, no. 10. (October 1997): 1437–1446.

Zenios, Stavros A., and Pan Kang. "Mean-Absolute Deviation Portfolio Optimization for Mortgaged-Backed Securities." *Annals of Operations Research* 45 (1993): 433–450.

DynaPorte™ Model Examples

> The most advanced nations are always those who navigate the most.
>
> *Ralph Waldo Emerson*
> *Society and Solitude (1870)*

In this chapter, the DynaPorte model is applied to a number of investment portfolios. Many of the portfolios are evaluated over the interval of 1980 to 2001. This 22-year range of data should provide sufficient opportunity for discovery of relationships between investment returns and the macroeconomic factors considered to affect them. Using a longer time interval is possible but not advisable. There are suitable data back to 1960 to almost double the number of data points evaluated. However, it is felt that the impact of market participants and the influence of the Federal Reserve Board were not consistent over the longer interval of 1960 to 2001. The influence of day traders, especially during the 1990s, has likely intensified the reaction of the stock market to certain macroeconomic factors. And as shown in Chapter 5 on interest rates, the factors influencing the Fed's policy reaction function were certainly not the same before and after the early 1980s. For these reasons, it seems best to build models to project performance after 1999 from data no further back than 1980.

In this chapter, we evaluate a number of portfolio combinations involving stocks, bonds, and cash. Each combination of investments considered would normally present a challenge to discover the logical set of macroeconomic factors that seem to influence the investment returns. In order to avoid confounding the results by using changing factors as well as changing investments, the factor set is held constant for most of the investment combinations considered. This isolates the impact on the portfolio performance attainable to just the changing investment combinations.

For each combination of investments, the unleveraged asset allocation solution targeting the highest return is obtained. In addition to the average return generated for each portfolio, various measures of risk are also reported. These statistical measures are considered sufficient to summarize the nature of the portfolio performance.

U.S. STOCKS AND T-BILLS MODEL

The first portfolio considered is the same one employed by most of the market timing evaluations presented in Chapter 8. This portfolio consists of large-cap stocks, represented by the S&P 500 index with dividends reinvested, and a cash component, represented by 90-day U.S. Treasury bills. Using the DynaPorte solution incorporating time-varying fractional allocations allows us to compare the results of dynamic asset allocation with those of the market timing methodologies requiring 100 percent allocation to either stocks or cash at each month. This investment combination grossly underutilizes the power of the DynaPorte formulation since it only involves two investments. The main reason for generating such a simplified portfolio is to provide a comparison against market timing solutions that involve 100 percent switching. This simplistic portfolio will also be used as a gauge to measure the effectiveness of other portfolios containing different combinations of stock and bond investment types. Data are used from January 1980 to December 2001.

The macroeconomic factors used are based on factors found influential on stocks, bonds, and T-bills as identified in previous chapters. The precise set of factors employed for this first model is shown in Table 11–1. This same set of factors will also be employed for other models to follow.

T A B L E   11-1

Macroeconomic Factors Used in Stocks, Bonds, T-Bills
Optimizations

Factor Name	Factor Description	Begin Lag	End Lag	Operator
Div. yield (1, 1)	S&P composite common stock: dividend yield	1	1	
Div. yield (2, 17)	S&P composite common stock: dividend yield	2	17	Average
T-bill (1, 3)	Treasury bills, 90 days, yield	1	3	Average
T-bill (4, 21)	Treasury bills, 90 days, yield	4	21	Average
S&P 500 (1, 23)	S&P 500, price only, 1-month return	1	23	Average
Baa − 10 yr (1, 2)	Baa corporate bond yield − 10-year government bond yield	1	2	Average
Cap. util. (1, 2)	Capacity utilization, manufacturing	1	2	Average
Cap. util. (3, 17)	Capacity utilization, manufacturing	3	17	Average
Indus. cap. (1, 2)	Industrial capacity, manufacturing 6-month percent change	1	2	Average
5-yr. bond (1, 1)	5-year Treasury bond yield	1	1	
Baa − Aaa (1, 8)	Baa corporate bond yield − Aaa corporate bond yield	1	8	Average
Baa − Aaa (9, 21)	Baa corporate bond yield − Aaa corporate bond yield	9	21	Average
January	January Boolean	0	0	
GDP defl. (1, 60)	12-month percent change in GDP implicit price deflator	1	60	Average
Unemploy. (1, 6)	Unemployment rate, civilian labor	1	6	Average
M3 chg. (1, 60)	M3 money supply, 12-month percent change	1	60	Average

All the factors in Table 11–1 except the January Boolean involve a time lag of at least 1 month in order to develop true forecasting models. Those factors involving a lag range greater than 1 month indicate that the factor is to be averaged over the months specified. For example, the factor T-bill (4, 21) is the T-bill rate averaged from 4 months ago to 21 months ago when determining the allocations for the current month. The January Boolean has a value of 1 in all months that are January and 0 for all other months. This factor does not require a lag for forecasting purposes because the timing of the occurrence of January is always known with certainty.

Many of the factors employed in this model are similar to factors affecting the 1-month regression returns of stocks and T-bills. The factor S&P 500 (1, 23) is a stock market mean-reversion factor. The factors Baa − 10 yr. (1, 2), Baa − Aaa (1, 8), and Baa − Aaa (9, 21) are credit spreads.

The selection of the specific lag range for each factor is determined by experimentation. The lags for factors developed through regression analysis are generally tried first. A range of lags near the regression lags are investigated for their impact on portfolio return as well as portfolio risk.

The resulting coefficients for the asset allocation functions in the stocks, T-bills model are displayed in Table 11–2. For this model, the coefficients are determined by maximizing the average

T A B L E 11-2

Stocks, T-Bills Model Asset Allocation Coefficients

Factor Name	Stocks Coefficient	T-Bills Coefficient	Factor Impact
Constant coefficient (alpha)	33.5250	66.4750	
Div. yield (1, 1)	56.2398	− 56.2398	294.1342
Div. yield (2, 17)	3.4911	− 3.4911	16.1746
T-bill (1, 3)	− 4.1918	4.1918	54.9266
T-bill (4, 21)	7.2626	− 7.2626	78.4607
S&P 500 (1, 23)	− 17.9470	17.9470	67.3785
Baa − 10 yr. (1, 2)	− 19.8372	19.8372	49.3947
Cap. util. (1, 2)	10.7989	− 10.7989	174.3324
Cap. util. (3, 17)	− 10.5225	10.5225	150.9156
Indus. cap. (1, 2)	32.4859	− 32.4859	112.8799
5-yr. bond (1, 1)	− 24.1633	24.1633	290.4427
Baa − Aaa (1, 8)	78.6262	− 78.6262	146.8344
Baa − Aaa (9, 21)	− 41.3193	41.3193	71.7685
January	2.7129	− 2.7129	2.7129
GDP defl. (1, 60)	− 15.4059	15.4059	98.7968
Unemploy. (1, 6)	1.0437	− 1.0437	6.7839
M3 chg. (1, 60)	1.8339	− 1.8339	18.3172

monthly arithmetic return irrespective of the risk levels involved. No leverage is employed in this model, and all allocations are limited to the range of 0 to 100 percent. A transaction cost is charged to changes in stocks allocations equal to 0.25 percent of the allocation change on both buy and sell transactions. No transaction cost is charged to changes in T-bills allocations. Note that in accordance with equation 10–10 from Chapter 10, the two constant (alpha) coefficients must sum to 100 since no leverage is employed. Similarly, the factor coefficients in each row must sum to zero in accordance with equation 10–11. In this chapter, all asset allocations are expressed as percentages, in the range of 0–100 percent and higher if leveraged. The original formulation in Chapter 10 treats allocations as fractions such as 0.0–1.0.

It would be useful to know how significant each one of the asset allocation coefficients is. The amount that each factor can contribute to the changing asset allocations is the issue. The magnitude of the coefficient itself is somewhat useful to estimate its significance but is not sufficient on its own. The product of the coefficient and the range of that factor's values would indicate the maximum historical impact exerted by that factor. This product is reported as the *factor impact*. For example, the Aaa − Baa (1, 8) factor has an impact on stock allocations of 146.8344 from the lowest value of this factor to the highest value. The factor impact represents the largest influence that this factor has on controlling the allocation changes to stocks. This result is obtained from a highest value of Aaa − Baa (1, 8) of 2.4413 and a lowest value of 0.5737, generating a range of 1.8676. This range multiplied by the factor coefficient of 78.6262 produces a factor impact value of 146.8344. Obviously, a factor with a very small factor impact, such as Unemploy. (1, 6) at 6.7839, has little influence on the stock or T-bill allocation changes. Factors with low impact values are allowed to remain in this model because they prove to be useful in models with a wider range of investment types.

Factors with impact values greater than 100 would seem to indicate that they have an inordinate influence on the investment. For example, the factor impact for Div. yield (1, 1) has a value of 294.1342 on stocks. On its own, this would mean that this factor could change the allocation to stocks by nearly three times the maximum possible allocation to stocks. This observation would be true if movements in the factors were completely independent. When the dividend yield goes up, causing the allocation to stocks to increase, there must be some other factor related to dividend yield causing the allocation to stocks to move in the opposite direction. This must be true or the investment allocation to stocks would be pushed beyond its 0-to-100 bounds for the unleveraged case. The fact that we obtain factor impacts greater than 100 is direct evidence that the factors themselves are not independent.

The dynamic asset allocation model described by the coefficients in Table 11–2 changes the allocations to each investment on a monthly basis. For example, the dynamic allocation to stocks for this model is shown in Figure 11–1.

The allocations to stocks and T-bills change each month. These allocations provide the monthly weights to determine the portfolio return. The statistical performance of the dynamic asset allocation model returns with these changing allocations is shown in Table 11–3 along with the 100 percent buy-and-hold stock portfolio. The average annual geometric return for the dynamic model is just over 4 percent higher than the buy-and-hold return for stocks for the

F I G U R E 11–1

Allocation to Stocks for the Stock, T-Bill Model

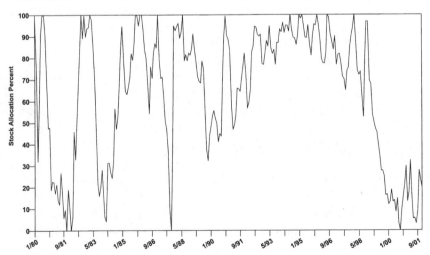

T A B L E   11-3

Statistical Performance of Dynamic Stock, T-Bills Model

Investments	Leverage Ratio	Max. or Min.	Monthly Arith. Average	Annual Geo. Average	Annual Arith. Std. Dev.	Max. Drawdown	Annual Sharpe Ratio	Average Deviation below 0
100% stocks	1.0	None	1.2688	14.9694	15.4011	30.4919	0.5438	1.1538
100% T-bills	1.0	None	0.5339	6.5948	0.7817	0.0	N/A	0.0
Dynamic stocks, T-bills	1.0	Max.	1.5059	19.1071	9.7022	7.9711	1.2896	0.4083

1980–2001 time interval. This compares favorably with the typical excess returns of 2 to 3 percent experienced by the market timing models using modest transaction costs as reported in Table 8–13 in Chapter 8. The maximum drawdown for the dynamic model is notably lower than for the stock portfolio. In fact, all the dynamic model risk measures dominate the risk values for the 100 percent stock portfolio. Considering that only two investments are available to the dynamic portfolio, this is a promising result for such a simple investment pair.

The growth of the dynamic portfolio and the pure stock portfolio is shown in Figure 11–2. Note that the dynamic portfolio

F I G U R E   11-2

Growth of $1 for the Dynamic Stock, T-Bills Model *vs* 100% Stocks

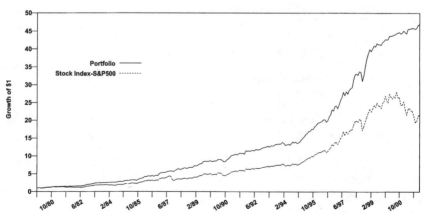

continues to grow after 1999 due to the strong reduction in the stock allocation after this time.

STOCKS, BONDS, AND T-BILLS MODEL

This model is an extension of the first model. Long-term government bonds are simply added to the portfolio. The total monthly return on long-term government bonds with a duration greater than 10 years is provided by Merrill Lynch.

An optimal dynamic portfolio is constructed using the same factors described in Table 11–1. By keeping the factors the same as the ones used for stocks and T-bills, the difference in performance between the two models can be attributed to the expanded investment set. Or it can be attributed to the difference in the ability of the factors to control the allocations to the expanded investment set.

The allocation factor model is derived using the following conditions:

The maximum achievable average monthly arithmetic return is targeted.

No leverage is employed.

Stock transaction costs are 0.25 percent for both purchases and sales.

Bond transaction costs are 0.10 percent for both purchases and sales.

No transaction cost is applied to T-bills.

Allocations for each investment are allowed to range from 0 to 100 percent.

The date range of monthly data employed is January 1980 to December 2001.

The coefficients for the three asset allocation functions of stocks, bonds, and T-bills for a model targeting maximum performance are shown in Table 11–4. Note that the factor coefficients for T-bills are all zero. This indicates that, for this

T A B L E   11-4

Stocks, Bonds, and T-Bills Model Maximum Performance
Coefficients

Factor Name	Stocks Coefficient	Govt. Bond Coefficient	T-Bills Coefficient	Maximum Impact
Constant coefficient	496.6958	−396.6958	0.0000	
Div. yield (1, 1)	66.0282	−66.0282	0.0000	345.3277
Div. yield (2, 17)	−10.3793	10.3793	0.0000	48.0885
T-bill (1, 3)	−3.7911	3.7911	0.0000	49.6754
T-bill (4, 21)	6.7481	−6.7481	0.0000	72.9023
S&P 500 (1, 23)	−7.4414	7.4414	0.0000	27.9372
Baa − 10 yr. (1, 2)	−30.1993	30.1993	0.0000	75.1962
Cap. util. (1, 2)	9.9930	−9.9930	0.0000	161.3224
Cap. util. (3, 17)	−12.9910	12.9910	0.0000	186.3193
Indus. cap. (1, 2)	24.2063	−24.2063	0.0000	84.1103
5-yr. bond (1,1)	−34.7731	34.7731	0.0000	417.9724
Baa − Aaa (1, 8)	161.3313	−161.3313	0.0000	301.2861
Baa − Aaa (9, 21)	1.8904	−1.8904	0.0000	3.2835
January	5.8113	−5.8113	0.0000	5.8113
GDP defl. (1, 60)	5.5303	−5.5303	0.0000	35.4656
Unemploy. (1, 6)	−35.7290	35.7290	0.0000	232.2387
M3 chg. (1, 60)	−7.9931	7.9931	0.0000	79.8365

maximum-return portfolio, no allocation is given to T-bills in any month from January 1980 to December 2001. The fact that there is no allocation to T-bills for the maximum-return portfolio does not mean that this investment would never be used at target rates of return less than the maximum return attainable. In fact, T-bills generally are used at other rates of return. Their absence from the maximum-return portfolio is an artifact of targeting the highest portfolio return and the fact that T-bills have the lowest rate of return of the three investments.

This turns out to be a very simple dynamic asset allocation model. Assets are shifted from stocks to bonds and back again to stocks as the values of the factors change. The dynamic allocation functions defined in Table 11-4 determine the allocations for each month of history. Because this is an unleveraged portfolio, the sum across investments of the constant coefficients is 100, and the sum of the coefficients for each factor is zero.

The "Maximum Impact" column reports the largest factor impact value evaluated over each of the investments. Factors with maximum impact less than 10 can typically be removed from any model with little detrimental effect. Factors with maximum impact greater than 50 would seriously affect the portfolio performance if removed from any model. The resulting dynamic allocation to stocks is shown in Figure 11–3.

The allocations given to stocks as shown in Figure 11–3 are similar, but not identical, to the stock allocations shown in Table 11–1. The statistical performance of the dynamic asset allocation model with these changing allocations is shown in the last row of Table 11–5 along with the 100 percent buy-and-hold investments and the performance of the dynamic stock, T-bills model for comparison. The maximum-performance dynamic model of stocks, bonds, and T-bills increases the excess return over 100 percent stocks by another 1.13 percent to a total excess return of 5.27 percent. While this increase in return suffers a little more risk compared with the stock, T-bills model, the new model still has much lower risk levels than 100 percent stocks. Nonetheless, the

F I G U R E 11–3

Maximum Performance Asset Allocation to Stocks in Stocks, Bonds, T-Bills Model

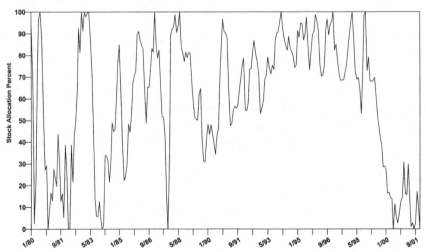

T A B L E 11–5

Statistical Performance of Dynamic Stocks, Bonds, T-Bills
Model

Investments	Leverage Ratio	Max. or Min.	Monthly Arith. Average	Annual Geo. Average	Annual Arith. Std. Dev.	Max. Drawdown	Annual Sharpe Ratio	Average Deviation below 0
100% stocks	1.0	None	1.2688	14.9694	15.4011	30.4919	0.5438	1.1538
100% government bonds	1.0	None	0.9057	10.7827	10.9256	19.2140	0.3833	0.7890
100% T-bills	1.0	None	0.5339	6.5948	0.7817	0.0	N/A	0.0
Dynamic stocks, T-bills	1.0	Max.	1.5059	19.1071	9.7022	7.9711	1.2896	0.4083
Dynamic stocks, bonds, T-bills	1.0	Max.	1.6018	20.2378	11.5479	10.6956	1.1814	0.6435

stocks–bonds portfolio, as shown in Figure 11–4 grows to a
significantly higher level of terminal wealth than the stocks–T-bills
portfolio.

All the dynamic portfolios determined to this point are based
on *in-sample* evaluations. That is, they only involve the *fitting* of
models. It would be worthwhile to determine how well a dynamic
model can forecast *out of sample*. To measure the success of the

F I G U R E 11–4

Growth of $1 for Dynamic Stocks, Bonds, T-Bills Model *vs*
100% Stocks

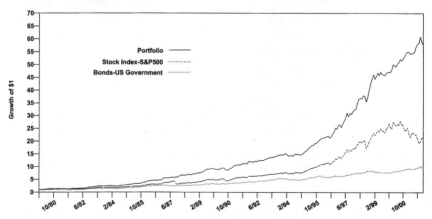

dynamic model, we need another asset allocation procedure to compare against. An experiment using stocks, bonds, and T-bills is designed to compare the forecasting performance of an out-of-sample dynamic model against an out-of-sample Markowitz model using an expanding data procedure. The procedure consists of the following steps:

Use historical monthly data from 1980 to 1985 to fit a maximum-return dynamic factor model based only on these data.

Record the standard deviation of this model as a measure of risk for the fit time interval.

Use this model to forecast individual monthly returns for 1986. These are the forecasts from the dynamic model. The dynamic model is not revised during the 1986 calendar year.

Construct an efficient frontier for a Markowitz mean-variance model using the same historical monthly data from 1980 to 1985 to determine expected returns, standard deviations, and correlation coefficients.

Select the point from the mean-variance efficient frontier with the same standard deviation as the dynamic factor model based on the fit time interval. This imposes the same risk level on both models.

Use the mix at this point on the Markowitz mean-variance efficient frontier as out-of-sample allocations to determine the portfolio results for the next 12 months. These forecasts will be statistically compared with the forecasted dynamic model. The mean-variance model is not revised during the 1986 calendar year.

Expand the date range forward 1 year to include 1980 through 1986.

Repeat the whole process to forecast 1987 monthly returns by both models.

Continue this procedure until the date range is expanded to 1980–2000 to obtain forecasts for 2001.

T A B L E   11-6

Annualized Results of Out-of-Sample Stock, Bonds, T-Bills Model

Year to Forecast	History Used to Fit Both Models	Common Standard Deviation	100% Stocks Annual Return	Markowitz Model Return	Dynamic Model Return
1986	1980–1985	10.47	18.68	15.71	17.92
1987	1980–1986	10.61	5.27	5.25	7.58
1988	1980–1987	11.37	16.61	12.59	14.91
1989	1980–1988	11.24	31.68	24.23	29.16
1990	1980–1989	11.07	−3.12	1.03	3.66
1991	1980–1990	11.02	30.47	23.00	20.63
1992	1980–1991	10.88	7.64	7.16	3.40
1993	1980–1992	10.71	10.08	11.33	15.13
1994	1980–1993	10.52	1.32	−1.93	−5.41
1995	1980–1994	10.37	37.59	30.49	27.87
1996	1980–1995	11.21	22.96	12.99	20.71
1997	1980–1996	10.28	33.38	24.32	25.37
1998	1980–1997	11.86	28.57	24.42	32.72
1999	1980–1998	11.99	21.03	11.10	6.14
2000	1980–1999	11.90	−9.09	−3.12	5.25
2001	1980–2000	11.64	−11.88	−5.87	6.09

Table 11–6 displays the annualized returns generated from this procedure. Note that the performance of 100 percent stocks is included as a benchmark.

The question is whether one model forecasts better than the other. Neither model consistently dominates the other based on annual returns. Only more detailed performance statistics will provide the answer, as shown in Table 11–7. The Markowitz model and the dynamic model target the same standard deviation on an in-sample basis. It appears that the dynamic model results in lower out-of-sample standard deviations than the Markowitz model. The expanding dynamic model adds 2.42 percent return per year on average over the expanding Markowitz forecasting procedure. The dynamic model has nearly the same return as the pure stock portfolio. But the risk measures for the dynamic model are much better than those for the Markowitz approach or 100 percent stocks. The difference between the dynamic model and the Markowitz model is actually larger than shown. Transaction costs are charged

T A B L E   11-7

Statistical Comparison of Out-of-Sample Models (1986–
2001)

Investments	Monthly Arith. Average	Annual Geo. Average	Annual Arith. Std. Dev.	Max. Drawdown	Annual Sharpe Ratio	Average Deviation below 0
100% stocks	1.21	14.05	15.72	30.49	0.47	2.94
Markowitz mean-variance model	0.96	11.52	10.57	18.91	0.47	1.85
Dynamic factor model	1.13	13.94	9.06	11.21	0.81	1.35

for the evaluation of the dynamic model, and no transaction costs
are charged against the annual dynamic changes associated with
the Markowitz model.

Any success that the dynamic model might have depends
completely on how well the factor model performs in suggesting
asset allocation changes. A badly specified dynamic model may
show promise on an in-sample basis but is sure to perform poorly
on an out-of-sample basis. The factors in the model need to be
fundamentally sound in order to generate successful forecasts.

TWO STOCKS, TWO BONDS, AND T-BILLS MODEL

The third portfolio evaluated consists of growth stocks, value
stocks, government bonds, corporate bonds, and T-bills. The
indices used to represent these investment categories are the
Wilshire large-cap growth index, the Wilshire large-cap value
index, long-term U.S. government bond returns, A-rated corporate
bond returns, and 90-day U.S. Treasury bills. An optimal dynamic
portfolio is constructed using the same factors described in Table
11-1.

The allocation factor model is derived using the following
conditions:

The maximum achievable average monthly arithmetic return
is targeted.

No leverage is employed initially.

Additional evaluations are conducted at a maximum of 50 percent leverage.

Stock transaction costs are 0.25 percent for both purchases and sales.

Bond transaction costs are 0.10 percent for both purchases and sales.

No transaction cost is applied to T-bills.

Allocations for each investment are allowed to range from 0 to 100 percent.

The date range of monthly data employed is January 1980 to December 2001.

The coefficients for the five asset allocation functions of stocks, bonds, and T-bills for a model targeting maximum performance are shown in Table 11–8. Note that the factor coefficients for corporate bonds and T-bills are all zero. This indicates that, for this maximum-return portfolio, no allocation is given to corporate bonds or to T-bills in any month from January 1980 to December 2001. Just as the maximum-performance stocks, bonds, and T-bills model gave no allocation to T-bills, this does not mean that these two investments would never be used at other target rates of return.

The dynamic allocation functions defined in Table 11–8 determine the allocations for each month of history. Again, the sum across investments of the constant coefficients is 100, and the sum of the coefficients for each factor is zero. The resulting allocations to growth stocks, value stocks, and government bonds are shown in Figure 11–5.

Employing these dynamic asset allocations leads to portfolio performance characteristics that dramatically outperform each of the underlying individual investments when employed on a buy-and-hold basis. Table 11–9 contains the performance statistics on the individual investments as well as the dynamic portfolio. The dynamic portfolio outperforms the best of the underlying investments by over 6.5 percent on an annual return basis. The portfolio risk measures clearly outperform those for the stock

T A B L E   11-8

Two Stocks, Two Bonds, and T-Bills Model Maximum-Performance Coefficients

Factor Name	Growth Stock Coefficient	Value Stock Coefficient	Govt. Bond Coefficient	Corp. Bond Coefficient	Treasury Bills Coefficient	Maximum Impact
Constant coefficient	1473.1324	−595.5569	−777.5755	0.0000	0.0000	
Div. yield (1, 1)	62.2058	1.1124	−63.3181	0.0000	0.0000	331.1538
Div. yield (2, 17)	27.5489	−20.5066	−7.0423	0.0000	0.0000	127.6374
T-bill (1, 3)	−7.8013	1.4898	6.3115	0.0000	0.0000	102.2230
T-bill (4, 21)	12.2232	−5.8116	−6.4117	0.0000	0.0000	132.0515
S&P 500 (1, 23)	0.1787	−5.5413	5.3626	0.0000	0.0000	20.8039
Baa − 10 yr. (1, 2)	−25.3264	−5.0065	30.333	0.0000	0.0000	75.5291
Cap. util. (1, 2)	6.9005	1.9652	−8.8656	0.0000	0.0000	143.1224
Cap. util. (3, 17)	−21.7295	5.7405	15.989	0.0000	0.0000	311.6485
Indus. cap. (1, 2)	29.4388	−5.1042	−24.3346	0.0000	0.0000	102.2919
5-yr. bond (1, 1)	−26.6137	−5.8038	32.4175	0.0000	0.0000	389.6585
Baa − Aaa (1, 8)	121.1385	26.585	−147.7235	0.0000	0.0000	275.8737
Baa − Aaa (9, 21)	−25.9125	32.1808	−6.2683	0.0000	0.0000	55.8957
January	4.2881	−1.8758	−2.4123	0.0000	0.0000	4.2881
GDP defl. (1, 60)	−7.7087	13.0645	−5.3558	0.0000	0.0000	83.7814
Unemploy. (1, 6)	−58.3989	9.6626	48.7364	0.0000	0.0000	379.5931
M3 chg. (1, 60)	−6.1409	−2.6962	8.8371	0.0000	0.0000	88.2561

F I G U R E 11-5

Maximum Performance Dynamic Asset Allocations in the Two Stocks, Two Bonds, T-Bills Model

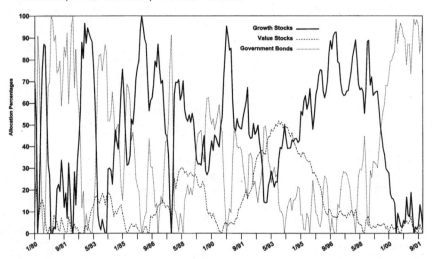

T A B L E 11-9

Maximum Unleveraged Performance of Dynamic Two Stocks, Two Bonds, T-Bills Model

Investments	Leverage Ratio	Max. or Min.	Monthly Arith. Average	Annual Geo. Average	Annual Arith. Std. Dev.	Max Drawdown	Annual Sharpe Ratio	Average Deviation below 0
100% growth stocks	1.0	None	1.2146	13.7053	18.1334	50.9926	0.3921	1.4672
100% value stocks	1.0	None	1.2261	14.5257	14.5935	27.7567	0.5435	1.0667
100% govt. bonds	1.0	None	0.9057	10.7827	10.9256	19.2140	0.3833	0.7890
100% corp. bonds	1.0	None	0.8581	10.4964	7.4864	14.0197	0.5212	0.4146
100% T-bills	1.0	None	0.5339	6.5948	0.7817	0.0	N/A	0.0
Dynamic 2 stocks, 2 bonds, T-bills	1.0	Max.	1.6686	21.1251	12.0139	11.5715	1.2095	0.6721

F I G U R E   11-6

Growth of $1 for the Maximum Unleveraged Two Stocks, Two Bonds, T-Bills Model

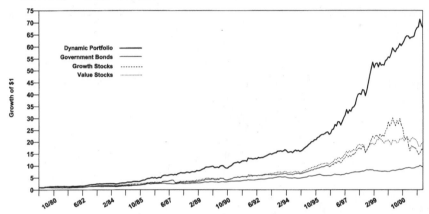

components. Except for standard deviation, the portfolio risk measures even outperform the risk statistics for government bonds.

Since the dynamic asset allocation switches to more than an 80 percent allocation to government bonds after late 1999, the portfolio does not suffer from the severe stock market losses during 2000 and 2001. This is evident from the graph showing growth of $1 in Figure 11-6.

Because the statistical performance of the unleveraged model shown in Table 11-8 so strongly dominates each of the underlying investments, it is tempting to evaluate the performance of a leveraged portfolio. In a leveraged portfolio, both the return and risk characteristics will be increased. The question is whether the increase in return justifies the increase in risk. It is assumed that riskless borrowing can be obtained at 0.75 percent above the broker call rate charged by investment firms to loan money to their customers investing on margin. According to regulations, up to 50 percent of the value of the portfolio can be borrowed. With borrowing at this maximum, an investor could be subject to margin calls during any unfavorable market move. To avoid most of this margin call problem, it is assumed that only 33.33 percent of the value of the portfolio is borrowed. For each $150 of invested money, $100 is provided by the investor and $50 is provided as a loan. To

T A B L E 11-10

Maximum-Leveraged Performance of a Dynamic Two Stocks, Two Bonds, T-Bills Model

Investments	Leverage Ratio	Max. or Min.	Monthly Arith. Average	Annual Geo. Average	Annual Arith. Std. Dev.	Max Drawdown	Annual Sharpe Ratio	Average Deviation below 0
100% growth stocks	1.0	None	1.2146	13.7053	18.1334	50.9926	0.3921	1.4672
100% value stocks	1.0	None	1.2261	14.5257	14.5935	27.7567	0.5435	1.0667
100% govt. bonds	1.0	None	0.9057	10.7827	10.9256	19.2140	0.3833	0.7890
100% corp. bonds	1.0	None	0.8581	10.4964	7.4864	14.0197	0.5212	0.4146
100% T-bills	1.0	None	0.5339	6.5948	0.7817	0.0	N/A	0.0
Dynamic stocks, bonds, T-bills	1.0	Max.	1.6686	21.1251	12.0139	11.5715	1.2095	0.6721
Dynamic stocks, bonds, T-bills	1.5	Max.	2.1367	27.1294	16.9975	16.6387	1.2081	0.9897

achieve this, a leverage ratio of 1.5 must be specified in the optimization. The result of this optimization is shown in the last row of Table 11–10. The unleveraged statistics are repeated for comparative purposes. Many investors would be willing to accept the performance of this maximum-leveraged portfolio since the annual return is 6 percent higher and the Sharpe ratio is virtually the same as the unleveraged portfolio. In addition, all the risk measures except for the arithmetic standard deviation compare favorably with the risk levels of the 100 percent stock investments.

The risk associated with this leveraged portfolio can be pared down to lower values by simply targeting lower rates of return. The coefficients generated in Table 11–8 are based on an optimization to maximize the portfolio return. It is possible to accept lower average returns as a trade-off for reducing the portfolio risk. If the average deviation below zero of the monthly performance numbers is adopted as the measure of risk, an efficient frontier of annual return versus average monthly deviation below zero can be traced out. To do this, a series of optimizations is performed. At each step, a specific annual return level is selected as a constraint. Then, the

T A B L E   11-11

Minimum Deviation Results for a Leveraged Two Stocks, Two Bonds, T-Bills Model at Various Target Returns

Investments	Leverage Ratio	Max. or Min.	Monthly Arith. Average	Annual Geo. Average	Annual Arith. Std. Dev.	Max. Drawdown	Annual Sharpe Ratio	Average Deviation below 0
Gro., Val., Govt., Corp., T-bills	1.5	Max.	2.1367	27.1294	16.9975	16.6387	1.2081	0.9897
Gro., Val., Govt., Corp., T-bills	1.5	Min.	2.1	26.9484	15.1164	11.3698	1.3465	0.7494
Gro., Val., Govt., Corp., T-bills	1.5	Min.	2.0	25.7747	13.2880	9.7696	1.4434	0.5759
Gro., Val., Govt., Corp., T-bills	1.5	Min.	1.9	24.4854	12.0612	8.7460	1.4833	0.4784
Gro., Val., Govt., Corp., T-bills	1.5	Min.	1.8	23.1643	11.0359	7.4155	1.5014	0.3952
Gro., Val., Govt., Corp., T-bills	1.5	Min.	1.7	21.8293	10.1364	6.0169	1.5029	0.3240
Gro., Val., Govt., Corp., T-bills	1.5	Min.	1.6	20.4738	9.4726	5.7680	1.4652	0.2628
Gro., Val., Govt., Corp., T-bills	1.5	Min.	1.5	19.1270	8.8056	5.2938	1.4232	0.2087
Gro., Val., Govt., Corp., T-bills	1.5	Min.	1.4	17.8043	7.9585	4.1340	1.4085	0.1610
Gro., Val., Govt., Corp., T-bills	1.5	Min.	1.3	16.4936	7.0263	3.0269	1.4088	0.1206
Gro., Val., Govt., Corp., T-bills	1.5	Min.	1.2	15.1778	6.2363	2.2970	1.3763	0.0835
Gro., Val., Govt., Corp., T-bills	1.5	Min.	1.1	13.8607	5.5863	2.4134	1.3007	0.0523
Gro., Val., Govt., Corp., T-bills	1.5	Min.	1.0	12.5608	4.7736	2.2796	1.2498	0.0284
Gro., Val., Govt., Corp., T-bills	1.5	Min.	0.9	11.2777	3.7133	1.2324	1.2611	0.0124
Gro., Val., Govt., Corp., T-bills	1.5	Min.	0.8	9.9957	2.6771	0.3736	1.2704	0.0032
Gro., Val., Govt., Corp., T-bills	1.5	Min.	0.7	8.7113	1.9305	0.0000	1.0964	0.0000

asset allocation functions are determined to minimize the average monthly deviation below zero while satisfying the return constraint. The performance statistics for optimized portfolios with monthly average returns from 2.1367 down to 0.70 are shown in Table 11–11. This is accomplished while maintaining a leverage ratio of 1.5.

In Table 11–11, the use of "Max." in the "Max. or Min." column indicates that the monthly rate of return is being maximized. The use of "Min." in this column indicates that average deviation below zero is being minimized at a target monthly return. Many of the investment portfolios below the maximum average return present attractive return-risk trade-offs. For example, the portfolio at a 2.0 monthly average return has an annual standard deviation lower than that of growth or value stocks and still generates annual returns at least 11 percent greater than stocks. Similarly, the portfolio at a 1.7 monthly average return has a standard deviation lower than that of government bonds and yet generates an annual return more than 11 percent over government bonds. In both these cases, the drawdown, Sharpe ratio, and deviation values are also better.

To make the same points graphically, Figures 11–7 to 11–10 show the efficient frontier of the leveraged portfolios using (respectively) standard deviation, maximum drawdown, Sharpe ratio, and deviation below zero as risk measures. The five underlying investments are also plotted in the risk-return space in order to show the optimized portfolio dominance over these investments. In this example, it is clear that the use of leverage along with dynamic optimization can provide higher returns and lower risk than the underlying investments used to construct the portfolio. This seems to be true irrespective of which statistical measure is selected to characterize the portfolio risk.

FOUR STOCK SECTORS, GOVERNMENT BONDS, AND CASH MODEL

In order to demonstrate the development of a more complex model, six investment categories are selected. Four of these categories represent stocks for different industrial sectors: financial services,

F I G U R E 11-7

Standard Deviation *vs* Annual Return for the Two Stocks, Two Bonds, T-Bills Model

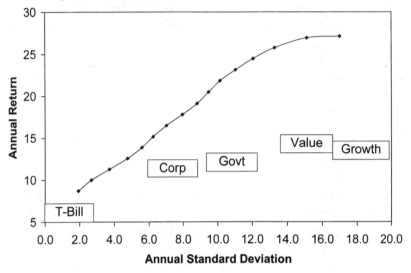

F I G U R E 11-8

Maximum Drawdown *vs* Annual Return for the Two Stocks, Two Bonds, T-Bills Model

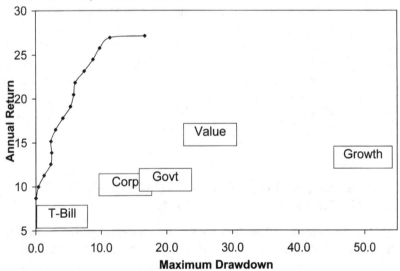

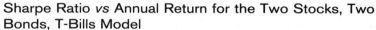

F I G U R E 11-9

Sharpe Ratio *vs* Annual Return for the Two Stocks, Two Bonds, T-Bills Model

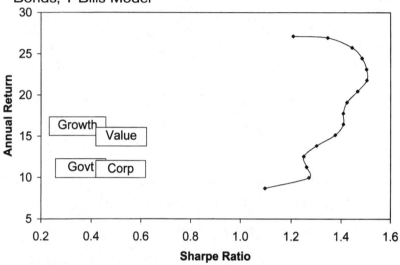

F I G U R E 11-10

Deviation below Zero *vs* Annual Return for the Two Stocks, Two Bonds, T-Bills Model

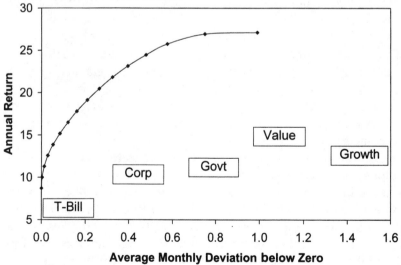

health care, technology, and utilities. Any institutional investor could easily construct portfolios of stocks representing these industrial sectors. The two other investment categories are government bonds and Treasury bills. In order to employ real-world investments representing these categories, six mutual funds are selected from the Fidelity Investments family of funds as surrogates for these six categories. The selected funds are:

Fidelity Select Financial Services Portfolio

Fidelity Select Health Care Portfolio

Fidelity Select Technology Portfolio

Fidelity Select Utilities Growth Portfolio

Fidelity Government Income Portfolio

Fidelity Cash Reserves Portfolio

These Fidelity Investments mutual funds are used because they each represent a real-world portfolio of stocks or government securities subject to actual commissions paid to maintain the portfolio. The Fidelity Select Portfolio funds for the four industrial sectors currently charge up to a 3 percent front-end load for all new capital additions and 0.75 percent trailing load for withdrawals of funds held less than 30 days. Because of transaction-size breakpoints, the front-end fees would not be charged to most institutional investors. For the purpose of this evaluation, these fees are not used, and no additional transaction costs are charged beyond the built-in commissions and the 12b-1 fees included in the mutual funds performance. This still produces a very conservative comparison against a Markowitz mean-variance model for which no transaction fees are charged at all.

The set of factors employed is based on the set used in the previous models, as shown in Table 11–1. But the factor set is altered and expanded. Some of the lags associated with the previous factors have been modified. In addition, new factors have been added. It is not surprising that additional factors would be required to control asset allocation changes among the four industrial sectors. The dividend yield for utility stocks and financial services stocks are particularly useful. The full set of factors employed in this model is shown in Table 11–12.

The allocation factor model is derived using the following conditions:

The maximum achievable average monthly arithmetic return is targeted.

One case of an unleveraged portfolio is evaluated.

A second case of leverage up to 50 percent (1.5 leverage ratio) is evaluated.

Annual interest on money borrowed is 0.75 percent above the broker call rate.

All transaction costs are 0.0 percent.

Allocations for each investment are allowed to range from 0 to 100 percent times the leverage ratio in effect for each month. This means that the sum of all allocations could be as high as 150 percent due to the availability of leverage.

The date range of monthly data employed is January 1982 to December 2001.

The coefficients for the asset allocation functions for the six investments and for the leverage function applied to a model targeting maximum performance are shown in Table 11–13.

Table 11–14 shows the average performance of each Fidelity Investments fund considered. This table also shows the average performance of the maximum-performance portfolio, both un-leveraged and leveraged. The utilities stock fund has the lowest return of the four stock funds. And the cash reserves fund has the lower return of the two securities funds. Since the coefficients displayed in Table 11–13 represent the highest-return model, it is not surprising that these two funds should receive zero allocations for all months of history for both leveraged cases.

What is surprising is the level of the average return that the DynaPorte formulation can abstract from the underlying invest-ments. Obtaining an annualized return over 35 percent for an unleveraged portfolio and 50 percent for a leveraged portfolio from

T A B L E 11-12

Macroeconomic Factors Used in Four Stock Sectors, Bonds, T-Bills Optimizations

Factor Name	Factor Description	Begin Lag	End Lag	Operator
Div. yield (1, 1)	S&P composite common stock: dividend yield	1	1	
Div. yield (2, 8)	S&P composite common stock: dividend yield	2	8	Average
T-bill (1, 4)	Treasury bills, 90 days, yield	1	4	Average
T-bill (5, 36)	Treasury bills, 90 days, yield	5	36	Average
S&P 500 (1, 23)	S&P 500, price only, 1-month return	1	23	Average
Baa − 10 yr. (1, 11)	Baa corporate bond yield − 10-year government bond yield	1	11	Average
Cap. util. (1, 2)	Capacity utilization, manufacturing	1	2	Average
Cap. util. (3, 20)	Capacity utilization, manufacturing	3	20	Average
Indus. cap. (1, 1)	Industrial capacity, manufacturing 6-month percent change	1	1	
Indus. cap. (2, 2)	Industrial capacity, manufacturing 6-month percent change	2	2	Average
5-yr. bond (1, 2)	5-year Treasury bond yield	1	2	Average
Baa − Aaa (1, 7)	Baa corporate bond yield − Aaa corporate bond yield	1	7	Average
Baa − Aaa (8, 21)	Baa corporate bond yield − Aaa corporate bond yield	8	21	Average
January	January Boolean	0	0	
GDP defl. (1, 61)	12-month percent change in GDP implicit price deflator	1	61	Average
Unemploy. (1, 4)	Unemployment rate, civilian labor	1	4	Average
Unemploy. (5, 16)	Unemployment rate, civilian labor	5	16	Average
M3 chg. (1, 60)	M3 money supply, 12-month percent change	1	60	Average
Turnover (1, 12)	NYSE, 1-month turnover ratio	1	12	Average
Turnover (13, 24)	NYSE, 1-month turnover ratio	13	24	Average
Util. div. (1, 1)	Utilities stocks: dividend yield	1	1	
Util. div. (2, 8)	Utilities stocks: dividend yield	2	8	Average
Fin. div. (1, 1)	Financial stocks: dividend yield	1	1	
Fin. div. (2, 8)	Financial stocks: dividend yield	2	8	Average

T A B L E 11-13

Four Stock Sectors, Government Bonds, and T-Bills Model Maximum-Leveraged Performance Coefficients

Factor Name	Financial Stock Sector	Health Stock Sector	Tech Stock Sector	Util. Stock Sector	Govt. Income	Cash Reserves	Leverage Function
Constant	1755.52	−952.42	968.95	0.00	−1179.31	0.00	5.9274
Div. yield (1, 1)	17.16	−54.23	49.86	0.00	−9.81	0.00	0.0298
Div. yield (2, 8)	18.14	96.21	−112.13	0.00	−4.87	0.00	−0.0265
T-bill (1, 4)	−5.35	19.69	0.63	0.00	−12.77	0.00	0.0220
T-bill (5, 36)	−1.47	6.74	−4.63	0.00	0.37	0.00	0.0102
S&P 500 (1, 23)	−6.21	−4.99	−18.06	0.00	17.45	0.00	−0.1181
Baa−10 yr. (1, 11)	−89.91	−1.67	162.35	0.00	−55.98	0.00	0.1479
Cap. util. (1, 2)	13.04	19.05	−19.45	0.00	−9.30	0.00	0.0334
Cap. util. (3, 20)	−30.06	−7.23	9.83	0.00	20.03	0.00	−0.0743
Indus. cap. (1, 1)	−175.51	5.00	275.02	0.00	−74.88	0.00	0.2962
Indus. cap. (2, 2)	163.44	−33.83	−210.31	0.00	61.18	0.00	−0.1952
5-yr. bond (1, 2)	0.74	−8.77	−16.62	0.00	20.40	0.00	−0.0425
Baa−Aaa (1, 7)	46.06	−83.05	30.38	0.00	15.31	0.00	0.0870
Baa−Aaa (8, 21)	41.41	−206.01	−63.52	0.00	150.36	0.00	−0.7776
January	0.01	6.30	−4.26	0.00	−1.38	0.00	0.0068
GDP defl. (1, 61)	−13.09	43.93	−99.30	0.00	37.08	0.00	−0.3138
Unemploy. (1, 4)	29.36	29.70	−61.51	0.00	4.67	0.00	0.0222
Unemploy. (5, 16)	−74.45	−45.55	108.39	0.00	14.47	0.00	0.0286
M3 chg. (1, 60)	−10.02	2.22	30.73	0.00	−13.19	0.00	0.0974
Turnover (1, 12)	39.53	62.29	−137.81	0.00	22.05	0.00	−0.1395
Turnover (13, 24)	−32.00	−39.43	14.62	0.00	38.82	0.00	−0.1800
Util. div. (1, 1)	5.38	21.52	−14.11	0.00	−8.07	0.00	0.0473
Util. div. (2, 8)	10.06	−17.49	48.71	0.00	−29.16	0.00	0.1212
Fin. div. (1, 1)	−16.46	−11.94	20.71	0.00	6.03	0.00	−0.0167
Fin. div. (2, 8)	1.41	2.33	−3.15	0.00	−1.07	0.00	−0.0048

dynamic allocations to investments having annualized returns under 21 percent is a powerful result, even when it is accomplished on an in-sample basis.

The dynamic allocations undergo large changes over the course of this 20-year interval. Figures 11–11a through d show that each one of the investments has several peaks of high allocations. The technology fund has several intervals of large allocations including a very long interval during the late 1990s. All the equity funds are then suppressed during 2001 as the majority of the allocation is given to bonds.

Note that several of the technology fund peaks are well over 100 percent. These coincide with an expansion in the leverage ratio

T A B L E   11-14

Maximum Performance of a Dynamic Four Stock Sectors, Government Bonds, T-Bills Model

Investments	Leverage Ratio	Max. or Min.	Monthly Arith. Average	Annual Geo. Average	Annual Arith. Std. Dev.	Max. Drawdown	Annual Sharpe Ratio	Average Deviation below 0
100% financial services	1.0	None	1.5507	17.9496	19.8014	46.9274	0.5734	1.5796
100% health care	1.0	None	1.7071	20.3394	19.1016	34.7716	0.7196	1.3413
100% technology	1.0	None	1.6463	15.7138	31.7550	74.0865	0.2872	2.6586
100% utility	1.0	None	1.1891	14.2175	13.4181	43.7506	0.5681	0.9808
100% govt. bonds	1.0	None	0.7555	9.3231	4.9063	7.3296	0.5561	0.2654
100% T-bills	1.0	None	0.5250	6.4833	0.6682	0.0	N/A	0.0
Dynamic stocks, bonds, T-bills	1.0	Max.	2.7168	35.8720	18.1381	11.7268	1.6141	0.7634
Dynamic stocks, bonds, T-bills	1.5	Max.	3.7355	50.2909	27.0251	17.5203	1.6169	1.2198

F I G U R E   11-11a

Dynamic Allocation to Financial Stocks in Four Stock Sectors, Government Bonds, T-Bills Model

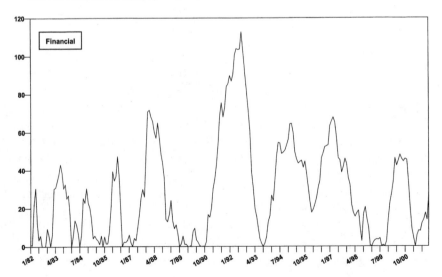

F I G U R E 11–11b

Dynamic Allocation to Health Stocks in Four Stock Sectors, Government Bonds, T-Bills Model

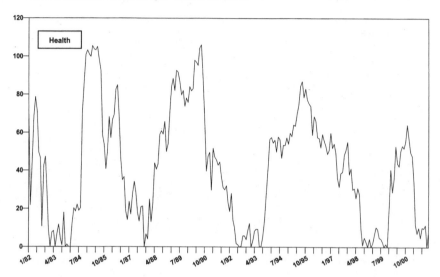

F I G U R E 11–11c

Dynamic Allocation to Technology Stocks in Four Stock Sectors, Government Bonds, T-Bills Model

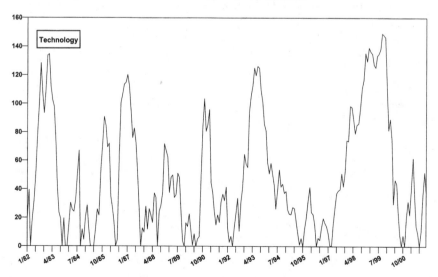

F I G U R E   11–11d

Dynamic Allocation to Bonds in Four Stock Sectors,
Government Bonds, T-Bills Model

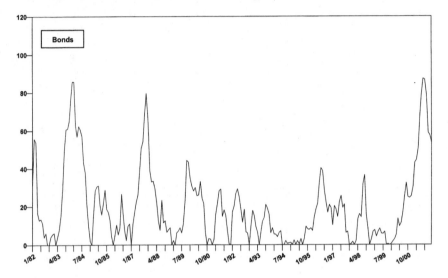

F I G U R E   11–12

Dynamic Leverage Ratio for the Four Stock Sectors,
Government Bonds, T-Bills Model

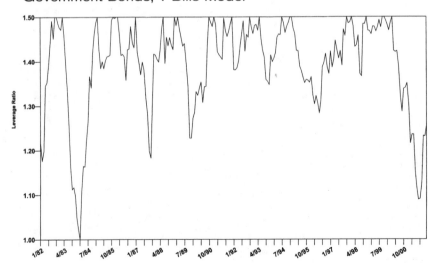

up to 1.5 percent. Figure 11–12 traces the leverage ratio over time. During all the 1990s the leverage ratio stayed very close to the 1.5 maximum value except for a brief run down to 1.3 during 1996. Allowing the leverage ratio to be a function of the macroeconomic factors provides a great deal of flexibility for achieving additional profitability. The sinking stock market in 2000 and 2001 coincides with a reduction in the leverage ratio back toward the 1.1 region.

The risk levels associated with this leveraged, maximum-return portfolio compare favorably with the risk levels of the underlying equity mutual funds. In order to add a degree of additional safety to the portfolio, it would be desirable to select a point on an efficient frontier with even lower levels of risk. Table 11–15 displays the values of various return-risk points along an efficient frontier. Any of the points between a 2.0 and 3.0 monthly arithmetic return would provide very attractive returns at acceptable levels of risk. For example, the risk statistics associated with the 2.6 monthly return are better than all the risk statistics for the equity fund returns with the exception of the standard deviation for the utility fund. The maximum drawdown at 6.9452 is less than one-fifth of the individual equity fund drawdowns. This is especially noteworthy considering that the dynamic portfolio is leveraged up by 50 percent.

The dynamic efficient frontiers for four different risk measures are shown in Figures 11–13 to 11–16. The locations of the return-risk of each underlying investment fund are also displayed. All dynamic efficient frontiers dominate the underlying investments in a way different from the traditional Markowitz mean-variance approach. In the Markowitz model, the upper point of an unconstrained and unleveraged efficient frontier always coincides with the return and risk of the highest-return investment. In any dynamic portfolio model, the highest point on the efficient frontier can have both a higher return and a lower risk than the investment with the highest return.

All the results displayed so far for this multisector stock model have been for a dynamic, in-sample approach, suffering no additional transaction costs. It is worthwhile considering the effects of both these assumptions.

If an individual investor with less than $250,000 of total capital conducted a dynamic asset allocation actually using the Fidelity

T A B L E   11-15

Minimum-Deviation Results for a Leveraged Four Stock Sectors, Bonds, T-Bills Model at Various Target Returns

Investments	Leverage Ratio	Max. or Min.	Monthly Arith. Average	Annual Geo. Average	Annual Arith. Std. Dev.	Max Drawdown	Annual Sharpe Ratio	Average Deviation below 0
Fin., health, tech, util., bonds, cash	1.5	Max.	3.7355	50.2909	27.0251	17.5203	1.6169	1.2198
Fin., health, tech, util., bonds, cash	1.5	Min.	3.6	48.9110	24.3208	13.7102	1.7399	0.8763
Fin., health, tech, util., bonds, cash	1.5	Min.	3.4	46.2315	21.7726	12.7464	1.8205	0.7054
Fin., health, tech, util., bonds, cash	1.5	Min.	3.2	43.4565	19.5049	10.4675	1.8899	0.5895
Fin., health, tech, util., bonds, cash	1.5	Min.	3.0	40.5475	17.8017	9.6592	1.9073	0.4969
Fin., health, tech, util., bonds, cash	1.5	Min.	2.8	37.6869	15.9539	8.4794	1.9489	0.4152
Fin., health, tech, util., bonds, cash	1.5	Min.	2.6	34.7990	14.3433	6.9452	1.9664	0.3446
Fin., health, tech, util., bonds, cash	1.5	Min.	2.4	31.9203	12.8451	5.3885	1.9716	0.2797
Fin., health, tech, util., bonds, cash	1.5	Min.	2.2	29.0437	11.5674	4.1385	1.9407	0.2191
Fin., health, tech, util., bonds, cash	1.5	Min.	2.0	26.1889	10.4543	2.7265	1.8743	0.1637
Fin., health, tech, util., bonds, cash	1.5	Min.	1.8	23.3889	9.1894	3.2590	1.8275	0.1154
Fin., health, tech, util., bonds, cash	1.5	Min.	1.6	20.6687	7.4483	2.5716	1.8895	0.0766
Fin., health, tech, util., bonds, cash	1.5	Min.	1.4	17.9286	6.4001	1.6192	1.7709	0.0452
Fin., health, tech, util., bonds, cash	1.5	Min.	1.2	15.2445	5.1546	1.1178	1.6781	0.0186
Fin., health, tech, util., bonds, cash	1.5	Min.	1.0	12.6026	3.8527	0.2910	1.5594	0.0018

Investments funds employed in this model, there would be substantial transaction costs for changing portfolio allocations. At the end of calendar year 2002, all additions to the four Fidelity Investments equity funds actually carry front-end loads as high as

F I G U R E 11-13

Standard Deviation *vs* Annual Return for the Four Stock Sectors, Government Bonds, T-Bills Model

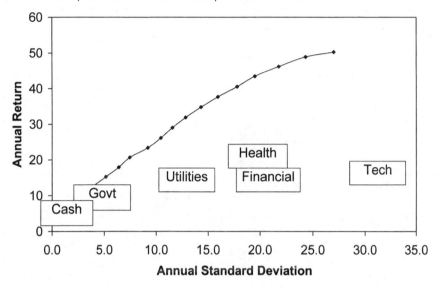

F I G U R E 11-14

Maximum Drawdown *vs* Annual Return for the Four Stock Sectors, Government Bonds, T-Bills Model

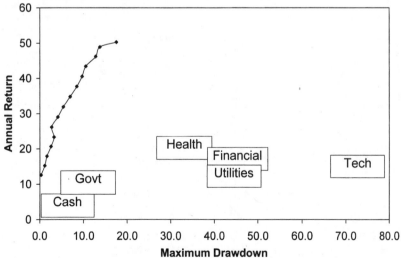

F I G U R E 11–15

Sharpe Ratio *vs* Annual Return for the Four Stock Sectors,
Government Bonds, T-Bills Model

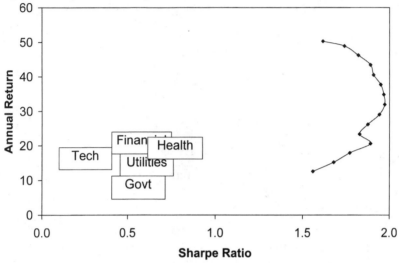

F I G U R E 11–16

Deviation below Zero *vs* Annual Return for the Four Stock
Sectors, Government Bonds, T-Bills Model

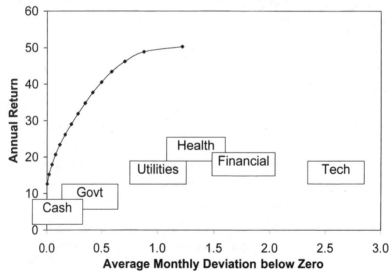

T A B L E   11–16

Front-End Transaction Fees for Fidelity's
Select Portfolio Funds

Transaction Amount	Fee Charged
$0 to $249,999	3%
$250,000 to $499,999	2%
$500,000 to $999,999	1%
$1,000,000 and greater	0%

3 percent. There is also a trailing load of 0.75 percent on all withdrawals of funds maintained less than 30 days.

The trailing load of 0.75 percent does not apply since all model holdings are for 30 days or more. But smaller investors applying the dynamic model might be subject to front-end fees. The front-end loads charged are subject to transaction-size breakpoints. Based on the amount of new additions, the breakpoints shown in Table 11–16 apply.

Using the same modeling assumptions as before, but allowing for this range of possible front-end loads on the Fidelity Sector funds, the adjusted results are shown in Table 11–17. Approximately a 2 percent return is lost for each 1 percent increase in fees. The dynamic portfolio risk gets slightly larger as the fees are increased. But even the model with the maximum fee level has an annual return over 44 percent. Small investors suffering the largest front-end loads could still receive very attractive returns.

Evaluating the effect of out-of-sample forecasts using an expanding data procedure is conducted using a procedure similar to the one applied in the case of stocks, bonds, and T-bills. The steps are:

Use historical monthly data from 1982 to 1986 to fit a dynamic factor model based only on this history while targeting a monthly return of 2.6. This 2.6 return level is selected in order to reduce portfolio risk. A maximum leverage ratio of 1.5 is allowed. Money borrowed to leverage is charged interest at 0.75 percent above the broker call rate.

T A B L E   11–17

Maximum-Leveraged Performance of a Dynamic Four Stock Sectors, Government Bonds, T-Bills Model Paying Various Levels of Front-End Loads on the Stock Funds

Investments	Leverage Ratio	Max. or Min.	Monthly Arith. Average	Annual Geo. Average	Annual Arith. Std. Dev.	Max. Drawdown	Annual Sharpe Ratio	Average Deviation below 0
Dynamic model with 0% load	1.5	Max.	3.7355	50.2909	27.0251	17.5203	1.6169	1.2198
Dynamic model with 1% load	1.5	Max.	3.6139	48.2546	26.8162	17.5510	1.5535	1.2405
Dynamic model with 2% load	1.5	Max.	3.5034	46.4073	26.6535	18.3363	1.4937	1.2707
Dynamic model with 3% load	1.5	Max.	3.4006	44.6405	26.7124	18.5425	1.4243	1.3077

Record the standard deviation of this model as a measure of risk of the fit time interval.

Use this model to forecast individual monthly returns for 1987. These are the forecasts from the dynamic model. The dynamic model is not revised during the 1987 calendar year.

Construct a leveraged efficient frontier for a Markowitz mean-variance model using the same historical monthly data from 1982 to 1986 to determine the required expected returns, standard deviations, and correlation coefficients. Borrowing up to 50 percent is allowed for this mean-variance model, with any money borrowed carrying interest at the same level of 0.75 percent above the broker call rate.

Select the point from the leveraged mean-variance efficient frontier with the same standard deviation as that of the dynamic factor model. This indicates that both models are evaluated at a point with the same level of risk.

Use the mix at this point on the Markowitz efficient frontier as out-of-sample allocations to determine the portfolio results for the next 12 months. These forecasts will be compared statistically with those of the dynamic model. The mean-variance model is not revised during the 1987 calendar year.

Expand the date range forward 1 year to include 1982 through 1987.

Repeat the whole process to forecast 1988 monthly returns by both models.

Continue this procedure until the date range is expanded to 1982–2000 to obtain forecasts for 2001.

Table 11–18 displays the annualized returns generated from this procedure. Note that the performance of 100 percent unleveraged stocks is included as a benchmark.

A statistical summary of the performance histories of the out-of-sample portfolios resulting from the Markowitz and dynamic models is presented in Table 11–19. The performance of the S&P 500 is also provided as a benchmark. The S&P 500 performance is based on an unleveraged evaluation. Leveraging up the S&P 500 by a leverage ratio that increases the standard deviation to the same value as that of the dynamic model (16.93), while including the cost of borrowing, leads to an average return still below that of the

T A B L E   11-18

Annualized Results of Out-of-Sample Leveraged Four Stocks, Bonds, T-Bills Model Comparisons

Year to Forecast	History Used to Fit Both Models	Common Standard Deviation	100% Stocks Annual Return	Markowitz Model Return	Dynamic Model Return
1987	1982–1986	11.71	5.27	−10.39	22.31
1988	1982–1987	11.80	16.61	12.42	15.10
1989	1982–1988	16.32	31.68	48.59	22.33
1990	1982–1989	12.47	−3.12	2.40	−0.35
1991	1982–1990	14.18	30.47	39.44	65.87
1992	1982–1991	12.94	7.64	−1.62	9.18
1993	1982–1992	13.94	10.08	10.94	24.77
1994	1982–1993	14.20	1.32	−6.53	2.10
1995	1982–1994	14.96	37.59	43.25	43.14
1996	1982–1995	14.07	22.96	13.68	20.75
1997	1982–1996	14.47	33.38	34.77	37.97
1998	1982–1997	14.83	28.57	47.78	38.03
1999	1982–1998	14.29	21.03	17.02	11.86
2000	1982–1999	14.17	−9.09	−6.51	−12.02
2001	1982–2000	14.17	−11.88	−18.84	5.33

T A B L E 11-19

Statistical Comparison of Out-of-Sample Leveraged Four
Stocks, Bonds, T-Bills Models (1987 – 2001)

Investments	Monthly Arith. Average	Annual Geo. Average	Annual Arith. Std. Dev.	Max. Draw-down	Annual Sharpe Ratio	Average Deviation below 0
100% S&P 500 stocks (not leveraged)	1.18	13.74	15.62	30.49	0.4577	2.9344
100% S&P 500 stocks (leveraged)	1.23	14.10	16.93	33.18	0.4435	3.2040
Markowitz model (leveraged)	1.11	13.03	14.08	36.19	0.4572	2.4962
Dynamic factor model (leveraged)	1.57	18.95	16.93	31.10	0.7297	2.6992

dynamic factor model. This leveraged performance of the S&P 500
is also shown in Table 11–19.

STOCKS, BONDS, AND FIVE HEDGE FUND CATEGORIES MODEL

This model incorporates five hedge fund categories into a stock and
bond portfolio. The five hedge fund categories evaluated in
Chapter 6 are all considered.

The allocation factor model is derived using the following
conditions:

The maximum achievable average monthly arithmetic return
is targeted.

A leverage level of 50 percent is allowed (a leverage ratio up to
1.5).

Annual interest on money borrowed is 0.75 percent above the
broker call rate.

No transaction costs are considered.

Allocations for each investment are allowed to range from 0 to
40 percent.

The date range of monthly data employed is January 1990 to December 2001.

The factors employed in the model are shown in Table 11-20.

The coefficients for the seven asset allocation functions for stocks, bonds, and the hedge fund categories of convertible arbitrage, fixed-income arbitrage, event-driven, global macro, and market-neutral are displayed in Table 11-21 for a model targeting

T A B L E   11-20

Macroeconomic Factors Used in Stocks, Bonds and Five Hedge Fund Categories Model

Factor Name	Factor Description	Begin Lag	End Lag	Operator
S&P yld. (1, 1)	S&P composite common stock: dividend yield	1	1	
S&P yld. (2, 17)	S&P composite common stock: dividend yield	2	17	Average
T-bill (1, 3)	Treasury bills, 90 days, yield	1	3	Average
T-bill (4, 21)	Treasury bills, 90 days, yield	4	21	Average
S&P 500 (1, 23)	S&P 500, price only, 1-month return	1	23	Average
Baa − 10 yr. (1, 3)	Baa corporate bond yield − 10-year government bond yield	1	3	Average
Cap. util. (1, 2)	Capacity utilization, manufacturing	1	2	Average
Cap. util. (3, 17)	Capacity utilization, manufacturing	3	17	Average
Indus. cap. (1, 2)	Industrial capacity, manufacturing 6-month percent change	1	2	Average
5-yr bond (1, 1)	5-year Treasury bond yield	1	1	
Baa − Aaa (1, 8)	Baa corporate bond yield − Aaa corporate bond yield	1	8	Average
Baa − Aaa (9, 21)	Baa corporate bond yield − Aaa corporate bond yield	9	21	Average
January	January Boolean	0	0	
GDP defl. (1, 60)	12-month percent change in GDP implicit price deflator	1	60	Average
Unemploy. (1, 6)	Unemployment rate, civilian labor	1	6	Average
M3 chg. (1, 60)	M3 money supply, 12-month percent change	1	60	Average
Crude oil (1, 3)	Cost of imported crude oil	1	3	Average
Currencies (1, 1)	Trade-weighted dollar-denominated currency index	1	1	
Fin. div. yld. (1, 1)	Financial stocks dividend yield	1	1	
SMB (1, 12)	Small-minus-big stock return differential	1	12	Average
HML (1, 7)	High-minus-low-value stock return differential	1	7	Average

T A B L E 11–21

Stocks, Bonds, and Five Hedge Fund Categories Model–Maximum-Performance Coefficients

Factor Name	Stocks Coefficient	Govt. Bond Coefficient	Convertible Arbitrage	Fixed-Income Arbitrage	Event-Driven	Global Macro	Market-Neutral	Maximum Impact
Constant coefficient	−1490.5113	741.9650	329.5654	520.5738	−950.4519	714.4475	284.4115	
S&P yld (1, 1)	58.7649	−52.8680	−8.3393	57.0329	−3.6064	−33.7473	−17.2368	114.3956
S&P yld (2, 17)	22.6683	−9.2209	−29.4300	−37.4695	−1.0776	139.3848	−84.8551	224.1191
T-bill (1, 3)	−10.0789	27.9336	10.1581	−7.2054	−42.3682	−10.7800	32.3408	157.6097
T-bill (4, 21)	0.8457	−6.3216	−7.8551	−7.0273	25.3982	−8.7421	3.7023	84.6795
S&P 500 (1, 23)	−27.0899	−3.9747	12.8265	25.1764	−10.4767	−20.6482	24.1866	65.5048
Baa − 10 yr (1, 3)	30.7060	−22.8053	−24.1469	3.6045	38.2013	−26.5831	1.0234	49.6618
Cap. util. (1, 2)	10.2180	−2.8489	−3.0690	−10.6399	9.3545	2.0077	−5.0224	76.8378
Cap. util. (3, 17)	5.2340	−10.5508	1.7777	4.0912	5.0714	−5.1617	−0.4618	46.9580
Indus. cap. (1, 2)	31.7979	20.3701	−15.7385	−5.7236	−10.2501	3.3739	−23.8296	73.6594
5-yr bond (1, 1)	−18.7509	8.0090	−3.4903	−5.7197	8.9816	10.1941	0.7762	60.7530
Baa − Aaa (1, 8)	198.6078	−97.9561	14.3085	50.7998	76.4405	−137.1985	−105.0021	87.5530
Baa − Aaa (9, 21)	338.5093	−232.0713	−9.9730	102.5588	77.4765	−161.0012	−115.4991	123.2521
January	0.6687	−0.7468	1.2042	12.4662	1.1237	−14.9715	0.2556	9.9810
GDP defl. (1,60)	−198.0586	90.1202	15.7826	37.1716	4.5832	−14.0546	64.4557	240.5115
Unemploy. (1, 6)	10.8070	38.2720	4.9197	−52.1980	−41.6133	9.2539	30.5588	125.2751
M3 chg. (1, 60)	−20.6950	20.4005	3.8560	−19.1317	−20.8837	38.0343	−1.5805	205.6583
Crude oil (1, 3)	−2.0621	−0.3638	−0.0294	1.5519	1.0919	1.5394	−1.7278	28.9012
Currencies (1, 1)	2.8614	0.5014	−1.4807	2.2703	0.2563	−5.2511	0.8424	99.5266
Fin. div. yld. (1, 1)	23.7923	14.3077	−0.9843	−3.4588	−13.1678	−39.8396	19.3505	129.0803
SMB (1, 12)	1.4430	4.1031	0.6268	2.4017	−4.2950	−11.9885	7.7089	40.2146
HML (1, 7)	−0.0073	−0.4269	−1.7919	−1.9918	−0.7104	1.7659	3.1624	28.5944

T A B L E 11–22

Maximum-Leveraged Performance of a Dynamic Stocks, Bonds, and Five Hedge Fund Categories Model

Investments	Leverage Ratio	Max. or Min.	Monthly Arith. Average	Annual Geo. Average	Annual Arith. Std. Dev.	Max. Drawdown	Annual Sharpe Ratio	Average Deviation below 0
Stocks, bonds, and five hedge funds	1.5	Max.	2.1880	29.2644	7.9890	4.3114	2.8376	0.2058

maximum performance. Using a threshold value of 25 in the "Maximum Impact" column in Table 11–21 to judge the significance of each factor, only the January factor appears to be a low contributor to the model performance. Using a maximum impact threshold of 25 means that the range of experienced values of the factor multiplied by the factor coefficient will move the allocation by 25 percent or less.

Setting the maximum allocations to 40 percent of capital employed prohibits any single investment from dominating the portfolio. While this will restrict the attainable portfolio average return, it will also reduce the standard deviation, drawdown, and deviation below zero. The performance statistics for this stock, bonds, and hedge funds model are shown in Table 11–22.

REVIEW OF THE DYNAPORTE DYNAMIC MODELS PERFORMANCE

The stocks and T-bills model evaluated in this chapter obtains performance similar to that of the market timing investigations obtained by other researchers. This is a kind of reality check on the capability of the DynaPorte formulation. One should not expect to obtain excess returns greater than 4 percent over stocks when only using stocks and T-bills as underlying investments in a dynamic approach.

The stocks, bonds, and T-bills model subsequently ekes out only another 1 percent. This now takes the dynamic portfolio to 5 percent excess return over stocks. This level is a very reasonable amount considering that only three investments are employed.

The addition of more investments and the use of leverage as applied in the other models lead to portfolio results that signal the possibility of much higher returns with in-sample determinations. However, we are brought back to reality by considering the differences between in-sample fits and out-of-sample results. The out-of-sample evaluations still indicate that 5 percent excess returns are attainable. The thought of obtaining 5 percent excess returns on an out-of-sample basis by employing dynamic asset allocation should be attractive to most institutional investors.

Given the practical limits imposed by some hedge funds concerning the frequency of additions and withdrawals, it might be reasonable to question the feasibility of dynamic asset allocation using hedge funds. Many hedge funds impose lockup intervals as long as 2 years. Other funds require 3- or 6-month notification in order to withdraw funds. Given these types of restrictions, it may present a challenge to change allocations on a monthly basis.

Several suggestions have been proposed to circumvent the impact of these limitations. There are many funds that do allow monthly additions and withdrawals with very short notification. These funds would be the most practical to employ for dynamic asset allocation. Additionally, hedge funds tracking a hedge fund category index have recently been implemented. These funds are less likely to have severe limitations on additions and withdrawals. They too could prove useful. Finally, a number of funds of hedge funds have liberal policies regarding contributions and redemptions.

Even funds that only allow redemptions every 3 months might prove to be useful if several could be identified that have staggered redemption months. Fund A allowing redemptions in January could be combined with fund B allowing redemptions in February, and so forth.

It is worthwhile to compare the performance attainable by the inclusion of different investment types at various levels of leverage. Table 11–23 summarizes the performance attainable under a variety of conditions. The date ranges used to construct these comparisons are not identical. The evaluation date range for hedge

T A B L E 11-23

Dynamic Portfolio Performance for Models Composed of Various Investment Combinations

Investments	Leverage Ratio	Max. or Min.	Monthly Arith. Average	Annual Geo. Average	Annual Arith. Std. Dev.	Max. Drawdown	Annual Sharpe Ratio	Average Deviation below 0
Stocks, T-bills	1.0	Max.	1.5059	19.1071	9.7022	7.9711	1.2896	0.4083
Stocks, bonds, T-bills	1.0	Max.	1.6018	20.2378	11.5479	10.6956	1.1814	0.6435
Stocks, bonds, T-bills	1.5	Max.	2.1367	27.1294	16.9975	16.6387	1.2081	0.9897
Fin., health, tech, util., bonds, T-bills	1.5	Max.	3.7355	50.2909	27.0251	17.5203	1.6169	1.2198
Fin., health, tech, util., bonds, T-bills	1.5	Min.	2.4000	31.9203	12.8451	5.3885	1.9716	0.2797
Stocks, bonds, hedge funds	1.5	Max.	2.1880	29.2644	7.9890	4.3114	2.8376	0.2058

funds in a portfolio (1990–2001) is considerably shorter than that of the other evaluations. But these performance statistics are still instructive of the types of returns attainable for different investment combinations.

The last two rows in Table 11–23 describe dynamic portfolio models with the highest Sharpe ratios shown. These high reward-to-risk ratios result from having a number of independent investments available to the portfolio. The hedge fund portfolio obtains a reasonably high return, with all risk measures having the lowest comparative values.

The dynamic portfolios constructed and evaluated in this chapter demonstrate the potential for superior out-of-sample forecasting based on dynamic allocation functions. The degree of success in constructing worthwhile portfolio realignment mechanisms depends completely on the fundamental validity of the variables used in the factor models. The factors must be logically sound, or the transition from in-sample fit to out-of-sample forecasting will be in jeopardy.

The DynaPorte formulation of linear factor models controlling the asset allocation process is just a tool. The success or failure of the tool is in the hands of the user. A sculptor combines personal skill with the intrinsic capabilities of the tools employed. Without study, training, practice, and insight, the sculptor cannot create a work of art that bridges the gap between concept and reality. A good tool simply makes it easier for someone skilled in the art.

So it is with the DynaPorte formulation. This chapter has shown that the tool can be used to construct useful models. The degree of success in using the DynaPorte tool will depend on the user's diligence in uncovering the relationships between macroeconomic factors and dynamic asset allocations among multiple investments.

Mean Absolute Deviation

> One of the brightest gems in the New England
> weather is the dazzling uncertainty of it.
>
> *Mark Twain*
> *New England Weather, Speech to the New England Society (1876)*

Assume a multifactor model of the form

$$R_t = \sum_{k=1}^{K} f_{kt} b_k + e_t \qquad (12\text{-}1)$$

where R_t and f_{kt} are known time series with values at each time
period t, and one of the f_{kt} could be a constant-value time series
which would allow a constant coefficient in the equation. In
attempting to fit this model, the unknown coefficients b_k are
determined in such a way that some chosen function of the error
terms e_t is made as small as possible. The goal is to make the fit
value for all values of t be as close as possible to the actual value.
The selected objective function simply allows us to develop a single
measure of closeness that incorporates all the error terms in some
way. The choice of the function of the error terms to be minimized is
not mandated by any universal statistical law. For example, how
should you choose the best objective function among the following
possibilities?

Minimize the result with the largest single error term.

Minimize the difference between the largest and smallest error
term.

Minimize the sum of the absolute values of the error terms.

Minimize the sum of squares of the error terms.

Minimize the sum of the fourth power of the error terms.

The first three of these are called L_1 norms because they involve measurements of the first power of the errors. The fourth is an L_2 norm, and the fifth is an L_4 norm.

Traditionally, minimizing the sum of the squares of the errors has been used in many standard statistical procedures. For example, multivariate regression analysis minimizes the sum of squares of the errors representing the difference between the actual and the fit values. The use of the sum of squares probably has more to do with the history of mathematical statistics than with a purposeful selection of sum of squares as the best method. Minimizing the sum of squares turns out to be the most convenient to deal with, given the mathematical tools at hand in the early development of statistical procedures.

This chapter seeks to evaluate the use of the mean absolute deviation as an acceptable measure of closeness when fitting a model of the form of (12–1). The mean absolute deviation is defined as the average of the absolute deviations of the predicted value from the actual value. Note that this measure goes by many other names in the literature, including minimum absolute deviation, least absolute error, least absolute residual, minimum sums of absolute error, minimum absolute errors, least absolute deviations, and least absolute values. The name *mean absolute deviation*—or MAD, for short—is adopted for the discussion that follows. By whatever name we call it, we are interested in putting the use of the mean absolute deviation in perspective, especially in comparison with minimizing the sum of squares of the errors. We shall refer to minimizing the sums of squares of errors by the term *least squares*, or LS, for the remainder of this chapter.

ADVANTAGES AND DISADVANTAGES OF LEAST SQUARES

Before evaluating mean absolute deviation, we need to understand the reasons for using the least squares as an objective function for minimizing error. There are three main advantages for using the least squares as the objective function. The first is based on ease of calculation. Determining the values of the b_k in (12–1) in such a way that the sum of squares of the error terms e_t is minimized involves a simple application of calculus. The solution can be stated in a closed form requiring nothing more complicated than the inversion of a matrix. For example, the solution to (12–1) is accomplished in a regression analysis framework as follows:

Write (12–1) in matrix form

$$R = fb + e \qquad\qquad (12\text{–}2)$$

The objective is to minimize the sum of squares of the error e.

Thus, minimize

$$e'e = (R - fb)'(R - fb) \qquad\qquad (12\text{–}3)$$

Differentiating (12–3) with respect to each one of the coefficients b_k generates the *normal equations*

$$(f'f)b = f'R \qquad\qquad (12\text{–}4)$$

Solving the normal equations for b yields the values of b as a function of f and R.

$$b = (f'f)^{-1}f'R \qquad\qquad (12\text{–}5)$$

The result in (12–5) states that, in order to minimize the sum of squares, the values of the coefficients b_k of the errors are just simple functions of the values f_{kt} and R_t. There is no restriction on the distribution of the values of R_t or f_{kt} to arrive at this result.

The second reason to use the least squares has to do with procedures for establishing various tests on the results of the regression. For example, if the errors are assumed to be normally distributed, then a wealth of statistical inference tests such as confidence intervals on the values of the b_k can be established. These tests can provide additional insight into the usefulness of the calculated values of the b_k. For more information about regression analysis and the types of statistical inference tests that can be applied, see Draper and Smith (1998).

There is a third seemingly advantageous feature of LS. The penalty associated with each error is related to the square of the error. Thus, large potential errors are penalized more than small errors. For example, an error of 1 unit is penalized with a value of 1. But an error of 3 units is penalized with a value of 9. This feature means the coefficients of the model will be determined in such a manner that large errors will be avoided. Outliers in the resulting distribution will be heavily penalized by the use of LS.

While the sounds like a laudable goal, setting the coefficients to avoid these outliers may produce unsatisfactory results. Consider a case in which the periodic rates of return R_t are usually drawn from a distribution influenced by the factors f_k with very small error terms e_t. Assume some extraordinary event occurs in one time period that results in a very large negative return caused by a factor not included in the f_k factors. None of the f_k factors can really explain this event. But the values of the b_k will be warped to do their best to "fit" the extraordinary event while attempting, with less success than before, to retain the strong relationship that exists with the other time periods. This one time period could ruin the strong relationship that fits well for all but one period. This example shows that outliers caused by unconsidered factors can have a detrimental effect on the resulting b_k.

Because the solution in (12–5) is so easy to derive and apply, the use of LS as an objective function for fitting equation (12–1) has become an almost universal approach. But there is no reason to accept LS as the only legitimate approach.

ADVANTAGES AND DISADVANTAGES OF MEAN ABSOLUTE DEVIATION

Let us define the mean absolute deviation as the average value of the absolute deviation of each actual value from the value predicted by the model. The use of the mean absolute deviation is far from being a new idea. Galileo suggested the concept in establishing a procedure for determining the location of a newly discovered star. The concept was subsequently investigated by a number of well-known mathematicians including Laplace and Gauss. For more background on the history of the development of MAD procedures, see Dodge (1987).

The earliest use of MAD was frustrated by the lack of a simple procedure to determine the optimal value of the coefficients.

Complex geometric arguments were suggested that were difficult to implement. A systematic method for calculating the mean absolute deviation had to wait for the development of linear programming in the middle of the twentieth century. Charnes, Cooper, and Ferguson (1955) show that regression based on a MAD objective function is equivalent to a particular linear programming problem. Their formulation opens the door to a practical method for fitting models such as (12–1) using the mean absolute deviation of the errors as the objective function.

Using the same notation as equation (12–1) and solving for e_t

$$e_t = R_t - \sum_{k=1}^{K} f_{kt} b_k \qquad (12\text{--}6)$$

Since we wish to minimize the sum of the absolute values of the e_t, we make the following substitution for e_t:

$$e_t = v_t - z_t \qquad (12\text{--}7)$$

Solving the following linear program minimizes the sum of the absolute values of the errors, e_t. A positive error of any size v_t is counted equal to the negative error z_t of the same size.

Minimize

$$\sum_{t=1}^{M} v_t + \sum_{t=1}^{M} z_t \qquad (12\text{--}8)$$

subject to

$$v_t - z_t = R_t - \sum_{k=1}^{K} f_{kt} b_k \qquad (12\text{--}9)$$

$$v_t \geq 0 \qquad (12\text{--}10)$$

$$z_t \geq 0 \qquad (12\text{--}11)$$

$$-\infty \leq b_k \leq \infty \qquad (12\text{--}12)$$

The solution to the linear program defined by equations (12–8) to (12–12) generally results in the determination of the K nonzero coefficients b_k and $M - K$ nonzero values of the errors e_t represented by the variable pair v_t, z_t. Simultaneously, K of the values of the errors e_t will have a value of zero. Whenever v_t has a nonzero value, z_t will have a zero value. Conversely, whenever z_t has a nonzero value, v_t will have a zero value. For further analysis of MAD solution characteristics, see Taylor (1973).

The reason for using the MAD objective function is rooted in the shape of the distribution of the resulting errors. A distribution that has a larger percentage of values in its tails than the normal distribution is said to have *fat tails*. If the error terms come from a distribution with fat tails, then the mean absolute deviation is considered a more efficient procedure for determining the model coefficients. Any system that randomly generates a number of large disturbances could be better served by a MAD objective function rather than by least squares.

As noted by Dodge (1987), three features of mean absolute deviation have kept the procedure from achieving preference over least squares. First, there is no simple closed-form solution available for MAD as there is for the least squares solution shown in (12–5). The calculation of the coefficients under MAD cannot be written as an equation. The coefficients must be determined by a process, the linear programming problem defined in (12–8) to (12–12). Second, MAD does not have the wealth of statistical inference procedures for determining such measures as confidence intervals on the coefficients b_k. Third, there is not much empirical evidence to show that MAD is numerically preferable to least squares even in the presence of fat-tailed distributions.

But we do not need to show that there is a clear dominance of MAD over least squares in order to justify using MAD. If we can show that the two procedures yield nearly equivalent degrees of closeness in terms of fit and if we can show that the linear nature of the MAD procedure gives us some other advantage, then the use of the MAD objective function can be acceptable.

DO MAD AND LS OBTAIN SIMILAR MODEL COEFFICIENTS?

The mean absolute deviation and least squares methods both provide estimates of the optimal coefficients of the model in (12–1). There is no reason to believe that they will not produce the same estimates of the coefficients based on the same set of data. Since both methods have been shown to produce unbiased estimators of the true optimal coefficients, then the expected value of the coefficients should be the same even though individual realizations could be different.

An empirical approach to evaluating the difference in the coefficients determined by each method would be to use the same data to estimate both sets of coefficients. Then this process could be repeated using multiple series of data. The coefficients generated by the multiple data series could be evaluated using statistical procedures. Such a test is undertaken by Cornell and Dietrich (1978). In this test, 52 weekly returns over the course of 1 year for 100 different stocks are used to calculate the beta for the capital asset pricing model (CAPM) relative to the S&P 500 stock market index.

$$R_{it} - R_{ft} = \alpha_i + \beta_i(R_{mt} - R_{ft}) + u_t \qquad (12\text{--}13)$$

where:

R_{it} = rate of return for stock i for week t
R_{ft} = risk-free rate for week t
R_{mt} = rate of return for the stock market index for week t
u_t = error term for stock i for week t

and

α_i = alpha of stock i
β_i = beta of stock i

The values of alphas and betas for each stock are determined twice, once using MAD and once using LS. The question is then posed whether the betas using the LS method β_{LS} are any different from the betas using the MAD method β_{MAD}. Cornell and Dietrich repeat this process for a total of 13 years. They find that the average correlation between the β_{LS} and the β_{MAD} is very high, over 0.88 for each of the years evaluated. This means that stocks with a high value of β_{LS} have a high value of β_{MAD}. In addition, stocks with a low value of β_{LS} have a low value of β_{MAD}. They conclude that the coefficients determined by LS and MAD are not statistically different from one another.

It is true that for a given stock and a given year, there could be a significant difference. But when considered across all stocks over a number of years, the difference between β_{LS} and β_{MAD} is essentially random. If the difference is random, then the process of determining the betas from LS cannot be preferred over the process of determining the betas using MAD. They produce equally good estimates.

In another comparison of the difference between LS and MAD estimates of regression coefficients, Sharpe (1971) finds that "the two methods give similar results." Since the difference is so small, Sharpe concludes that the LS method may be the more preferable because it is easier to calculate. In the absence of any other reason to prefer MAD, this seems a reasonable conclusion.

DOES MAD PRODUCE BETTER FORECASTS THAN LEAST SQUARES?

A number of statistical tests can be made using the estimates of the coefficients based on least squares. Assuming the errors are normally distributed, we can determine a confidence interval on the coefficients determined using LS. We can even formulate hypotheses about the expected value of future returns for R_t as it relates to the coefficients found for equation (12–1). Not as much is known about the kinds of statistical inference tests that can be made on the coefficients determined using MAD. For a review of the statistical inference procedures that have been investigated for MAD, see Dodge (1987).

But there is one test that can be made for both MAD and LS. This test is a very practical one involving the accuracy of forecasts made using the two sets of coefficients. Meyer and Glauber (1964) undertake an evaluation of investment models by fitting their models using both MAD and LS objectives. They use these models to forecast performance out of sample. They conclude that the models developed with MAD coefficients produce forecasts superior to those produced by the models with LS coefficients in terms of fit during the out-of-sample intervals. This result is obtained in an evaluation of six different models. In five out of six cases, the forecasts generated from coefficients determined using

MAD outperform the forecasts using coefficients determined using least squares. This is true across a range of forecasting accuracy measures as well as a number of evaluation time intervals. While these results are anecdotal and very likely dependent on the particular data set employed, they do highlight the potentiality of the MAD objective function.

Subsequent research by Cornell and Dietrich (1978) evaluates the relationship between one year's beta and the following year's beta. Based on the same set of tests described in the previous section regarding a CAPM formulation, the β_{MAD} found for year t is regressed against the β_{MAD} found for year $t + 1$. The average correlation between the two successive years is 0.576 based on the MAD estimates. Next, β_{LS} for year t is regressed against β_{LS} for year $t + 1$. The average correlation between the two successive years using the LS estimates has a value of 0.573, a surprisingly close result to the MAD result. These results seem to indicate that neither method is to be preferred over the other when evaluating the ability to predict future betas.

SHOULD WE PREFER MAD TO LS?

We have seen that both mean absolute deviation and least squares produce coefficients for the model in (12–1) that are unbiased. Konno and Yamazaki (1991) show that if the rates of return are multivariate normally distributed, the MAD objective function and the LS objective function lead to equivalent solutions. For a large number of random draws of data from investments with nearly bell-shaped distributions, one would expect to determine similar coefficients from both the MAD and LS methodologies.

So it may simply come down to practicalities to decide which one of the methods to use. For a portfolio optimization model with a choice of MAD or LS as an objective function, there is some advantage in choosing the MAD approach because it represents a linear objective. Using LS requires quadratic programming procedures that can limit the size of the problem solved or incur unacceptable solution time. If the constraints utilized by the portfolio optimization problem are all linear, then it would appear that the MAD objective function is more practical.

If there is an overriding need to draw statistical inferences about the calculated coefficients based on sampling theory, and we are willing to assume that the error terms are normally distributed, then the LS methodology would be required. Calculations such as confidence intervals on the coefficients are not available to the MAD methodology.

On the other hand, predictability might be the overriding concern. There are some conflicting results concerning the predictability of models developed with coefficients using MAD and coefficients developed using LS. Meyer and Glauber (1964) show that the use of MAD may be a better approach. Cornell and Dietrich (1978) indicate that the two approaches may be equal in predictability. But in any case, MAD predictability does not appear to be worse than LS predictability.

For fat-tailed distributions of the error term e_t in equation (12–1), there is an assumption that coefficients produced by MAD are better estimates than the coefficients produced by LS. For a given set of data, R_t, and f_{kt}, the determination of whether the error term will have fat tails cannot be known in advance. The LS solution would need to be calculated first and the errors evaluated. If the errors were found to be fat-tailed, then the MAD solution would need to be calculated. This would require solving (12–1) using both LS and MAD objective functions. The effort would be simpler if only the MAD solution were calculated all the time.

Overall, it appears that using the MAD objective function is not worse than using the LS objective function. For the DynaPorte dynamic portfolio optimization model, the use of the MAD objective function allows the use of a pure linear programming approach with all its power and efficiency.

REFERENCES

Charnes, A., W. W. Cooper, and R. O. Ferguson. "Optimum Estimation of Executive Compensation by Linear Programming." *Management Science* 1 (1955): 138.

Cornell, Bradford, and J. Kimball Dietrich. "Mean-Absolute-Deviation versus Least-Squares Regression Estimation of Beta Coefficients." *Journal of Financial and Quantitative Analysis* (March 1978): 123–131.

Dodge, Yadolah. "An Introduction to Statistical Data Analysis L_1-Norm Based." In *Statistical Data Analysis Based on the L_1-Norm and Related Methods*, edited by Yadolah Dodge. North Holland: Elsevier Science Publishers B. V., 1987.

Draper, Norman R., and Harry Smith. *Applied Regression Analysis*. New York: John Wiley and Sons, 1998.

Konno, Hiroshi, and Hiroaki Yamazaki. "Mean-Absolute Deviation Portfolio Optimization Model and Its Applications to Tokyo Stock Market." *Management Science* 37, no. 5 (May 1991): 519–531.

Meyer, John R., and Robert R. Glauber. *Investment Decisions, Economic Forecasting and Public Policy*. Cambridge, Mass.: Harvard Business School Press, 1964.

Sharpe, William F. "Mean-Absolute Deviation Characteristic Lines for Securities and Portfolios." *Management Science* 18, no. 2 (October 1971): B1–B13.

Taylor, Lester D. "Estimation by Minimizing the Sum of Absolute Errors." In *Frontiers of Econometrics*, edited by P. Zarembka. New York: Academic Press, 1973.

INDEX

About the Author

Richard E. Oberuc is the CEO of Burlington Hall Asset Management, Inc., of Hackettstown, New Jersey. Since 1987 he has been the designer and developer of the LaPorte Asset Allocation System, a software product for the development of investment portfolios using modern portfolio theory.

In a wide-ranging career, Mr. Oberuc was once an engineer at the Manned Spacecraft Center in Houston designing training simulators for NASA astronauts. As a result he is one of the few true "rocket scientists" working in the financial community. Following that he spent nearly 20 years developing supply/demand price forecasting models for futures and currency markets for the M&M/Mars Corporation.

In his most recent endeavor, Richard Oberuc has invented a revolutionary portfolio development product called DynaPorte. DynaPorte determines the macroeconomic factors that influence investment performance and advises how to change allocations as these important factors change through time.